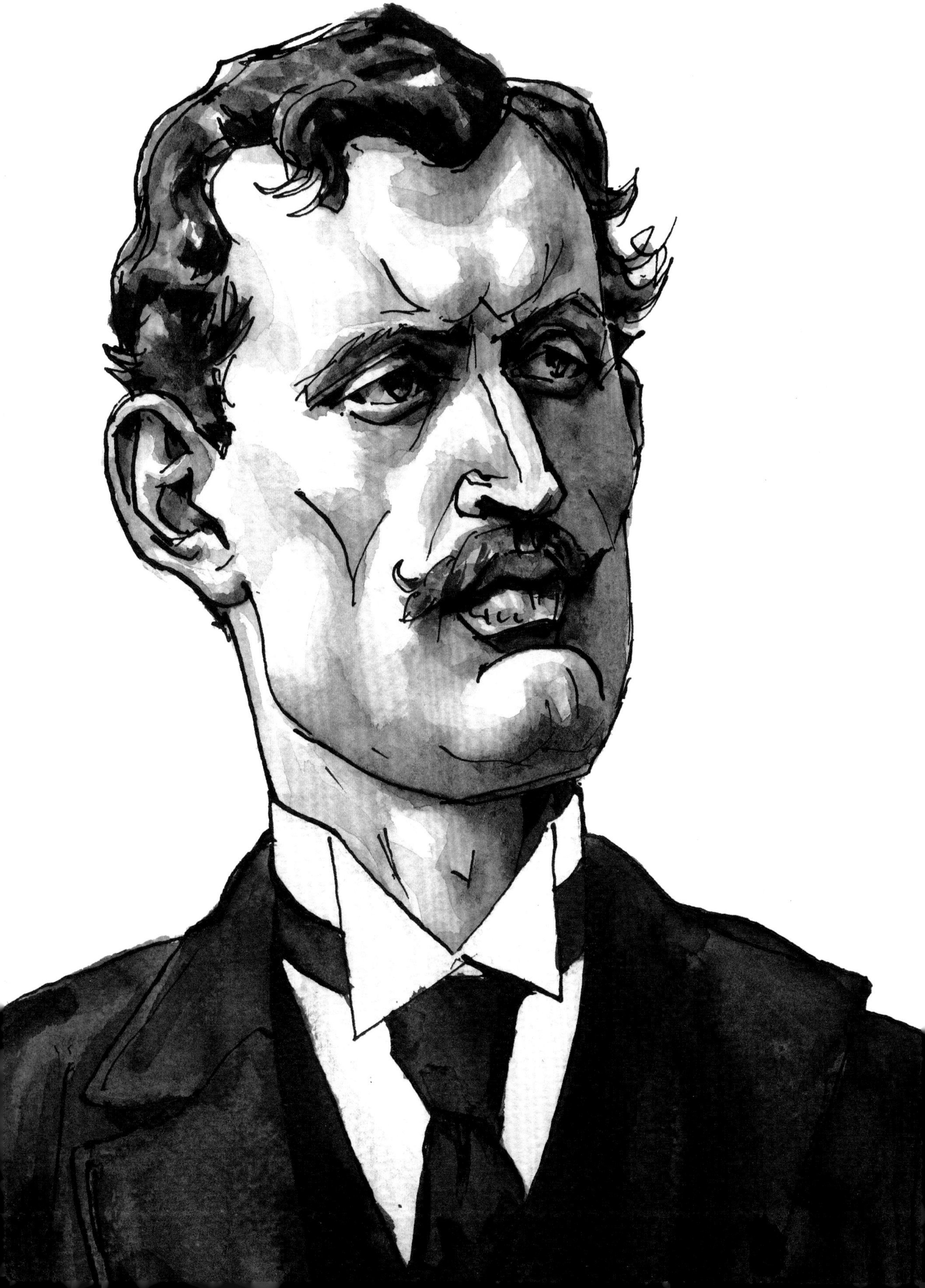

STEFFEN KVERNELAND

Munch

Translated by
Francesca M. Nichols

SELF
MADE
HERO

Published in English in 2016
by SelfMadeHero
139 –141 Pancras Road
London NW1 1UN
www.selfmadehero.com

The publication of this translation has been made possible through the financial support
of NORLA, Norwegian Literature Abroad.

Written and illustrated by Steffen Kverneland
Cover and book design by Steffen Kverneland
Translated from Norwegian by Francesca M. Nichols

Lettering and design by Txabi Jones
Marketing Manager: Sam Humphrey
Publishing Assistant: Guillaume Rater
Publishing Director: Emma Hayley
UK Publicist: Paul Smith
US Publicist: Maya Bradford

The publisher wishes to thank: Dan Lockwood
The author wishes to thank: Lars Fiske, Lasse Jacobsen, Gerd Woll, Liv Braathen,
Espen Holtestaul, Otto Ersland, Geir Atle Ersland and Pål Norheim

A CIP record for this book is available from the British Library.

ISBN 978-1-910593-12-7

10 9 8 7 6 5 4 3 2 1

Printed and bound in China

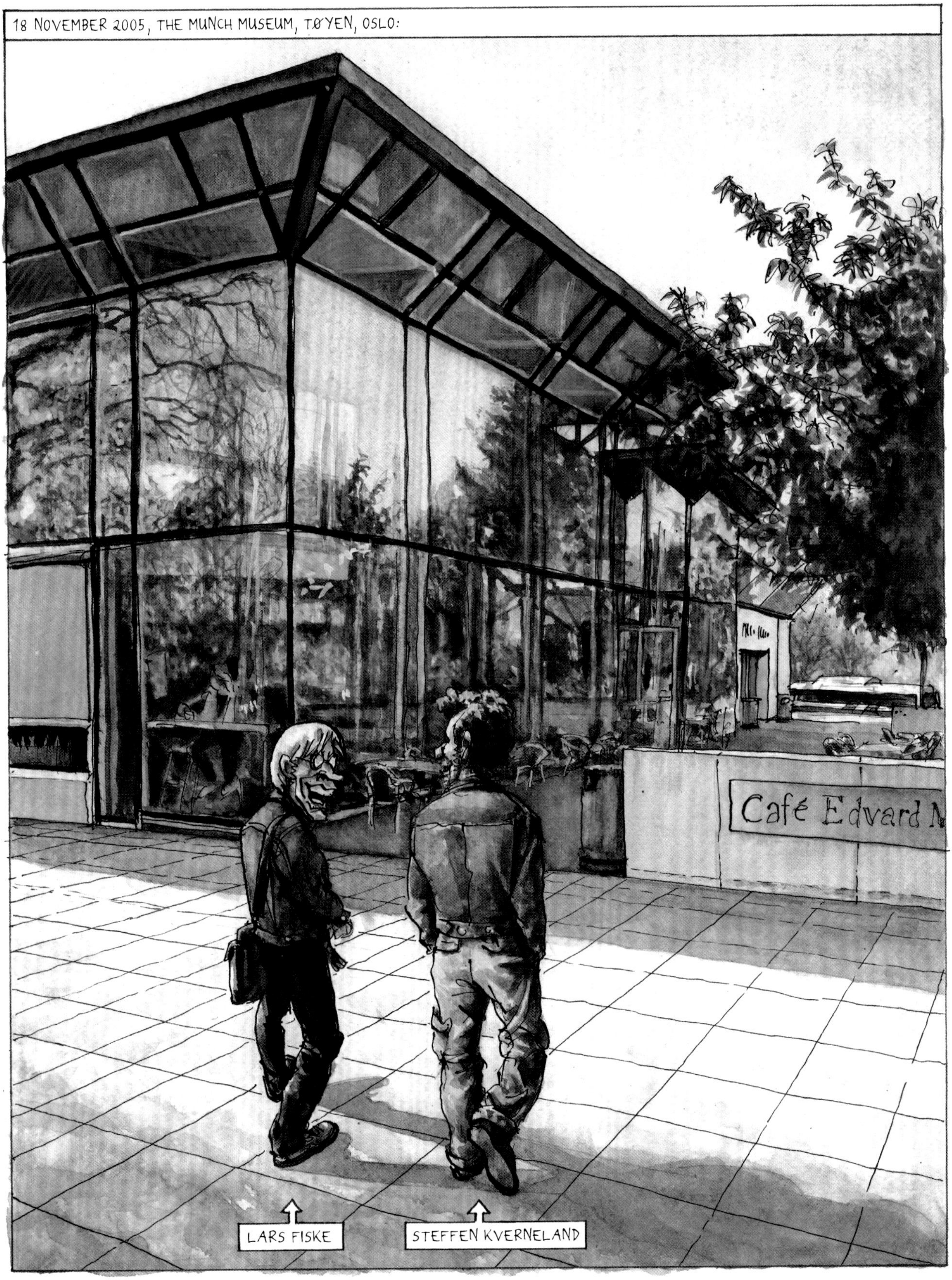
18 NOVEMBER 2005, THE MUNCH MUSEUM, TØYEN, OSLO:
Café Edvard M
LARS FISKE
STEFFEN KVERNELAND

THAT WENT STRAIGHT TO THE NOGGIN!

HIT THE SPOT!

WHAT D'YA KNOW, AIRPORT-STANDARD SECURITY CHECKPOINTS!

RIGHT ON!

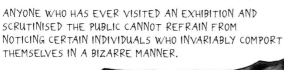

ANYONE WHO HAS EVER VISITED AN EXHIBITION AND SCRUTINISED THE PUBLIC CANNOT REFRAIN FROM NOTICING CERTAIN INDIVIDUALS WHO INVARIABLY COMPORT THEMSELVES IN A BIZARRE MANNER.

AUGUST STRINDBERG:
"HOW TO BECOME A CONNOISSEUR OF ART IN 60 MINUTES", 1877.

WHEN TWO SUCH TYPES MEET, THEIR BEHAVIOUR CAN BECOME QUITE ALARMING...

WOW! THAT'S RADICAL. HARDCORE SYMBOLISM. GUARANTEED 1890S.

PSYCHEDELIC NEW AGE SPIRITUAL PAINTING.

FACSIMILE

(IN AUTUMN 2005, A NEWLY DISCOVERED PAINTING BY MUNCH WAS EXHIBITED AT THE MUNCH MUSEUM.)

THEY TAKE EACH OTHER BY THE ARM AND WANDER FROM ROOM TO ROOM, HEADS TOGETHER, GESTICULATING AND TALKING EXCITEDLY.

THAT'S TOTALLY RETARDED! WHAT THE HELL WAS HE THINKING?

HE WAS PROBABLY SLOSHED ON PORT. WHAT AN ACID TRIP!

THESE GENTLEMEN ARE ART CONNOISSEURS.

THE ONE ON THE LEFT HAS TO BE A SELF-PORTRAIT WITH RED HAIR AND A BEARD.

OR AN AURA? TOADFACE ON THE RIGHT HAS GOTTA BE GUNNAR HEIBERG FOR SURE.

BUT WHO'S THE DUDE IN THE MIDDLE? A SCRAWNY, SUNBURNED CHRISTIAN KROHG WITH A GREEN BEARD?

THOSE ROMANTICISING INSIDE-MUNCH'S-HEAD BIOGRAPHIES IN THE PRESENT TENSE ARE FRIGGIN' BULLSHIT. NERDS WHO NEVER MET MUNCH SIT THERE A HUNDRED YEARS LATER SHOWING OFF.

NOTHING BUT PATHOLOGICAL LIES, SOAP OPERAS AND MASKED COPIES OF THE SOURCES.

IF I WERE GOING TO MAKE A MUNCH SERIES, THE MANUSCRIPT WOULD BE A COLLAGE OF PURE QUOTES!

BRILLIANT! LET THE SOURCES SPEAK FOR THEMSELVES!

GIMME THAT FLASK!

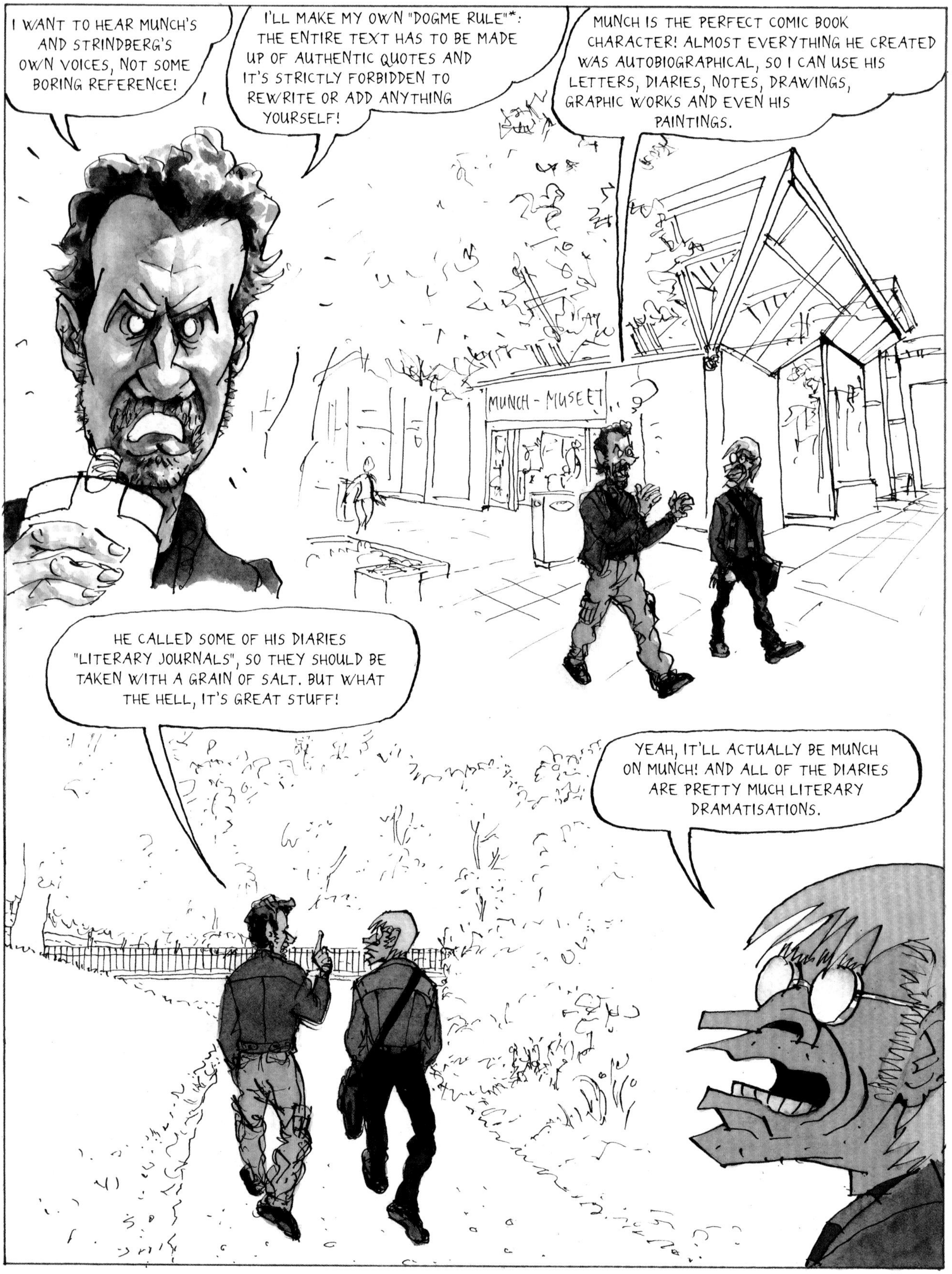
I WANT TO HEAR MUNCH'S AND STRINDBERG'S OWN VOICES, NOT SOME BORING REFERENCE!
I'LL MAKE MY OWN "DOGME RULE"*: THE ENTIRE TEXT HAS TO BE MADE UP OF AUTHENTIC QUOTES AND IT'S STRICTLY FORBIDDEN TO REWRITE OR ADD ANYTHING YOURSELF!
MUNCH IS THE PERFECT COMIC BOOK CHARACTER! ALMOST EVERYTHING HE CREATED WAS AUTOBIOGRAPHICAL, SO I CAN USE HIS LETTERS, DIARIES, NOTES, DRAWINGS, GRAPHIC WORKS AND EVEN HIS PAINTINGS.
MUNCH-MUSEET
HE CALLED SOME OF HIS DIARIES "LITERARY JOURNALS", SO THEY SHOULD BE TAKEN WITH A GRAIN OF SALT. BUT WHAT THE HELL, IT'S GREAT STUFF!
YEAH, IT'LL ACTUALLY BE MUNCH ON MUNCH! AND ALL OF THE DIARIES ARE PRETTY MUCH LITERARY DRAMATISATIONS.

* DOGME 95 FILM MANIFESTO.

* ARNE EGGUM (B.1936), NORWEGIAN ART HISTORIAN AND FORMER DIRECTOR OF THE MUNCH MUSEUM.

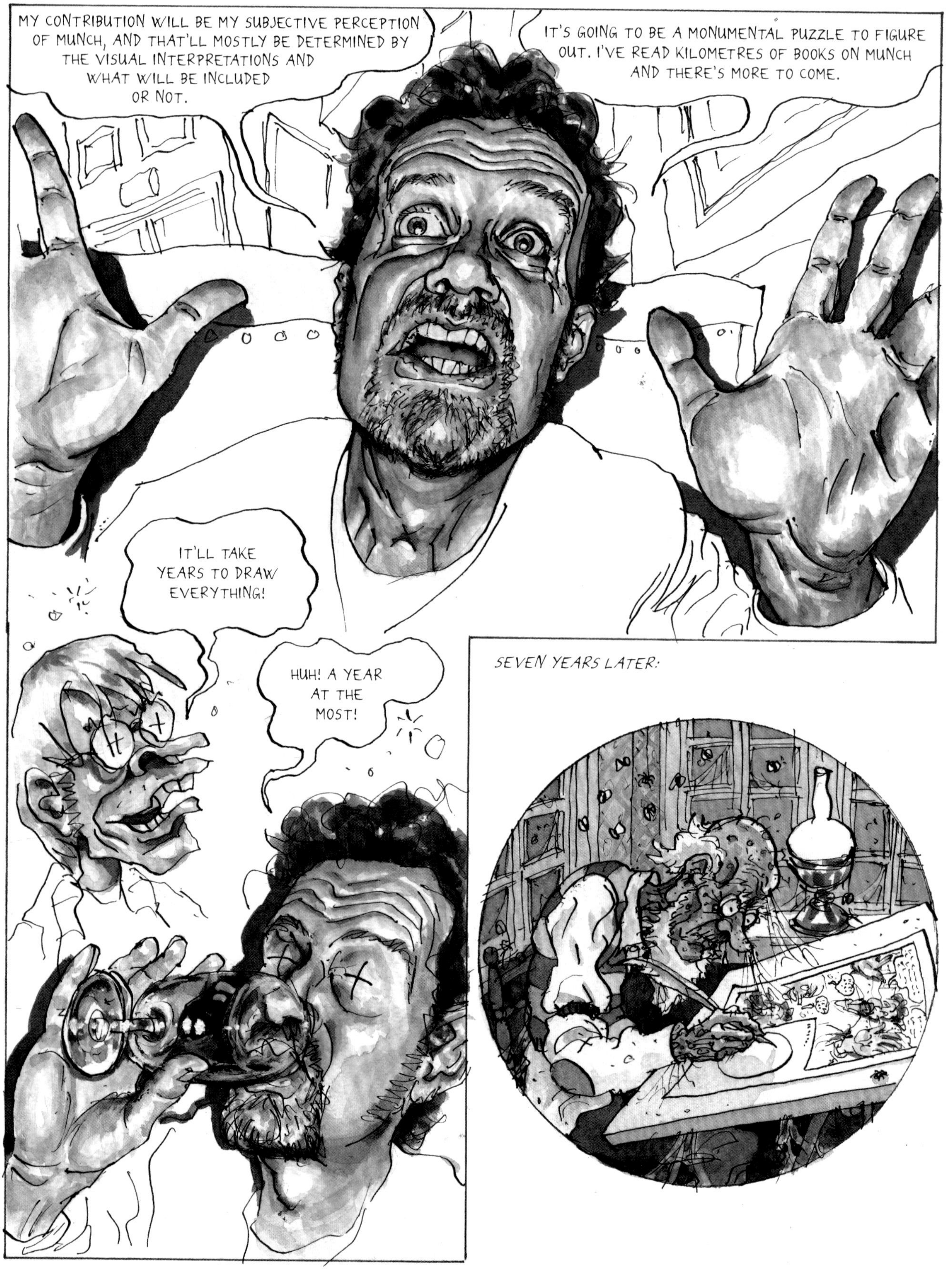
MY CONTRIBUTION WILL BE MY SUBJECTIVE PERCEPTION OF MUNCH, AND THAT'LL MOSTLY BE DETERMINED BY THE VISUAL INTERPRETATIONS AND WHAT WILL BE INCLUDED OR NOT.
IT'S GOING TO BE A MONUMENTAL PUZZLE TO FIGURE OUT. I'VE READ KILOMETRES OF BOOKS ON MUNCH AND THERE'S MORE TO COME.
IT'LL TAKE YEARS TO DRAW EVERYTHING!
HUH! A YEAR AT THE MOST!
SEVEN YEARS LATER:

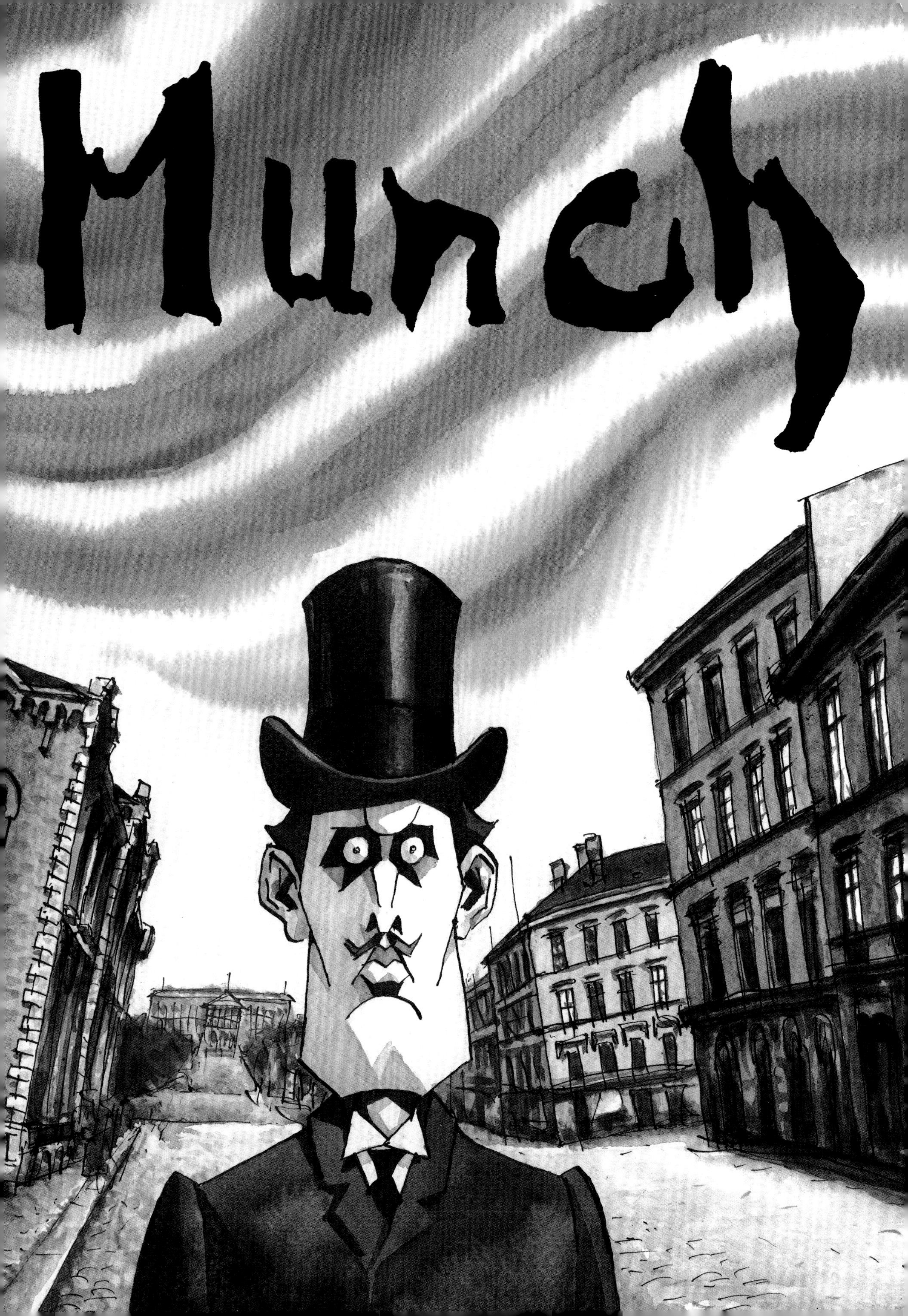
Munch

EILERT ADELSTEEN NORMANN: NORWEGIAN NATIONAL ROMANTIC PAINTER AND MEMBER OF THE BERLIN ARTIST GUILD.

SEPTEMBER 1892, TOSTRUPGÅRDEN, KRISTIANIA*.

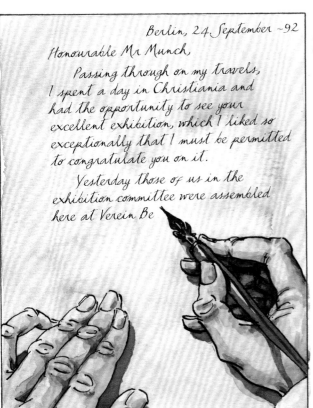

Berlin, 24 September ~92

Honourable Mr Munch,

Passing through on my travels, I spent a day in Christiania and had the opportunity to see your excellent exhibition, which I liked so exceptionally that I must be permitted to congratulate you on it.

Yesterday those of us in the exhibition committee were assembled here at Verein Be

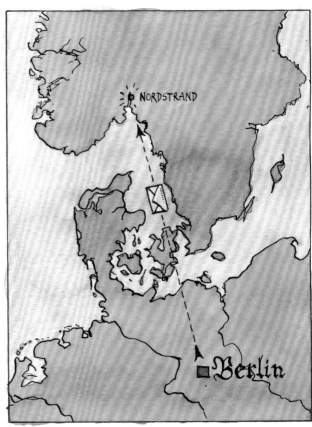

to exhibit your collected pictures in the Verein Berliner Künstler, which was unanimously approved.

I therefore take the liberty to ask you, if you have not already disposed of your pictures, if you might be willing to exhibit them here and under what conditions.

With best regards and respectfully,
A. Normann

CHRISTIAN KROHG:

WHEN MUNCH WAS BORN, HE WAS IN SUCH FAILING HEALTH THAT THEY WONDERED WHETHER IT WAS WORTH THE BOTHER TO "PUT HIM TO THE BREAST".

THEY DID NEVERTHELESS, AND HE IMMEDIATELY CAME DOWN WITH ALL THE MAJOR DISEASES IN SUCCESSION, SO THAT THEY WERE CONSTANTLY PRAYING FOR HIM IN CHURCH.

NEARLY EVERY TIME HE WAS ENTIRELY GIVEN UP ON BY THE DOCTORS; BUT HE LIVED ON, IN MOCKERY OF ALL SCIENCE, AS HE CONTINUED TO BE HAUNTED BY ILLNESS AND LAY CLOSE TO DEATH FROM TIME TO TIME.

HE IS STILL A BIT ON THE LEAN SIDE.

HIS VIEWS ON ART WERE ALWAYS THE SAME AND CULMINATED IN A HATRED OF REALISM.

ONE SHOULD NOT PAINT AS ONE SEES, BUT AS ONE SAW.

IT WAS THE EMOTIONAL IMPRESSION AND ONLY THIS THAT HE STROVE TO REPRODUCE, NOT AN IMAGE OF RANDOM NATURE.

IF, FOR EXAMPLE, THE CLOUDS LOOKED LIKE BLOOD WHEN ONE WAS IN A DISTURBED EMOTIONAL STATE, THERE'S NO POINT IN PAINTING PROPER CLOUDS.

ONE MUST TAKE THE DIRECT ROUTE — *PAINT THE CLOUDS LIKE BLOOD.*

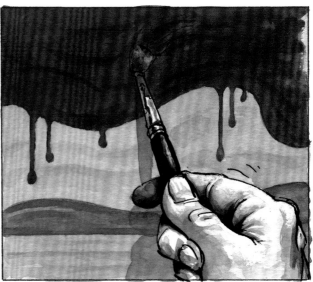

I MET HIM ONE DAY WHEN HE WAS ABOUT TO LEAVE FOR BERLIN.

YOU NATURALLY DO NOT BELIEVE ANYONE ELSE PAINTS WELL ASIDE FROM YOURSELF.

WELL, NO, I HONESTLY DO NOT THINK SO.

OH WAIT, AS A MATTER OF FACT WERENSKIOLD* DRAWS PRETTY WELL.

WHAT DO YOU THINK OF ME?

HE LAUGHED:

ONE IS NOT ALWAYS IN THE MOOD TO CHASTISE.

*ERIK WERENSKIOLD (1855–1938), NORWEGIAN PAINTER.

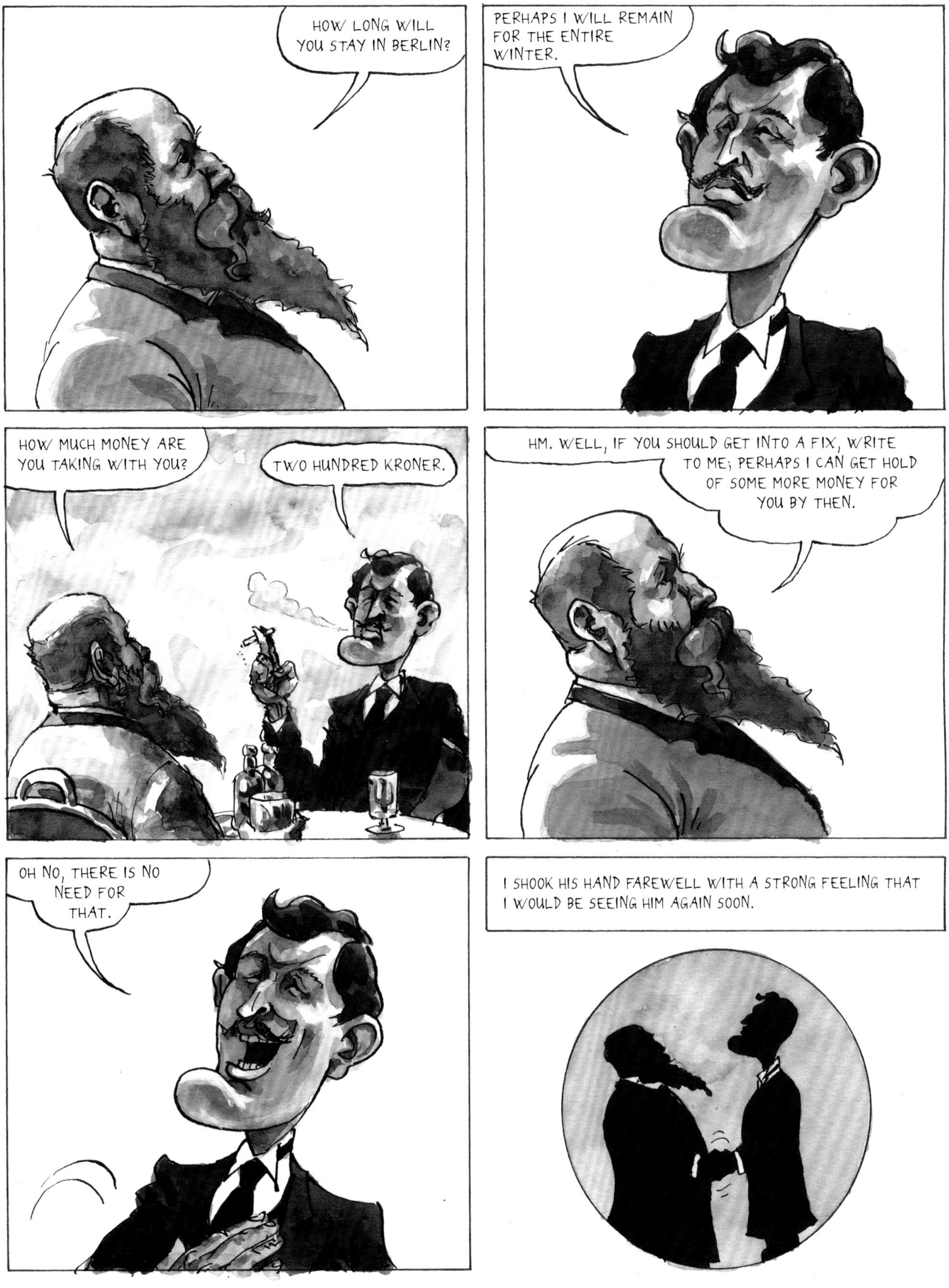
HOW LONG WILL YOU STAY IN BERLIN?
PERHAPS I WILL REMAIN FOR THE ENTIRE WINTER.
HOW MUCH MONEY ARE YOU TAKING WITH YOU?
TWO HUNDRED KRONER.
HM. WELL, IF YOU SHOULD GET INTO A FIX, WRITE TO ME; PERHAPS I CAN GET HOLD OF SOME MORE MONEY FOR YOU BY THEN.
OH NO, THERE IS NO NEED FOR THAT.
I SHOOK HIS HAND FAREWELL WITH A STRONG FEELING THAT I WOULD BE SEEING HIM AGAIN SOON.

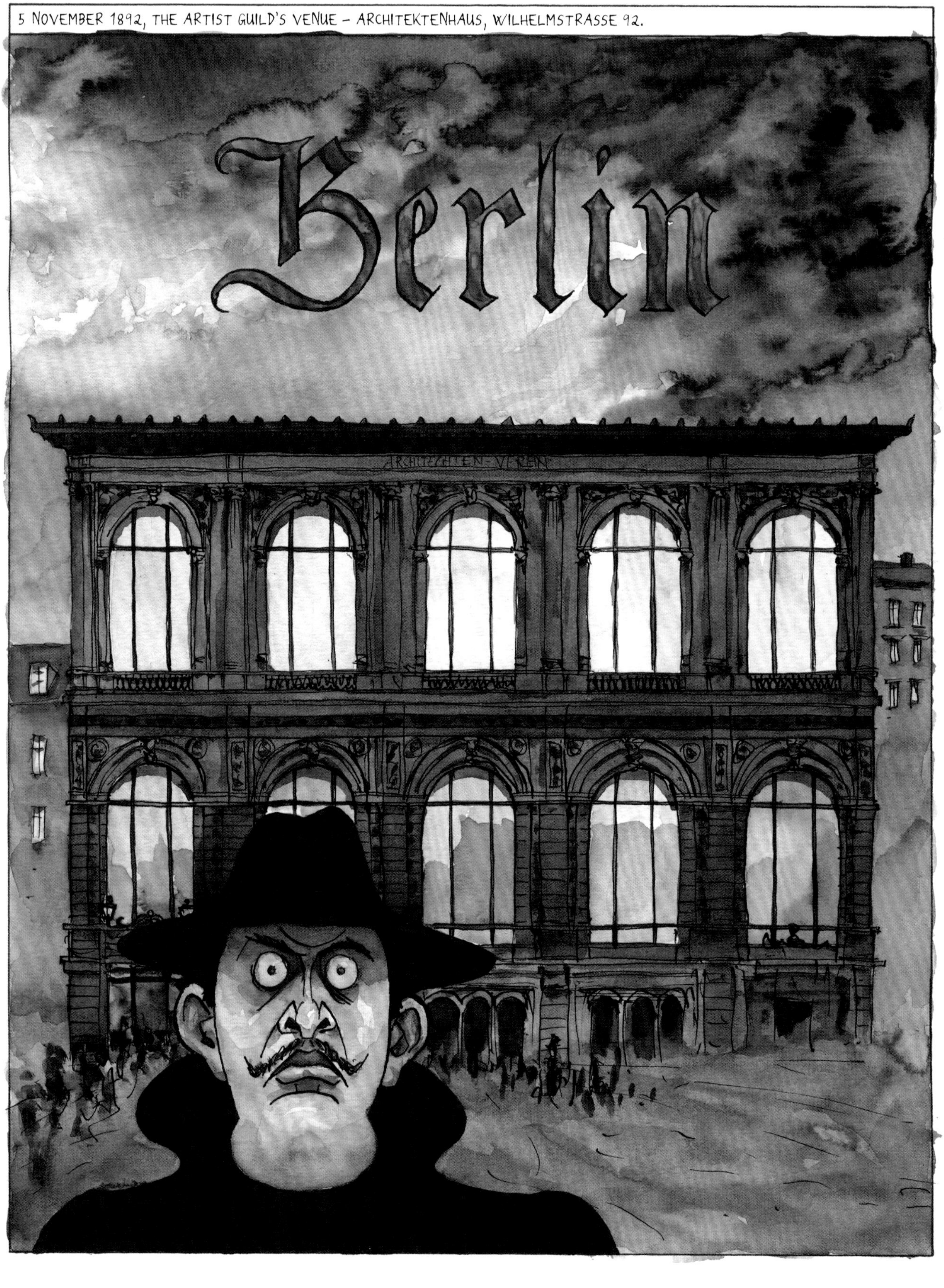
5 NOVEMBER 1892, THE ARTIST GUILD'S VENUE - ARCHITEKTENHAUS, WILHELMSTRASSE 92.
Berlin

THE DOORS OPENED PRECISELY AT THE STROKE OF 10, AND THEY MARCHED INTO THE EXHIBITION ROOM IN PROCESSION.

"THE PAINTER OF UNIFORMS AND BOOTS", ANTON VON WERNER, CHAIRMAN OF THE ARTIST GUILD.

MUNCH HAD BEEN ADVISED TO KEEP AWAY, AS IT WAS ASSUMED THAT THE OLDER PAINTERS WOULD CREATE "A GREAT UPROAR".

AND UPROAR THERE WAS.

MUNCH'S WORKS WERE PERCEIVED AS A DIRECT INSULT TO ART, AN ANARCHISTIC PROVOCATION.

IT WAS NOT THE MOTIFS THAT TRIGGERED THE NEGATIVE EMOTIONAL OUTBURSTS, BUT THE PAINTERLY AND TECHNICAL EXECUTION.

MUNCH WAS VIEWED AS A LIVING EXAMPLE OF WHAT WOULD HAPPEN TO A GERMAN PAINTER IF HE ALLOWED HIMSELF TO BE INFLUENCED BY THE HEDONISTIC FRENCH IMPRESSIONISM.

ALL FRENCH INFLUENCE WAS UNDESIRABLE. ON THE BASIS OF THIS, AN EXTRAORDINARY MEETING OF THE ARTIST GUILD WAS CONVENED, WHERE A PROPOSAL TO REMOVE MUNCH'S PICTURES WAS APPROVED, WITH 120 VOTES FOR AND 104 AGAINST.

THE SCULPTOR MAX KRUSE RECOUNTS:
ANTON VON WERNER DECLARED THAT THE EXHIBITION WAS CLOSED – IT MADE A MOCKERY OF ART, WAS OBSCENE AND IMMORAL.

WE DECLARED THAT IT WAS UNFITTING TO THROW OUT A GUEST. WERNER'S REPLY:

I DON'T GIVE A DAMN, THE EXHIBITION SHALL REMAIN CLOSED!

AND THEN ALL PANDEMONIUM BROKE LOOSE, WITH BOOING AND SHOUTING, FINALLY ENDING IN A PROPER SCUFFLE.

21

THE YOUNGEST AMONG US WISHED TO LEAVE THE ROOM, BUT THE OLDER ARTISTS BLOCKED OUR WAY. IN THE END, WE FORMED A WEDGE AND BROKE THROUGH THE WALL OF OPPONENTS.

INTOXICATED BY VICTORY, WE LEFT WILHELMSTRASSE...

ONLY ONE WEEK AFTER THE OPENING, AFTER THE GREATEST SCANDAL IN GERMANY'S MODERN ART HISTORY, THE PICTURES WERE TAKEN DOWN FROM THE WALLS.

THIS IS THE BEST THING THAT COULD HAPPEN. THE PUBLICITY COULD NOT HAVE BEEN BETTER.

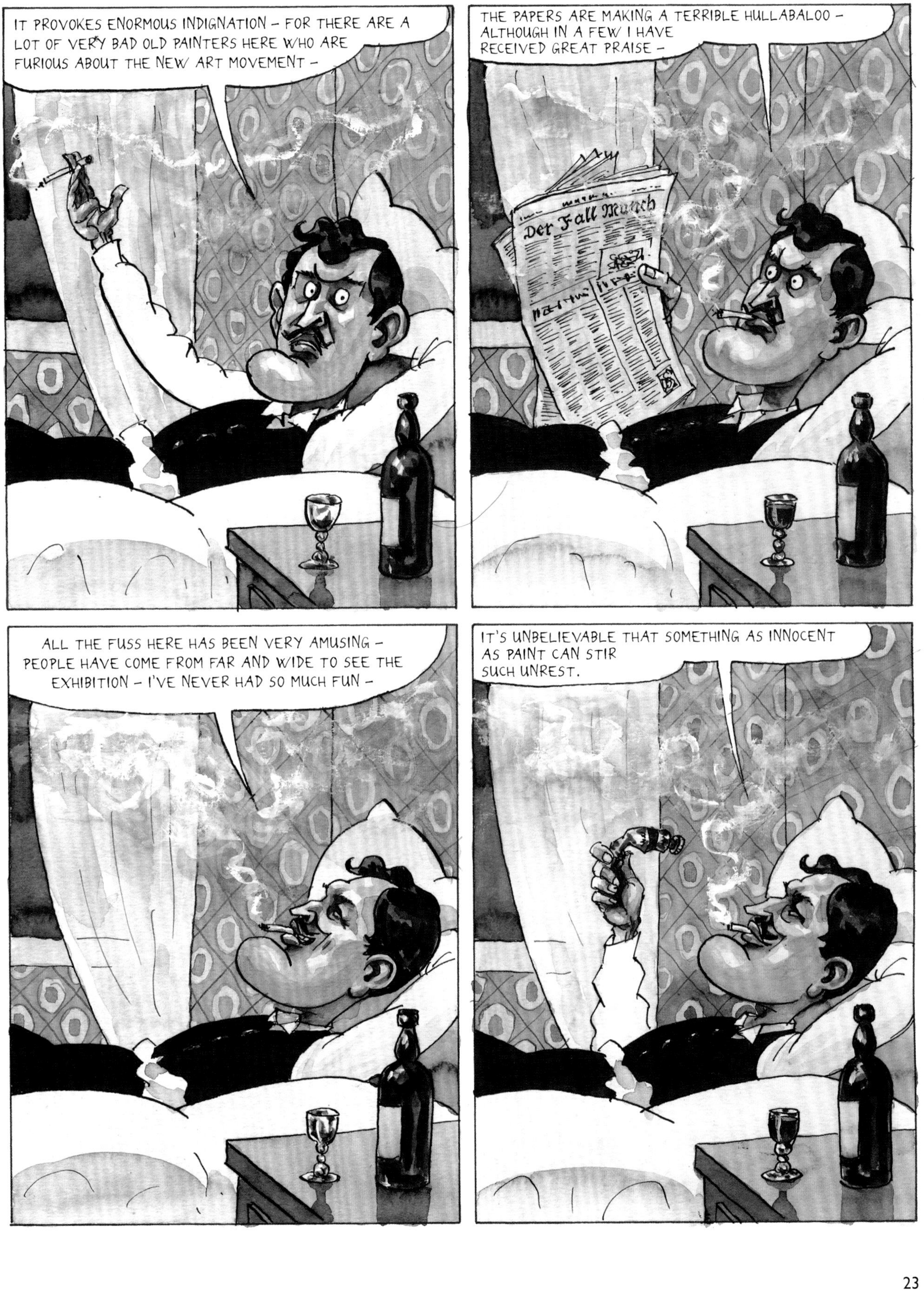
IT PROVOKES ENORMOUS INDIGNATION – FOR THERE ARE A LOT OF VERY BAD OLD PAINTERS HERE WHO ARE FURIOUS ABOUT THE NEW ART MOVEMENT –
THE PAPERS ARE MAKING A TERRIBLE HULLABALOO – ALTHOUGH IN A FEW I HAVE RECEIVED GREAT PRAISE –
Der Fall Munch
ALL THE FUSS HERE HAS BEEN VERY AMUSING – PEOPLE HAVE COME FROM FAR AND WIDE TO SEE THE EXHIBITION – I'VE NEVER HAD SO MUCH FUN –
IT'S UNBELIEVABLE THAT SOMETHING AS INNOCENT AS PAINT CAN STIR SUCH UNREST.

AFTER THE PUBLICITY SURROUNDING THE SCANDAL, MUNCH SUDDENLY BECAME ALL THE RAGE IN BERLIN.

HE BECAME CAUGHT UP IN THE SOCIAL LIFE OF WELL-TO-DO JEWISH ART CONNOISSEURS, WHERE HE INCIDENTALLY ALSO MET AUGUST STRINDBERG.

HE WENT SKATING WITH LIEBERMANN'S LOVELY DAUGHTERS, AND WILLINGLY RETURNED THE FLIRTATIONS OF BEAUTIFUL YOUNG LADIES.

HE SIGNED A CONTRACT WITH THE ART DEALER EDOUARD SCHULTE TO MOUNT THE EXHIBITION IN COLOGNE AND DUSSELDORF, AND SECURED HIMSELF ONE THIRD OF THE TICKET REVENUES.

THE PUBLIC FLOCKED TO SEE THE EXHIBITION THAT HAD SHAKEN THE IMPERIAL STATE CAPITAL.

THE EXHIBITION RETURNED TO BERLIN AGAIN IN DECEMBER.

HE SENT A TELEGRAPH TO KRISTIANIA ORDERING THE LARGEST POSSIBLE "PLAIN" NORWEGIAN FLAG*, RENTED AN EXHIBITION VENUE IN FRIEDRICHSTRASSE ON THE CORNER OF LEIPZIGERSTRASSE AND, DURING CHRISTMAS WEEK, MOVED IN WITH HIS CRATES.

* RATHER THAN THE CURRENT FLAG SHOWING THE SYMBOL OF NORWAY'S UNION WITH SWEDEN.

HE HAD A FLAGPOLE ERECTED OUT FRONT, RAISED THE ENORMOUS FLAG AND OPENED THE EXHIBITION!

MUNCH FORGOT TO INCLUDE THE DATE AND YEAR ON THE CATALOGUE, REMEMBERING ONLY THE TIME OF DAY.

HE KNEW WHAT HE WAS DOING WHEN HE CHOSE A THIRD OF THE TICKET REVENUES RATHER THAN AN ADVANCE OF 200 MARKS.

THE INCOME FROM THE ENTRANCE TICKETS CAME TO 1,800 MARKS* – BUT THE PROFIT WILL UNFORTUNATELY BE SMALL, SINCE THE EXPENSES WERE TERRIBLY HIGH.

*THE AMOUNT A LOWER MIDDLE CLASS GERMAN FAMILY EARNED IN A YEAR.

AT LEAST ONE NEW PICTURE WAS INCLUDED IN THIS EXHIBITION: THE PORTRAIT OF STRINDBERG.

WHEN MUNCH DONATED THE PAINTING TO THE NATIONAL MUSEUM IN STOCKHOLM 40 YEARS LATER, HE WROTE:

I MUST ADMIT THAT THERE IS AN EMPTY SPOT IN MY SITTING ROOM WHERE STRINDBERG HAS HUNG FOR 20 YEARS – IT IS FOR ME THE INCARNATION OF THE TWO STRANGE YEARS I SPENT IN BERLIN.

IN 1928, MUNCH TOLD RAGNAR HOPPE* "HOW HE PAINTED THE PORTRAIT OF STRINDBERG IN THE PLAYWRIGHT'S HOTEL ROOM ONE MORNING AFTER A VERY EXHILARATING NIGHT."

"IF STRINDBERG LOOKED A BIT PALE AND FATIGUED, IT WAS DUE TO THE COLD WINTER DAY AND THE 'DAY AFTER' ATMOSPHERE."

JENS THIIS**: IT WAS PRECISELY THIS PICTURE I STOOD IN FRONT OF ONE GREY CHRISTMAS DAY, WHEN TWO MEN ENTERED THE PREMISES...

JENS THIIS

* RAGNAR HOPPE (1885–1967), SWEDISH ART HISTORIAN AND CRITIC.
** JENS THIIS, NORWEGIAN ART HISTORIAN AND FIRST DIRECTOR OF THE NATIONAL GALLERY.

BOTH WERE DRESSED IN THOSE VOLUMINOUS BLUE RAINCOATS THAT WERE THE POOR MAN'S FASHION THEN.

IT WAS MUNCH AND STRINDBERG.

MUNCH INTRODUCED ME TO HIM.

WE LEFT THE EXHIBITION AND WALKED ABOUT THE CITY IN THE MOST DISMAL RAIN.

TO ME, STRINDBERG SEEMED DEFINITELY SYMPATHETIC. THERE WAS A STYLISH SWEDISH *GRANDEZZA* ABOUT THE WAY HE COMPORTED HIMSELF, QUITE DIFFERENT FROM MUNCH'S FORTHRIGHT NORWEGIAN CHARACTER, BUT THE TWO GOT ALONG MAGNIFICENTLY AND THERE WAS CERTAINLY AN EXCHANGE OF IDEAS ALREADY DURING THIS EARLY BERLIN PERIOD.

MUNCH WANTED TO DRAW STRINDBERG. IT WAS MID-AFTERNOON, A TIME OF DAY WHEN "FERKEL"* WAS EMPTY.

LET'S GO THERE. WE WON'T BE DISTURBED AT THIS HOUR.

* ZUM SCHWARZEN FERKEL, A TAVERN IN BERLIN.

WE EACH HAD A "SCHOPPEN"** OF MOSEL AND STRINDBERG POSED FOR MUNCH.

** A GLASS OR SMALL MUG.

MUNCH DREW AT LENGTH AND WITH GREAT INTENSITY.

I SAT IN A DARK CORNER AND, AS I HAD NOTHING BETTER TO DO THAN SIT AS QUIET AS A MOUSE, TOOK UP MY MUSEUM PAD AND STROVE, WITH A PENCIL, I RECALL, TO FURTIVELY MAKE AN OUTLINE OF THE SAME MODEL.

WHEN MUNCH WAS DONE, THE DEEP VOICE UTTERED:

LET ME SEE.

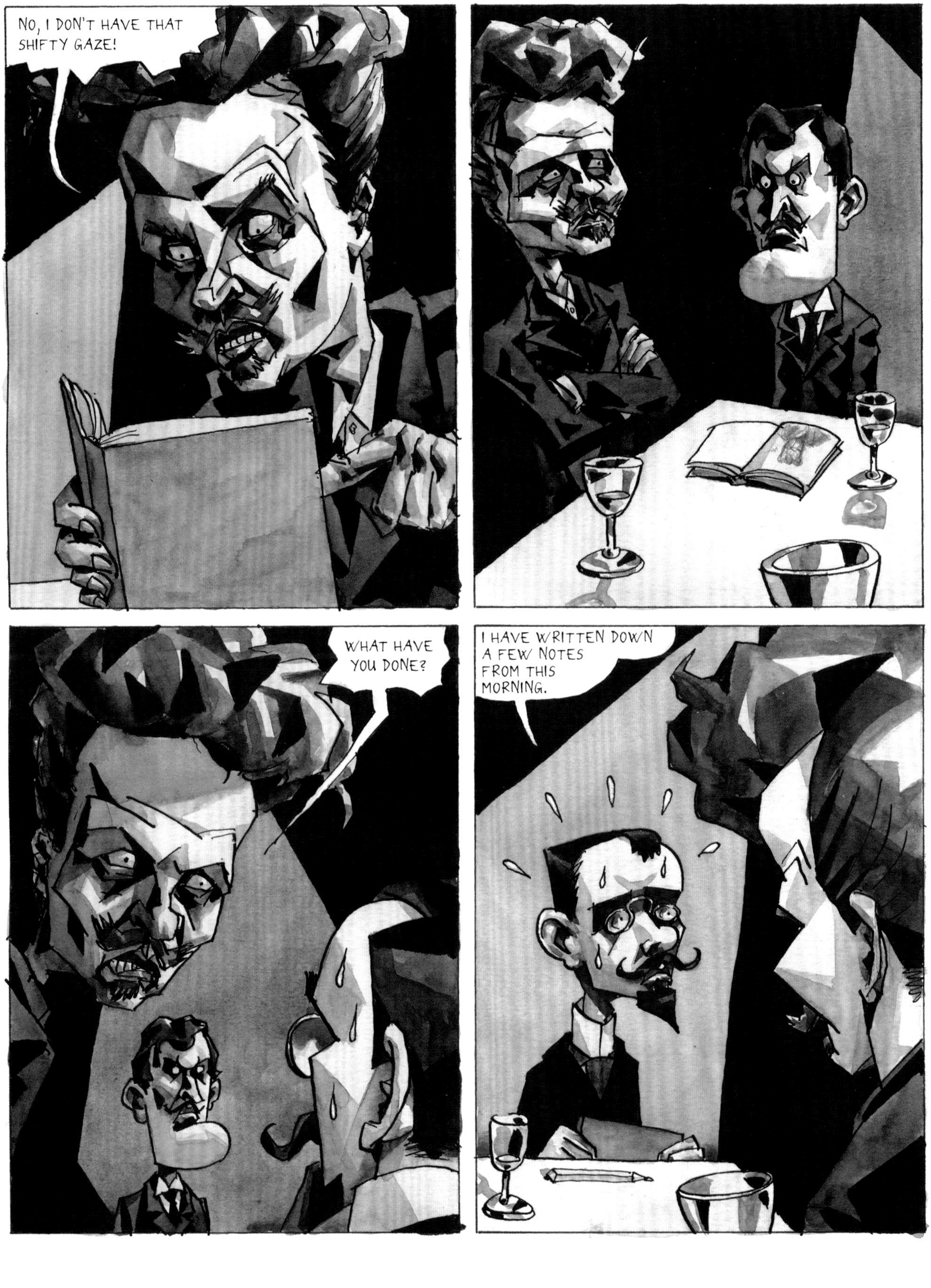
NO, I DON'T HAVE THAT SHIFTY GAZE!
WHAT HAVE YOU DONE?
I HAVE WRITTEN DOWN A FEW NOTES FROM THIS MORNING.

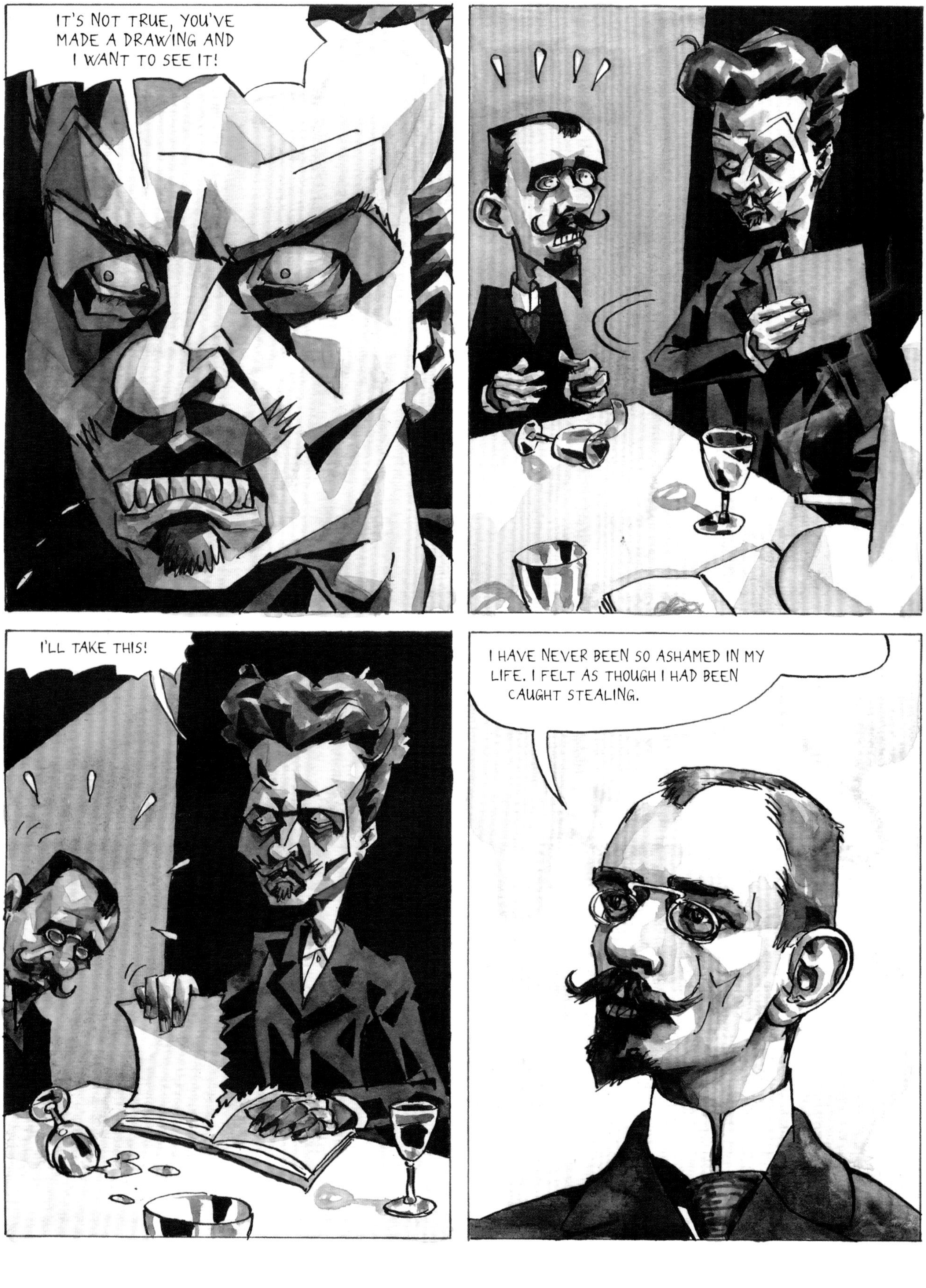
IT'S NOT TRUE, YOU'VE MADE A DRAWING AND I WANT TO SEE IT!
I'LL TAKE THIS!
I HAVE NEVER BEEN SO ASHAMED IN MY LIFE. I FELT AS THOUGH I HAD BEEN CAUGHT STEALING.

OH YES, STRINDBERG, I REMEMBER HIM WELL. HE USED A REPULSIVE FELLOW NAMED PAUL* AS A VALET AND DOORMAT.

* ADOLF PAUL, FINNISH WRITER AND JOURNALIST.

"FETCH MY COAT," HE'D SAY, AND PAUL WOULD RUN.

STRINDBERG PAINTED, TOO. EVOCATIVE PICTURES OF STORMS AND GREY WEATHER. SMALL AND VIGOROUS IN BLACK, WHITE AND GREY.

"NIGHT OF JEALOUSY", OIL ON CARDBOARD, 41 X 32CM, 1893.

ONE EVENING, HE SAID TO ME:

I'M THE GREATEST PAINTER IN SCANDINAVIA.

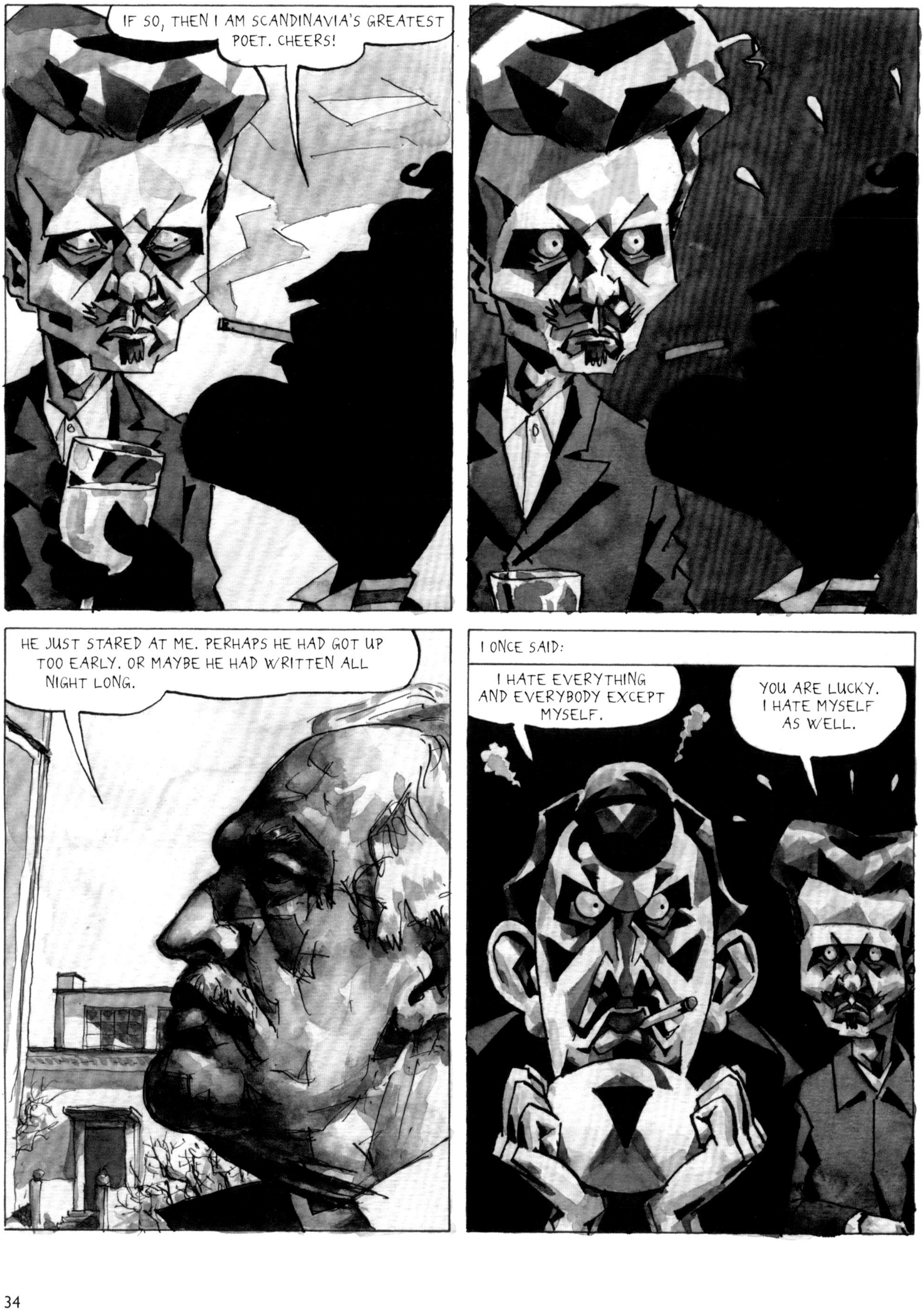
IF SO, THEN I AM SCANDINAVIA'S GREATEST POET. CHEERS!
HE JUST STARED AT ME. PERHAPS HE HAD GOT UP TOO EARLY. OR MAYBE HE HAD WRITTEN ALL NIGHT LONG.
I ONCE SAID:
I HATE EVERYTHING AND EVERYBODY EXCEPT MYSELF.
YOU ARE LUCKY. I HATE MYSELF AS WELL.

MUNCH WAS BY NO MEANS A LEARNED MAN. HE BELIEVED IN STRANGE SPIRITS AND THAT THE EARTH ONCE HAD TWO MOONS. STRINDBERG HAD SAID SO.

ONE MIGHT FIND THE SECOND MOON IF ONE SEARCHED IN THE VICINITY OF THE NORTH POLE. IT HAD EVIDENTLY FALLEN DOWN THERE.

ODDLY ENOUGH, THEY BECAME FRIENDS, EVEN THOUGH STRINDBERG WAS ALSO DIFFICULT, OBSTINATE AND DISTRUSTFUL. THEY WERE VERY DIFFERENT, AND YET THEY SHARED MANY OF THE SAME IDIOSYNCRASIES.

AMONG OTHER THINGS, THEY HAD A RELATIVELY SIMILAR VIEW ON WOMEN. DESPITE THE FACT THAT STRINDBERG HAD MARRIED THREE TIMES.

THEY ALSO BELIEVED IN "SUPERNATURAL POWERS" AND WOULD LOOK STEALTHILY ABOUT BEFORE ENTERING A NEW ROOM. WAS IT "COFFIN-SHAPED" OR PERHAPS "EVIL"?

MUNCH TOLD A FRIEND THAT STRINDBERG HAD "THE HABIT... OF SUDDENLY TRIPPING ME, SO THAT I LAY FLAT ON MY FACE IN THE STREET."

WHEN IT HAPPENED AGAIN, MUNCH THREATENED TO GIVE HIM A BEATING...

"SO HE GAVE UP THAT BAD HABIT."

ADOLF PAUL:
"ZUM SCHWARZEN FERKEL" {THE BLACK PIGLET} WAS LOCATED IN THE NOW DEMOLISHED BUILDING ON THE CORNER OF NEUE WILHELMSTRASSE AND UNTER DEN LINDEN.

ABOVE THE ENTRANCE HUNG THREE STUFFED ARMENIAN WINESKINS THAT CREAKED IN THEIR IRON CHAINS.

AND BECAUSE THE OWNER WAS THE FORTUNATE PROPRIETOR OF AT LEAST NINE HUNDRED DIFFERENT TYPES OF LIQUOR, IT WAS NOT DIFFICULT TO FIND A SUITABLE FLUID SUBSTANCE FOR EVERY CONCEIVABLE MOOD.

LISTEN, THE PIGLET IS WELCOMING US WITH HIS GRUNTING. LET US ENTER.

SQUEAL!

THE HOST READILY APPROVED THE NEW NAME FOR HIS ESTABLISHMENT INVENTED BY STRINDBERG, "THE BLACK PIGLET", AND HE HAD A YOUNG, SLENDER, BEAUTIFUL, BLONDE AND UTTERLY CHARMING WIFE.

ALL ALONG THE WALLS LINING THE SHOP, STORED FROM FLOOR TO CEILING ON INNUMERABLE SHELVES, WERE BOTTLES IN THE MOST FANTASTIC SHAPES AND COLOURS.

EVEN THE WINDOWS WERE SO CLUTTERED WITH THEM THAT WE LITERALLY SAW THE SUN RISE THROUGH THE BOOZE!

STRINDBERG DEPOSITED HIS GUITAR THERE ON THE FIRST NIGHT, DELIGHTED AND PLEASED TO HAVE FINALLY FOUND A PLACE IN BERLIN WHERE HE FELT AT HOME.

LETTER FROM STRINDBERG DATED 22 DECEMBER 1892:

My good man Paul!

Was sitting at the Ferkel. That sweet Frau Türke* had put on a new dress and a red neckerchief, the colour of love.

* THE PROPRIETOR GUSTAV TÜRKE'S WIFE.

She sat waiting despondently for Munch, who did not arrive, that unfaithful Liebhaber*.

* GERMAN FOR "LOVER".

39

THROUGHOUT HIS LIFE, EDVARD MUNCH HAD A TREMENDOUS INFLUENCE OVER WOMEN.

THE FACT THAT HE WAS RESERVED AND QUIET ONLY INCREASED HIS APPEAL.

MANY OF THE MOST BEAUTIFUL WOMEN OF THE TIME PURSUED HIM.

BUT HE NEVER WISHED TO MARRY.

IF A RELATIONSHIP BECAME TOO INVOLVED, HE WAS QUICK TO EXTRICATE HIMSELF.

HE SIMPLY FLED.

ADOLF PAUL:
A BEAUTIFUL YOUNG NORWEGIAN GIRL, DARK-EYED AND WITH LOCKS AS BLACK AS NIGHT, WAS TO BE IMMORTALISED BY MUNCH. AND NATURALLY IT COULD ONLY TAKE PLACE IN THE FERKEL!

STRINDBERG WAS ALSO PRESENT, STRUMMING HIS GUITAR, SIPPING FROM HIS PUNCH GLASS.

HE ROLLED ONE CIGARETTE AFTER ANOTHER, LIT ONE SACRIFICIAL SMOKE AFTER THE OTHER FOR THE BEAUTY AND ENTERTAINED THE COMPANY.

AND THE YOUNG MAIDEN SET GREAT STORE BY HIS GALLANTRY!

MUNCH TOOK OUT HIS SKETCHBOOK AND BEGAN DRAWING.

BUT SHE ONLY HAD EYES FOR THE FAMOUS "WOMAN-HATER", WHOSE "HATE" COULD HAVE SUCH CHARMING MANIFESTATIONS!

MUNCH CARRIED ON AT LENGTH WITH HIS DRAWING BUT COULD NOT TEAR HIMSELF AWAY FROM HER BLACK EYES

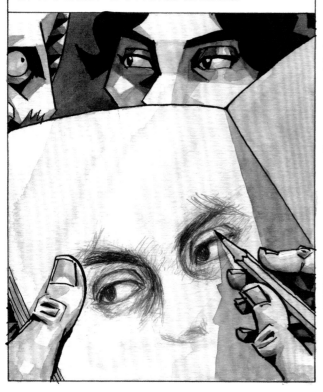

AND THUS CREATED A PORTRAIT WITHOUT CONTOURS, ONLY THE EYES, NOSE AND MOUTH!

AND THE SMILE ON THE MOUTH WAS NOT INTENDED FOR HIM!

THE EMISSARY OF POETRY HAD ALL THE CARDS IN HIS HAND THAT EVENING, AND THE EMISSARY OF PAINTING WAS FORCED TO RESIGN!

43

EDVARD MUNCH:
I WANDERED DOWN THERE ALONG THE GREYISH WHITE SHORE –

1885:   21 YRS.

IT WAS HERE THAT I FIRST BECAME FAMILIAR WITH A NEW WORLD — THE WORLD OF LOVE —

YOUNG AND INEXPERIENCED — FROM A CLOISTER-LIKE HOME — NEVER HAVING EXPERIENCED THE INTOXICATING POWER OF A KISS —

HERE I MET THE YOUNG TWO-YEAR-OLDER SALON LADY FROM KRISTIANIA — EVERYONE KNEW THE BEAUTIFUL COQUETTE MADAME T* —

* "MRS T", "MRS HEIBERG": MILLIE THAULOW, MARRIED TO CAPTAIN CARL THAULOW.

I STOOD BEFORE THE MYSTERY OF WOMAN – I GAZED INTO AN UNDREAMED-OF WORLD –

I DON'T FANCY THE LIGHT – I PREFER THE MOON WHEN IT'S BEHIND A CLOUD LIKE THAT –

SO DELICIOUSLY INDISCREET.

WHAT DID THIS MEAN – THIS GAZE ISSUED FROM A DREADFUL STRANGE – AND MAGNIFICENT WORLD – WHAT WAS THIS WORLD –

AND LAUGHTER ISSUED FORTH – WHICH I HAD NEVER HEARD BEFORE –

TITILLATING, AROUSED – TERRIBLE AND DELIGHTFUL –

STAND LIKE THIS A MINUTE — LET ME HAVE A LOOK AT YOU.

HOW WORTHY OF A PAINTING YOU ARE NOW IN THIS LIGHT.

YOU ARE TALLER THAN ME — I STAND ON A TUFT OF GRASS SO THAT I CAN LOOK INTO YOUR EYES.

WHEN WE STOOD FACING ONE ANOTHER AND YOUR EYES GAZED INTO MY EYES I FELT AS THOUGH INVISIBLE THREADS LED FROM YOUR EYES INTO MINE AND TRUSSED OUR HEARTS TOGETHER

HOW LOVELY SHE WAS IN THE SOFT WARM GLOW FROM THE HORIZON – SHE SAW HIM ADMIRING HER – AND SMILED AGAIN THAT PECULIAR SMILE ON ONE SIDE – AND ONCE AGAIN HE FELT THAT TITILLATING HEAT RUSHING THROUGH HIS VEINS

ON EVENINGS LIKE THIS, I MIGHT DO ANYTHING AT ALL – SOMETHING TERRIBLY NAUGHTY –

YOU DON'T KNOW HOW ANXIOUS I AM AT NIGHT.

I HAVE SUCH TERRIBLE NIGHTMARES AND I WALK IN MY SLEEP.

WHAT WOULD YOU SAY IF I CAME TO YOU?

THEY BOTH SMILED

HE IMAGINED HER COMING TO HIM IN THE WHITE CHEMISE WITH EYES CLOSED AND BARE LEGS AND IT TITILLATED HIM

HE WENT TO BED BUT COULD NOT SLEEP – AN IMAGE OF HER AS SHE HAD STOOD THERE IN THE LIGHT SUMMER NIGHT WITH THE PALE MOON ABOVE – CAME TO HIM

HER EYES IN SHADOW YET HOW THEY GAZED AT HIM – AS THOUGH SHE WAS WAITING FOR SOMETHING

"THE VOICE/SUMMER NIGHT", OIL ON CANVAS, 1893.

THEY ENTERED AN OPENING IN THE FOREST — THE ATMOSPHERE AROUND THEM WAS SOLEMN AS IN A CHURCH —

IT'S GETTING DARK.

YES.

MY GAZE FELL UPON A NAKED THROAT — A NAKED ARM —

I SAW THE HIP THAT SWAYED —

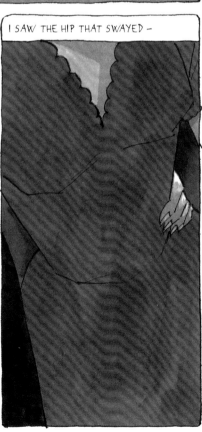

SHE ROSE UP TO MEET HIM –

AND HE COULD NO LONGER SEE –

NO LONGER THINK –

THE TREES AND THE AIR DISAPPEARED –

WE LEFT THE MURKY FOREST – FULL OF FLOWERS – OUT INTO THE LIGHT NIGHT –

I LOOKED AT HER FACE AND UNDERSTOOD... I HAD COMMITTED FORNICATION –

A MEDUSA HEAD –

I LEANED OVER AND SAT DOWN... I FELT AS THOUGH OUR LOVE... LAY THERE ON THE HARD STONES...

"STUDY/THE SICK CHILD", 1885-86.

SOMEONE KNOCKED ON THE DOOR.

GOOD AFTERNOON.

COME HERE!

AND HE RESTED HIS HEAD ON HER BREAST –

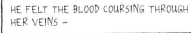

HE LISTENED TO HER HEARTBEAT –

HE BURIED HIS FACE IN HER LAP –

HE FELT TWO BURNING LIPS AGAINST HIS NECK –

IT SENT A SHIVER THROUGH HIS BODY — A FREEZING VOLUPTUOUSNESS — SO THAT HE CONVULSIVELY PRESSED HER TO HIM.

SHE CREPT UP AND CAST HER WHITE NAKED BODY OVER HIM —

THE PAUSE WHEN THE WHOLE WORLD STOPPED IN ITS TRACKS

YOUR FACE ENCOMPASSES ALL OF THE EARTH'S BEAUTY

YOUR LIPS CRIMSON LIKE RIPENING FRUIT

PART AS THOUGH IN PAIN THE SMILE OF A CORPSE.

NOW LIFE OFFERS DEATH ITS HAND
THE CHAIN CONNECTING THE MILLENNIUM OF GENERATIONS THAT ARE DECEASED TO THE
MILLENNIUM OF GENERATIONS THAT ARE TO COME HAS BEEN SECURED.

IF ONLY I KNEW — WHETHER YOU CARED FOR ME OR NOT —

WHEN I SAW YOU RECENTLY IN THE GRAND* — PALE AND DRESSED IN BLACK —

YOU RESEMBLED A MADONNA —

IF ONLY I KNEW WHETHER IT WAS YOUR FAULT — THAT IT WAS OVER —

I DO NOT WISH TO COME TO YOU — FOR I KNOW THAT YOU ARE DECEITFUL —

YOUR DETACHMENT IS A TORTURE — IT MAKES ME CRAZY —

* THE GRAND HOTEL.

I KNOW IT WAS I WHO ASKED YOU NOT TO COME — SO OFTEN —

FOR I WAS NOT AWARE THAT I CARED FOR YOU —

NOW THAT I HAVE LOST YOU I LOVE YOU —

IF ONLY I KNEW WHETHER IT WAS TO PUNISH ME THAT YOU WENT TO SOMEONE ELSE OR WAS IT BECAUSE YOU WISHED TO LEAVE ME — IF I KNEW IT WAS MY FAULT THEN WE COULD MAKE AMENDS —

THIS UNCERTAINTY IS AFFECTING ME — MAKING ME MAD.

HERE SHE CAME — HE FELT AN ELECTRIC
SHOCK PASS THROUGH HIM —

MISTAKEN AGAIN — HOW THEY ALL
RESEMBLE HER —

AND THEN SHE FINALLY ARRIVED. HE HAD NEVER SEEN HER SO LOVELY.

SUCH LOVELY SKIN, SUCH SOFT FEATURES.

SHE SMILED TENDERLY AND WALKED ON.

WHY HAD HE NOT STOPPED HER AND TOLD HER THAT SHE WAS THE ONLY ONE AND THAT HE WAS MAD AND AN IDIOT –

SHE LOOKED SO SAD – PERHAPS IT IS SHE WHO BELIEVES THAT I AM NOT FOND OF HER AND IT IS MY OWN FAULT –

WHAT A PATHETIC MISERABLE IDIOT YOU ARE –

A COWARDLY WRETCH COWARDLY COWARDLY COWARDLY WRETCH – YOU ARROGANT FOOL. HE WORKED HIMSELF IN TO A VERITABLE FRENZY.

THEN EVERYTHING BECAME QUIET. NOISE FROM THE STREET WAS SO
DISTANT — AS THOUGH IT CAME FROM ABOVE. HE COULD NOT FEEL
HIS LEGS — AS THOUGH THEY WOULD NOT BEAR HIS WEIGHT —

PEOPLE WHO PASSED BY LOOKED SO FOREIGN AND STRANGE AND HE
FELT THEY WERE STARING INTENSELY AT HIM — STARING AT HIM —

ALL THESE FACES — PALE IN THE EVENING LIGHT.

63

HE WANTED TO FIND A GIRL IMMEDIATELY – A PLACE WHERE HE COULD REST HIS HEAD – FEEL HER HEART PULSE –

HE DID NOT CARE ABOUT MRS HEIBERG –

THEIR HANDS MET – HE SHUDDERED
SLIGHTLY –

HOW LUMPY AND ROUGH IT WAS – IT
ACTUALLY SCRATCHED HIM –

THEN SHE SANG — IT WAS MEANT TO
BE TOUCHING —

THERE WERE DRAWLING NOTES —
SOMETIMES SCREECHING AND SOMETIMES
WITH LONG TRILLS —

SHE LEANED TOWARDS HIM AND PLACED
HER CHEEK NEXT TO HIS —

HOW REPULSIVE HE THOUGHT SHE WAS.

WAS IT BECAUSE SHE WAS THE FIRST ONE I KISSED THAT SHE TOOK THE FRAGRANCE OF LIFE FROM ME –

WAS IT BECAUSE SHE LIED – DECEIVED – THAT SHE ONE DAY UNEXPECTEDLY REMOVED THE SCALES FROM MY EYES SO THAT I SAW THE MEDUSA HEAD – SAW LIFE AS A GREAT TERROR –

SO THAT EVERYTHING WHICH BEFORE HAD HAD A ROSY HUE – NOW APPEARED EMPTY AND GREY

THE RELATIONSHIP MARKED HIM FOR MANY YEARS TO COME, AND THE VISUAL MEMORIES OF THESE PAINFUL INCIDENCES BECAME THE BASIS OF A NUMBER OF PICTURES THAT TOGETHER WOULD BECOME HIS MAJOR WORK, "THE FRIEZE OF LIFE".

"EVENING ON KARL JOHAN", OIL ON CANVAS, 1892.

ONE NEED NOT GO VERY FAR TO EXPLAIN HOW "THE FRIEZE OF LIFE" CAME INTO BEING – FOR IT HAS ITS ORIGINS IN THE BOHEMIAN PERIOD – IT WAS A QUESTION OF PAINTING LIFE AS IT WAS LIVED AND ONE'S OWN LIFE –

FURTHERMORE I HAD THE ENTIRE FRIEZE OF LIFE COMPLETED LONG AGO IN LITERARY FORM SO IT WAS ALREADY THOROUGHLY PREPARED MANY YEARS BEFORE I ARRIVED IN BERLIN.

KVERNELAND 2007

EVERYTHING EDVARD MUNCH PAINTED WAS A MIRROR IMAGE OF HIS OWN MIND. EVEN WHEN SOMEONE SAT FOR HIM, THE PICTURE SAYS MORE ABOUT EDVARD MUNCH.

HE WAS NOT INTERESTED IN PAINTING "A FACE IN THE STREET", WHAT MOST PEOPLE PERCEIVE AS A TRUE LIKENESS.

THE PICTURE SHOULD NOT RESEMBLE REALITY. IT SHOULD BE A GOOD PICTURE.

"THE FRIEZE OF LIFE" TOOK OVER MORE AND MORE SPACE IN MY WORK AND I WAS ALSO SUPPORTED BY THE CONTEMPORARY TRENDS IN PAINTING AND LITERATURE.

SYMBOLISM. THE SIMPLIFICATION OF LINES (WHICH DEGENERATED INTO ART NOUVEAU). IRON CONSTRUCTIONS –

A HINT OF ENIGMATIC RAYS AND ETHEREAL UNDULATIONS AND WAVES.

"WOMAN MAKING LOVE/MADONNA", OIL ON CANVAS, 1893.

ORIGINALLY THERE MUST HAVE EXISTED AT LEAST TWO DIFFERENT VERSIONS OF THE PAINTING "WOMAN MAKING LOVE/ MADONNA". ONE OF THEM WE KNOW AS MUNCH'S CLASSIC VERSION; THE OTHER HAS BEEN LOST. THERE ARE AS MANY AS FIVE PRESERVED VARIATIONS OF THE MOST FAMOUS VERSION.

A DRYPOINT ETCHING AND A CARICATURE OF THE LOST PAINTING IN THE SATIRICAL MAGAZINE *TYRIHANS* PROVIDE US WITH KEYS FOR A RECONSTRUCTION.

KVERNELAND'S ATTEMPT AT A RECONSTRUCTION.

CERTAIN DETAILS SUCH AS THE MOTHER AND THE EMBRYO — WHICH REPRESENT IN WORDS AND DRAWING THE LOFTIEST MOMENTS IN A HUMAN BEING'S LIFE — OR ONE OF THE THREE LOFTIEST — BIRTH — CONCEPTION — AND DEATH — IT SHOULD LIKE BIRTH AND DEATH BE ENSHRINED ON AN ALTAR —

THE DRAWING THAT THE UNKNOWN VERSION OF "MADONNA" WAS BASED ON LOOKED A HELL OF A LOT LIKE OTHER MUNCH PAINTINGS: "THE KISS OF DEATH", FOR EXAMPLE.

YOU MEAN LIKE A RECYCLED SKETCH?

YEAH, AND THE MUGS IN "MADONNA" AND "THE DAY AFTER" ARE BLOODY LOOKALIKES. IT'S THE SAME MODEL, I SWEAR!

HMM... A LITTLE SPECULATIVE, MAYBE?

YOU MEAN À LA TOR BOMANN*? HUH! NO, THIS IS SERIOUS! FIRST THEY PROBABLY GOT DRUNK; HE DRANK LIKE CRAZY THEN, YA KNOW.

* TOR BOMANN-LARSEN: LAUNCHED HIS BIOGRAPHY ON NORWEGIAN ROYALTY IN 2004, WITH AN UNFOUNDED THEORY ABOUT KING OLAV V'S PATERNITY, BASED ON CIRCUMSTANTIAL EVIDENCE AND "EVIDENCE" BASED ON A PHOTO.

THEN THEY PROBABLY HAD SEX. ALL THE MODELS WERE WHORES IN THOSE DAYS.

AND JUST AS HE WAS COMING, HE HAD A FLASHBACK TO THE TIME HE HAD SEX WITH MILLIE THAULOW*.

* SEE PAGE 57.

AND THAT'S HOW HE GOT THE IDEA FOR "MADONNA"; IT'S A DEPICTION OF ORGASM AND CONCEPTION, YA SEE.

AFTER THAT THEY MUST'VE SNOOZED, AND THE DAY AFTER HE GOT THE IDEA FOR "THE DAY AFTER".

FINALLY HE SLAPPED A HALO ON MADONNA, AND PRESTO, HE HAD A SYMBOLIST WHORE-AND-MADONNA PAINTING AND AN IMPRESSIONIST BOHEMIAN PAINTING. A SURE WINNER IN TWO OF THE HIPPEST ART MOVEMENTS OF THE TIME.

CHEERS, PROFESSOR KVERNELAND!

NOTE: "MADONNA" WAS PAINTED IN 1893, "THE DAY AFTER" IN 1894...

AND IT ISN'T A COINCIDENCE THAT SHE'S A BRUNETTE, CAUSE HE LIKED THEM BEST, EVEN THOUGH HE ALLOWED HIMSELF TO BE SEDUCED BY REDHEADS.

OH, JEEEZ! WHAT A MASOCHIST.

"HATE", 1907.

EDVARD MUNCH:
MY MISFORTUNE WAS TO HAVE MET WOMEN WITH BLONDE OR FLAMING RED TUFTS OF HAIR ON ELONGATED SKULLS — AND EYES LIKE BLUEBERRIES ON PINS —

TULLA LARSEN, WHOM HE ALMOST MARRIED IN 1899.

HAD I FOUND THE MIRROR IMAGE OF MY SOUL — IN TWO CHARCOAL-BLACK EYES —

WHAT KIND OF PAINTER WOULD I HAVE BECOME —

EVA MUDOCCI, WHOM HE FELL IN LOVE WITH, 1903.

ADOLF PAUL:
I WENT ONE DAY TO VISIT HIM IN BERLIN.

HE WAS PAINTING... A MODEL... WITH FLAMING RED HAIR THAT SPILLED DOWN HER BODY LIKE BLOOD.

KNEEL DOWN IN FRONT OF HER!

LEAN YOUR HEAD INTO HER GROIN!

SHE LEANED DOWN OVER ME,

AND PRESSED HER LIPS AGAINST MY NECK AS HER HAIR FELL DOWN AND STROKED ME.

MUNCH CONTINUED TO PAINT AND IN NO TIME HE HAD PAINTED HIS "VAMPIRE", WHICH HE LATER OFTEN REPEATED IN WOODCUTS AND LITHOGRAPHS.

AUGUST STRINDBERG COMMENTED ON THE MOTIF, WHICH HE CALLED "RED HAIR":

A SHOWER OF GOLD SPILLS OVER THE MISERABLE MAN, WHO KNEELING IN FRONT OF HIS WORST HALF BEGS FOR A MERCIFUL DEMISE BY NEEDLES.

A SHOWER OF BLOOD SPILLS OVER THE INSANE MAN, WHO SEEKS CALAMITY, THAT DIVINE CALAMITY WHICH IS TO BE LOVED, OR RATHER TO LOVE

"LOVE AND PAIN" WAS THE MOTIF'S FIRST TITLE. THE TITLE "VAMPIRE" IS MOST LIKELY ATTRIBUTABLE TO STANISLAW PRZYBYSZEWSKI*.

PRZYBYSZEWSKI BECAME ACQUAINTED WITH MUNCH AND HIS ART IN DECEMBER.

*POLISH AUTHOR (1867–1927) WHO PUBLISHED THE FIRST BOOK ON MUNCH IN 1894, "THE WORKS OF EDVARD MUNCH".

AT LAST, AN ARTIST WHO INTUITIVELY TURNED HIS BACK ON THAT DESPICABLE REALISM, AN IDEOLOGUE WHO CREATED HIS WORKS BASED ON VISION, VOM INNEN HERAUS!*

* FROM THE INSIDE OUT!

LIKE STRINDBERG AND SO MANY OTHERS AT THE TIME, PRZYBYSZEWSKI WAS A MYSTIC PREOCCUPIED WITH OCCULT PHENOMENA, WHO CULTIVATED DEMONIC AND MACABRE FORCES AND CONSIDERED HIMSELF A "SATANIST".

A PROSTRATE MAN AND A VAMPIRE BITING HIS NECK.

THE MAN REELS DEEPER AND DEEPER INTO THE ABYSS, UNRESISTING, POWERLESS AND REJOICING AT THE PROSPECT OF BEING ABLE TO TUMBLE AS PASSIVELY AS A STONE.

AND YET HE CANNOT ESCAPE THE VAMPIRE, NOR THE PAIN,

AND THE WOMAN WILL BE THERE FOR ALL ETERNITY BITING HIM WITH A THOUSAND SERPENT TONGUES, WITH A THOUSAND VENOMOUS FANGS.

THERE ARE MOMENTS WHEN THE WOMAN CEASES TO BE THE VAMPIRE.

IN GIVING HERSELF ABSOLUTELY TO A MAN THE DIRT IS WASHED OFF AND HER LUST TO DESTROY AND HER SHAME DISAPPEAR WITHOUT A TRACE,

HER FACE SHINES IN CONCEPTION'S TERRIFYING BEAUTY.

THERE IS A MOMENT IN THE WOMAN'S SOUL WHEN SHE FORGETS HERSELF AND EVERYTHING AROUND HER AND TRANSFORMS HERSELF INTO A FORMLESS, TIMELESS AND DIMENSIONLESS CREATURE,

A MOMENT WHEN SHE CONCEIVES IN VIRGINITY: "MADONNA".

AROUND 1933, MUNCH FORMULATED IT AS FOLLOWS:

THE TITLE "VAMPIRE" IS ACTUALLY WHAT GIVES THE PICTURE A LITERARY QUALITY, WHEN IN REALITY IT IS SIMPLY A WOMAN KISSING A MAN ON THE NECK.

HERMANN SCHLITTGEN*:
I GOT TO KNOW HIM {MUNCH}. A DISTINGUISHED, CULTIVATED PERSON WITH A MODEST APPEARANCE AND A STRONG CHARACTER, SOMEWHAT ADDICTED TO DRINK.

✳ GERMAN CARICATURIST AND PAINTER.

HE WAS PERPETUALLY PENNILESS.

YES, WELL, YOU'RE ALWAYS TELLING ME THAT YOU'VE RECEIVED OFFERS FOR YOUR PICTURES. WHY DON'T YOU SELL THEM?

MY PRICES ARE TOO HIGH.

HE ALWAYS STAYED IN BOARDING HOUSES AND WAS CONSTANTLY ON THE MOVE; THE LANDLADIES COULD NOT ABIDE HIS PAINTINGS.

THEY WERE SCATTERED AROUND THE ROOM, ON THE SOFA, ON TOP OF THE WARDROBES,

ON ALL THE CHAIRS,

ON THE WASHSTAND,

ON THE STOVE:

HERE A DISTORTED FACE MIGHT STARE AT YOU,

ONE BECAME UNNERVED BY THE CHAOS OF COLOURS.

HE OFTEN PAINTED AT NIGHT WHEN HE RETURNED LATE, IN ORDER TO CAPTURE SOME IMPRESSION OR OTHER.

IF ONE VISITED HIM THE NEXT MORNING, ONE MIGHT STUMBLE ON A PALETTE OR BRUSH AGAINST A FRESHLY PAINTED PICTURE THAT WAS LEFT IN AN IMPOSSIBLE PLACE.

HE WAS AN IMPRACTICAL MAN AND HELPLESS AS A CHILD WHEN IT CAME TO EVERYDAY TASKS.

AUGUST STRINDBERG:
THE FAMOUS CAFÉ "ZUM SCHWARZEN FERKEL" ON THE CORNER OF LINDEN IS THE HABITUAL HAUNT OF ARTISTS AND WRITERS.

A GALLEY FULL OF DAMNED SOULS, IF EVER THERE WAS ONE.

THERE IS NOT ONE AMONG THEM WHO DOES NOT DRAG A BALL AND CHAIN OF HARSH FATE BEHIND THEM; HERE A STORM OF CURSES RAGES, A HAILSTORM OF PROFANITIES.

OFTEN A PASSERBY WILL LINGER IN THE NIGHT.

THROUGH THE WINDOW, WHERE BOTTLES ARE DISPLAYED, THEIR HOWLING AND RAGING CAN BE HEARD IN THE QUIET STREET.

THE BYSTANDER HURRIES ON HIS WAY, SAYING TO HIMSELF:

WHAT A DEN OF CUTTHROATS!

EDVARD MUNCH:
AT THE END TABLE IN THE "SCHWARZEN FERKEL", SURROUNDED BY GERMANS, DANES, SWEDES, FINNS, NORWEGIANS AND RUSSIANS – ROWDILY CELEBRATED

BY THE YOUNG GERMAN POETS – DEHMEL* IN PARTICULAR – WHO CLIMBED ONTO THE TABLE AND CAUSED THE BOTTLES TO TOPPLE – TO SING HIS PRAISE.

* RICHARD DEHMEL (1863–1920), GERMAN POET.

AND THE FIRST READING OF HIS PIECES
 – THE LINES STRUCK LIKE THE THRUSTS OF BLADES
 – WORDS DEFTLY ARTICULATED – NOW LIKE A SWORD,
NOW LIKE A DAGGER –

BEFORE YOU KNEW IT THE AIR FROTHED LIKE THE WINE ON THE TABLE
 – RED HOT WHITE HOT
DRIPPING SWEATING
 – BLAZING –

YOU ROSE UP HOLDING IN YOUR HANDS THE INFERNO AND OFFERED
IT TO US

 – AND LEGENDS
 – PERHAPS THE STRANGEST NOVELS SINCE "CRIME AND PUNISHMENT".

IT BEGAN WITH "THE RED ROOM" FOR US NORWEGIANS – THAT
UNIVERSE CALLED STRINDBERG.

FRIDA STRINDBERG*:
STRINDBERG IN THE "FERKEL" HAS BECOME ONE OF BERLIN'S ATTRACTIONS. YOU HAVE TO FIGHT FOR A SEAT.

WOMEN WILL NOW BE ALLOWED IN THE GROUP.

* BORN UHL, ENGAGED TO STRINDBERG ON 11 APRIL 1893.

WHO ARE THE WOMEN? ARE THEY BEAUTIFUL?

UNTIL NOW THERE HAS ONLY BEEN TALK OF ONE, CHRISTIAN KROHG'S WIFE, AND SHE IS BEAUTIFUL. ONE MORE WAS ANNOUNCED. SHE IS A FRIEND OF THE PAINTER MUNCH.

20 YRS.

43 YRS.

THE TWO OF THEM HAVE BEEN SEEN TOGETHER, BUT HE KEEPS HER HIDDEN LIKE A MISER AND DOES NOT WISH TO BRING HER TO THE "FERKEL", WHERE THE GANG IS DROOLING IN ANTICIPATION OF SEEING HER AND GRUMBLING UNTIL THEY ARE HOARSE.

I UNDERSTAND MR MUNCH VERY WELL.

BUT IT IS FUTILE. YOU HAVE NO IDEA HOW MANY BEAUTIES ARE ATTRACTED BY INQUISITIVENESS AND MY REPUTATION AS A MISOGYNIST.

* ASPASIA (CA. 470-410 AD), LOVER OF PERICLES. ONE OF THE MOST BEAUTIFUL AND CONTROVERSIAL WOMEN OF HER TIME.

AND SHE LIVED UP TO HER NAME. PORTRAITS WERE PAINTED OF HER AND SHE WAS CELEBRATED, BOTH ADMIRED AND MALIGNED.

DAGNY JUEL, BORN JUELL, 1867–1901.

ONE OF MUNCH'S MOST ACCOMPLISHED PORTRAITS OWES ITS EXISTENCE TO HER.

SHE WAS QUITE ORIGINAL FOR HER TIMES, A KIND OF SOLO DANCER, THE ONLY ONE AMONG THEIR CIRCLE OF FRIENDS.

THERE WAS SOMETHING SPELLBINDING AND INTANGIBLE ABOUT HER DANCING, SOMETHING STRANGE AND MAGICAL WHICH MESMERISED HER AUDIENCE.

FRIDA STRINDBERG:
SHE WAS A VIRTUOSO ON BOTH THE PIANO AND THE MALE SOUL, AND NOT ONLY KNEW HOW TO SPEAK, BUT ALSO HOW TO LISTEN.

SHE WAS MILDLY POSSESSIVE, AND STRINDBERG'S ESCAPADES HAD PROVOKED HER FOR A LONG TIME. FROM NOW ON, SHE ONLY SAW HIM AND RUTHLESSLY DROPPED MUNCH.

WHAT HAPPENED BETWEEN DAGNY JUEL AND STRINDBERG IS VEILED IN DARKNESS.

VERSION A (ADOLF PAUL):
FROM HER PLACE AT THE TABLE RESERVED FOR THE REGULARS SHE LISTENED, ENTHRALLED, TO THE TUNES FROM STRINDBERG'S GUITAR, WHICH AWAKENED THE PRIMORDIAL MYSTERIES TO LIFE IN HER SOUL!

ONLY TO FIND THEM FALSE THE FOLLOWING DAY, COMPARED TO THE ARDENT SONG OF A NEW ADMIRER!

STRINDBERG FEARED HER MORE THAN "MRS BLUEBEARD" AND DESPISED HER LIKE THE DEVIL, WHILE HE ALSO LOVED HER DESPITE HIMSELF!

VERSION B (FRIDA STRINDBERG):
BEER, WINE, TODDY, SWEDISH PUNCH, ABSINTHE!

HALF-ANAESTHETISED HE ACCOMPANIED HER HOME!

STRINDBERG KNOWS HOW TO BEHAVE PROPERLY!

HE FOLLOWED HER UP TO HER ROOM.

WHICH WAS NOT AT ALL PROPER...

BUT NOTHING WAS QUITE CLEAR TO HIM NOR WAS HIS MEMORY OF IT...

UNTIL THE MOMENT HE AWOKE FROM HIS STUPOR.

HE SUDDENLY REALISED THAT HE WAS IN A STRANGE, DISHEVELLED ROOM.

HE WAS FILLED WITH A COLD LOATHING.

AND THEN HE CAUGHT SIGHT OF A WOMAN IN A SHAMELESS POSITION NEXT TO HIM.

HE SPRANG UP,

GRABBED HER ROUGHLY BY THE NECK,

PULLED HER OUT OF BED IN HER NIGHTGOWN,

DRAGGED HER OUT OF THE ROOM,

AND SLAMMED AND LOCKED THE DOOR.

HE HAD LIVED IN HOTEL ROOMS SO OFTEN IN RECENT YEARS THAT IT DID NOT OCCUR TO HIM THAT IT WAS NOT HIS OWN ROOM HE HAD PURGED IN THIS WAY.

THE FAMOUS "DR KNEIPPS VINBAR" ON THE CORNER OF TORVBAKK STREET AND MARKVEIEN (IN OSLO) IS KVERNELAND AND FISKE'S HABITUAL HAUNT.

BEER AND AQUAVIT AND THE MENU!

THE SAME, THANKS!

A GALLEY FULL OF DAMNED SOULS, IF EVER THERE WAS ONE.

DID YOU KNOW THAT MUNCH MADE HIS OWN KIND OF AUTOBIOGRAPHICAL COMICS IN THE 1880S?

GEE, ALMOST 100 YEARS BEFORE CRUMB*!

*ROBERT CRUMB (B.1943), PIONEERING AMERICAN CARTOONIST.

YEAH, LISTEN TO THIS: "MUNCH HAD PLANS TO COMBINE PICTURES AND TEXTS EARLY ON. 'THE ILLUSTRATED JOURNAL' SUGGESTS THAT HE MAY HAVE INITIALLY PLANNED A LITERARY PUBLICATION WITH ILLUSTRATIONS SECONDARY TO THE TEXT."**!

AHA! PROTOCOMICS!

** ARNE EGGUM, "EDVARD MUNCH – THE FRIEZE OF LIFE FROM PAINTING TO GRAPHIC ART".

HE WAS INSPIRED BY HANS JÆGER'S BOHEMIAN COMMANDMENT. YOU KNOW, "THOU SHALT WRITE THINE OWN LIFE". THE IDEAS FOR MANY OF THE MOTIFS IN "THE FRIEZE OF LIFE" WERE FIRST DEVELOPED IN "THE ILLUSTRATED JOURNAL".

HE SHOULD'VE SLAPPED ON SOME SPEECH BALLOONS, SWEAT DROPS AND SPIRALS ABOVE THEIR HEADS!

ABSOLUTELY! I'VE USED AT LEAST 18 MUNCH MOTIFS MYSELF TO FILL THE PANELS IN THE FIRST 16 PAGES OF THIS EPISODE. PAINTINGS, DRAWINGS, GRAPHIC WORKS, SKETCHES...

IS THE HARD-ON ON PAGE 57 ALSO MUNCH'S?

YEAH, IT'S BASED ON AN ETCHING FROM 1914, "THE CAT". BUT WITH A LITTLE ADDITION: I THOUGHT, YA KNOW, YOUNG MAN + NAKED LADY = ERECTION.

AHA!

THE FAT WHORES ON PAGE 65 AND THE DETAIL ON PAGE 82 ARE "ROSE AND AMELIE",* RIGHT? THEY LOOK SO JAPANESE. WHAT A SICK PICTURE.

"THE DUMMY": LOOSE-LEAF SKETCHES AND FINISHED PAGES FOR PART 2.

✱ "ROSE AND AMELIE", OIL ON CANVAS, 1893.

OFTEN A PASSERBY WILL LINGER IN THE NIGHT.

BACK THEN, VISITING A WHOREHOUSE WAS STANDARD PRACTICE. BESIDES, WHORES WERE THE ONLY ONES WHO WOULD MODEL NAKED, SO IT WAS SPOT ON FOR MUNCH.

THROUGH THE WINDOW, WHERE BOTTLES ARE DISPLAYED, THEIR HOWLING AND RAGING CAN BE HEARD IN THE QUIET STREET.

AT A WHOREHOUSE, YOU COULD PAINT, DRINK AND FUCK AROUND THE CLOCK! MUNCH WAS EVEN THERE ON CHRISTMAS EVE!!

ISN'T CHRISTMAS WITHOUT A VISIT TO THE WHOREHOUSE!

"Christmas Eve at a brothel"
(Drawing by Munch)

MERRY CHRISTMAS, WHORES!

THE BYSTANDER HURRIES ON HER WAY, SAYING TO HERSELF:

WHAT A DEN OF CUTTHROATS!

ADOLF PAUL: WE HAD ARRANGED A "BIG NIGHT AT THE FERKEL".

| EDVARD MUNCH | CHRISTIAN KROHG | ADOLF PAUL | AUGUST STRINDBERG | ODA KROHG | GUNNAR HEIBERG* | HOLGER DRACHMANN** |

* GUNNAR HEIBERG (1857–1929), NORWEGIAN AUTHOR.   ** HOLGER DRACHMANN (1846–1908), DANISH AUTHOR.

MUNCH SAT IN A CORNER DREAMING OF ASPASIA'S BETRAYAL, NOW AND THEN INTERRUPTED BY HEIBERG'S SARCASTIC REMARKS.

THAT EVENING, ASPASIA HAD SETTLED UPON ANOTHER ESTABLISHMENT WITH HER TWO ARMOUR-BEARERS LIDFORSS*** AND PRZYBYSZEWSKI, TO THE GREAT DISMAY OF STRINDBERG, WHO IMMEDIATELY ASSUMED THAT SHE WAS HATCHING PLANS TO RETALIATE AGAINST HIM FOR HIS RECENT ENGAGEMENT!

*** BENGT LIDFORSS, SWEDISH BOTANIST AND FRIEND OF STRINDBERG.

HE EXPECTED THE WORST FROM HIS TWO FRIENDS, WHO WERE HER SERVILE ATTENDANTS AND FROM WHOM SHE COULD ATTAIN ANYTHING SHE WISHED.

MUNCH BEGAN TO REACT TO HEIBERG'S OUTBURSTS, BUT, ABSENT-MINDED AS ALWAYS, HE DIRECTED HIS COUNTERBLOWS AT THE WRONG PERSON, WHICH DID NOT EXACTLY IMPROVE THE MOOD OF THE OBJECT OF HIS RAGE.

IN ORDER TO PUT AN END TO THE BICKERING, STRINDBERG WISHED TO PERFORM A SONG, BUT FORGOT THE LYRICS

AND RELINQUISHED THE GUITAR TO MRS KROHG, WHO PROPOSED TO SING A DIFFERENT SONG.

FOR THAT REASON SHE BEGAN TO RETUNE THE GUITAR, WHICH WAS AN AFFRONT TO STRINDBERG'S DIGNITY, AS HIS INSTRUMENT HAD ITS OWN UNIQUE AND THEREFORE SACRED TONE!

THEN THEY ARGUED AT SUCH LENGTH ABOUT THIS THAT THE MOOD WAS DESTROYED.

DRACHMANN THEN ROSE AND BEGAN TO SPEAK.

AHEM!

LET US DRINK A TOAST TO OUR FRIEND STRINDBERG, WHOSE MISOGYNY HAS GONE BANKRUPT AND FORCED HIM TO HIS KNEE BEFORE THE MASTERPIECE OF CREATION, WOMAN!

FOR I AM NOT LIKE YOU, MRS KROHG, WHO SITS THERE DESPISING HIM IN SILENCE FOR ALL THE TERRIBLE THINGS HE HAS WRITTEN ABOUT THE WOMEN WHO WERE QUITE DESERVING OF IT!

NOR AM I LIKE KROGH, WHO HAS PAINTED STRINDBERG, AND MANAGED TO CREATE A PICTURE THAT TELLS US NOTHING ABOUT KROHG AND EVEN LESS ABOUT STRINDBERG, AND WHO BLAMES HIS MODEL FOR IT!

AND I AM NOT LIKE MUNCH, WHO ARRIVED HERE IN BERLIN AND MADE A SCANDAL AND A SUCCESS, AND IS NOW SO FILLED WITH IT THAT FOR HIS DIGNITY'S SAKE HE CAN NO LONGER BE HAPPY!

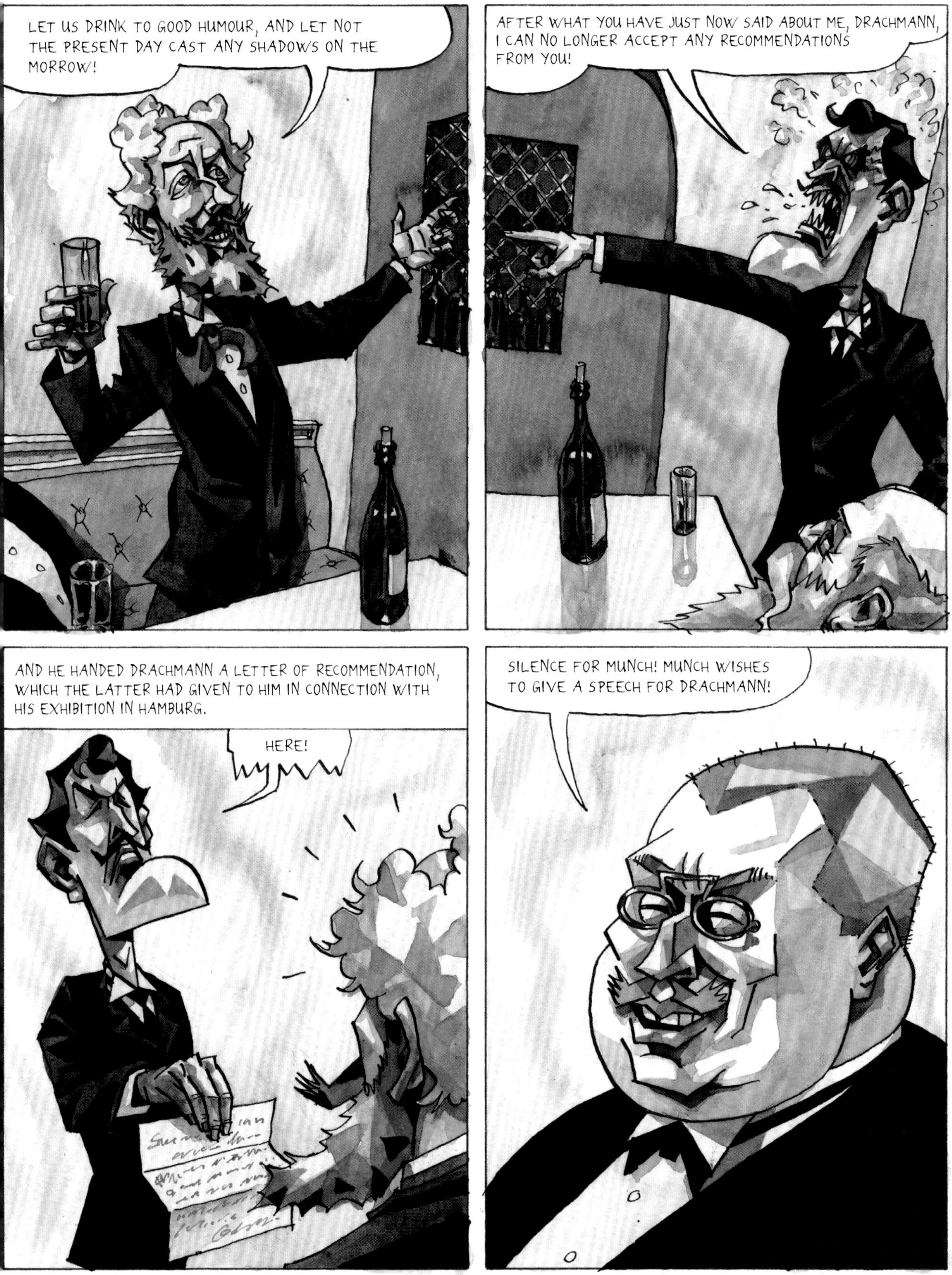
LET US DRINK TO GOOD HUMOUR, AND LET NOT THE PRESENT DAY CAST ANY SHADOWS ON THE MORROW!
AFTER WHAT YOU HAVE JUST NOW SAID ABOUT ME, DRACHMANN, I CAN NO LONGER ACCEPT ANY RECOMMENDATIONS FROM YOU!
AND HE HANDED DRACHMANN A LETTER OF RECOMMENDATION, WHICH THE LATTER HAD GIVEN TO HIM IN CONNECTION WITH HIS EXHIBITION IN HAMBURG.
HERE!
SILENCE FOR MUNCH! MUNCH WISHES TO GIVE A SPEECH FOR DRACHMANN!

THE ONLY WAY I CAN GIVE SUCH A SPEECH IS BY LEAVING!

!!

WHEREUPON KROGH, IN HIS CAPACITY AS AN OLDER COLLEAGUE AND FELLOW COUNTRYMAN, FELT CALLED UPON TO INFORM MUNCH HOW HE SHOULD BEHAVE AMONG CIVILISED PEOPLE.

MUNCH CALLED HIM "A DESPICABLE CLICHÉ OF A HUMAN BEING" AND GRABBED HIS HAT AND LEFT.

YOU ARE RIGHT, MUNCH! IF YOU HAD NOT GIVEN THAT SPEECH, THEN I WOULD HAVE!

WHEREUPON THE QUARREL BROKE OUT ANEW, THIS TIME WITH STRINDBERG AS THE SCAPEGOAT.

THE FRIENDSHIP BETWEEN STRINDBERG AND MUNCH WAS NOT ONLY BUILT UPON COMMON INTERESTS IN LITERATURE, PSYCHOLOGY, ETC, BUT ALSO ON VISUAL ART. FOR STRINDBERG, PAINTING WAS NOT MERELY A HOBBY.

HIS SPONTANEOUS AND TACHISTE* PAINTERLY STYLE AND COURBET-INSPIRED SEASCAPES WERE, ASIDE FROM MUNCH'S WORKS, PERHAPS THE MOST AVANT-GARDE ARTWORKS IN BERLIN.

*TACHISME: ABSTRACT MODERNIST STYLE OF PAINTING FROM THE 1950S.

"SNOWSTORM ON THE SEA", OIL ON CARDBOARD, 1894.

AS A VISUAL ARTIST, STRINDBERG APPEARS TO HAVE BEEN INSPIRED BY SPIRITISM, WHERE THE MEDIUM PLAYS A ROLE AS AN UNWITTING MESSENGER OF AN ALTERNATE REALITY.

"THE SOLITARY TOADSTOOL", OIL ON PAPER MOUNTED ON CANVAS, 1893.

THE ACCIDENTAL DETAILS THAT APPEARED IN A WORK OF ART DURING THE CREATIVE PROCESS SHOULD BE RETAINED, AS THIS FORM OF EXPRESSION MIGHT HAVE FAR GREATER IMPORTANCE THAN WHAT WAS DELIBERATELY PLANNED.

DESPITE DIFFERENCES IN THEIR PERCEPTION OF NATURE, STRINDBERG AND MUNCH CONCURRED COMPLETELY WHEN IT CAME TO CULTIVATING A SPONTANEOUS EXPRESSION, AND IN THEIR APPRECIATION OF THE ACCIDENTAL EFFECTS THAT AROSE DURING THE EXECUTION OF AN ARTWORK.

MUNCH WAS THE VERY FIRST PAINTER TO EXPERIMENT WITH SPRAYING PAINT DIRECTLY ONTO THE CANVAS AND ALLOWING THE COLOURS TO RUN IN ORDER TO ACHIEVE VERY SPECIAL EFFECTS.

"STANISLAW PRZYBYSZEWSKI", TEMPERA ON BOARD, PARTIALLY SPRAYED, 1893/95.

IT IS HARD TO BELIEVE THE EXPLOSION OF CREATIVITY THAT CHARACTERISED MUNCH'S WORK DURING THESE BERLIN YEARS. THE WORKS VIRTUALLY FLOWED FROM HIS HAND: DRAWINGS, PASTELS, WATERCOLOURS AND PAINTINGS, ONE AFTER THE OTHER, AS THOUGH HE WORKED IN A FEVERISH RAPTURE.

LETTER FROM EDVARD MUNCH TO KAREN BJØLSTAD:

Dear Aunt! There won't be much time for writing now – I have had so much to do – I am not earning as much money as hoped for, some unfortunate incident always gets in the way – the pictures are presently on their way to Breslau and Dresden and later to Munich so I should be getting something – I am working exceptionally well by the way, and will be able to have a new exhibition ready by autumn –

Dear Aunt — I made a very adventurous trip to Dresden, Leipzig, Magdeburg and Hamburg and made arrangements with art dealers in these places so I hope to be able to earn at least something — my pictures will be exhibited in all of these cities —

You must not pay heed to the nasty reviews which Aftenposten naturally picks out — I will make sure to send you some good ones — I was quite fortunate in Copenhagen — I visited a paper manufacturer and offered them some of my pictures for reproductions — for 4 pictures, I received 100 kroner on the spot and shall have an additional 100 kroner in a month.

LETTER TO PETER ANDREAS MUNCH, EDVARD MUNCH'S YOUNGER BROTHER:

Dear Andreas! I am extremely busy painting now — the two exhibitions I have in Frankfurt and Hamburg have brought me a bit of change — in Hamburg people were so enraged by my pictures that I had to leave the city in great haste followed by a shower of abuse — I didn't dare to show up at the exhibition —

BASED ON MUNCH'S EXHIBITION AND THE PICTURES HE HAD IN HIS STUDIO, STANISLAW PRZYBYSZEWSKI PUBLISHED THE FIRST BOOK ON MUNCH, "THE WORKS OF EDVARD MUNCH, FOUR CONTRIBUTIONS", COMPOSED OF IN-DEPTH ANALYSES WRITTEN BY PRZYBYSZEWSKI, FRANZ SERVAES*, WILLY PASTOR** AND JULIUS MEIER-GRAEFE***.

* FRANZ SERVAES (1862–1947), GERMAN AUTHOR. ** WILLY PASTOR (1867–1933), GERMAN AUTHOR AND JOURNALIST.
*** JULIUS MEIER-GRAEFE (1867–1935), GERMAN ART CRITIC.

WHAT THE FOUR AUTHORS APPEAR TO CONCUR UPON IS THAT MUNCH WAS A UNIQUE AND INSIGHTFUL PSYCHOLOGIST WHO HAD A DEEP UNDERSTANDING OF THE LIFE OF THE SOUL.

THAT MUNCH'S VISUAL IMAGERY HAD A PARTICULARLY CLOSE AND INTIMATE RELATIONSHIP TO LITERATURE WAS OFTEN POINTED OUT DURING HIS TIME.

ALMOST EVERYTHING THAT YOU SEE HAS ITS ORIGIN IN MANUSCRIPT FORM. A GREAT PORTION OF IT I WROTE DOWN TEN YEARS AGO.

HE WAS EVENTUALLY PERCEIVED AS A SOLITARY, EGOCENTRIC ARTIST PERSONA WHO KEPT A VIGILANT AND IRONIC DISTANCE FROM HIS SURROUNDINGS, EVEN WHEN HE FELL INTO THE "FERKEL" MILIEU'S DIABOLICAL PURSUIT OF INEBRIATION AND EROTIC LICENTIOUSNESS.

STACHU {STANISLAW PRZYBYSZEWSKI} AND DAGNY'S WEDDING ON 18 AUGUST 1893 CAME AS A SURPRISE TO THEIR FRIENDS AND ACQUAINTANCES, PERHAPS EVEN TO THEMSELVES.

WE MARRIED BECAUSE THE CIVIL WEDDING CEREMONY COST ONLY ONE MARK, AND ON THAT PARTICULAR DAY WE HAD ONE MARK COMBINED.

BOTH OF THEM, STACHU AND DAGNY, ENTERTAINED A BOTTOMLESS CONTEMPT FOR ALL KINDS OF ORDER. THEY FOUND THE THOUGHT OF TOMORROW RIDICULOUS AND UNNECESSARY.

IN THE SPRING, DAGNY PAWNED HER WINTER CLOTHES. SHE REDEEMED THEM IN THE AUTUMN, WHEN SHE LEFT HER SUMMER CLOTHES INSTEAD.

STACHU WAS A SERIOUS ALCOHOLIC. HIS OBSESSIONS WITH SATANISM, SEX AND DRINK DARKENED THEIR ENVIRONMENT.

EDVARD MUNCH: I STILL SEE HIM AS HE SAT THERE IN THE CORNER OF THE SOFA OF THAT LITTLE WINE HOUSE IN BERLIN, SLOUCHED AND WITH FEVERISH EYES.

THEN HE COULD SUDDENLY JUMP UP IN ECSTASY, AND RUN OVER TO THE PIANO SO FAST THAT HE SEEMED TO BE FOLLOWING AN INNER VOICE CALLING TO HIM.

AND IN THE DEATHLY QUIET FOLLOWING THE FIRST CHORD, CHOPIN'S IMMORTAL MUSIC SOUNDED THROUGH THE NARROW ROOM AND SUDDENLY CHANGED IT TO A RADIANT CONCERT HALL, A CONCERT HALL OF ART.

MEIER-GRAEFE: A RED KEROSENE LAMP BURNED IN LOUISENSTRASSE, IN A ROOM ON THE FIRST FLOOR, UNTIL THE EARLY MORNING HOUR... HERE LIVED THE PRZYBYSZEWSKI COUPLE... HE WAS A POLE, WHO WROTE HIS AUDACIOUS LITERARY WORKS IN GERMAN AND SUFFERED FROM HALLUCINATIONS. HE WAS CALLED STACHU...
THE COUNTRY IN THE WEST, HUYSMANS'* AND ROPS'** PARIS, PROVIDED THE BACKGROUND FOR STACHU'S DESCRIPTIONS OF PATHOLOGICAL EROTICISM. PROMISCUOUS FOREIGN WORDS WITH MURKY SIGNIFICANCE EVOKED AN ATMOSPHERE OF SATANISM.

* JORIS-KARL HUYSMANS (1848–1907), FRENCH WRITER. ** FÈLICIEN ROPS (1833–1898), BELGIAN GRAPHIC ARTIST.

SHE WAS CALLED DUCHA {POLISH FOR SPIRIT, SOUL} AND DRANK ABSINTHE BY THE LITRE WITHOUT BECOMING INTOXICATED...

HE PLAYED CHOPIN, OUT OF TUNE AND WITH FANTASTIC RHYTHM.

ONE OF THEM DANCED WITH DUCHA AND THE TWO SITTING AT THE TABLE LOOKED ON, ONE OF THEM WAS MUNCH, THE OTHER AS A RULE STRINDBERG. THE FOUR MEN WERE ALL IN LOVE WITH DUCHA, EACH IN THEIR OWN WAY, BUT DID NOT LET IT SHOW.

MEIER-GRAEFE

STRINDBERG DISCUSSED CHEMISTRY. MUNCH SAID NOTHING.

DUCHA HAD AN ENTICING WORD FOR EVERY ONE OF THEM, DREW THEM CLOSE TO HER ONLY TO TURN THEM AWAY AGAIN.

DURING THE DANCE, HER LONG, CLOSE-FITTING OUTFIT TURNED INTO AN ELECTRIFYING LINE, WHICH THE POOR CHAP EXPERIENCED IN SILENT PAIN ONCE SHE HAD DISCARDED HIM.

I DON'T KNOW HOW MY NERVES TOLERATED IT. I SAT THERE AT THE TABLE AND COULD NEVER BRING MYSELF TO SAY A WORD. STRINDBERG TALKED.

THE WHOLE TIME, I WAS THINKING:

DOESN'T THAT HUSBAND OF HERS UNDERSTAND ANYTHING? FIRST HE WILL TURN GREEN AND THEN HE WILL BECOME ANGRY.

MUNCH PAINTED THE HUSBAND GREEN. IT SHOULD HAVE BEEN HIMSELF OR STRINDBERG.

TOP: "JEALOUSY", OIL ON CANVAS, 1895. CENTRE: "JEALOUSY I", LITHOGRAPH, 1896.
BOTTOM: "JEALOUSY II", LITHOGRAPH, HAND-COLOURED, 1896.

LETTER FROM STRINDBERG TO ADOLF PAUL:

If the Pole [Przybyszewski] hates me because I had his Aspasia before she knew him, I can understand, but on the other hand I cannot base my sexual intercourses on all of his upcoming marriages!

The fact that he married her was a mere formality, a lad is a lad, a whore is a whore, married or not.

LETTER FROM PRZYBYSZEWSKI TO ADOLF PAUL:

She has been maligned in the most ignoble manner. Much of it is generally true, and I know about all of her former liaisons.

But what does that have to do with me? What do I care if a picture that I love has previously hung on a grimy wall in a pub?

Brother Paul,
The Pole is unhappy because Aspasia is presently only keeping company with Munch!! At the "Ferkel"? In other words, it ends as it began.

L. referred to the Pole's desperate attempts at coitus in second-class taxis,

and his revulsion in the face of Aspasia's own attempts at seduction with advances and by extinguishing the lights

and informed me rather open-mindedly of her decision to become a tart on Karstrasse.

117

SKOPPUM STATION, VESTFOLD COUNTY, 22 SEPTEMBER 2007.

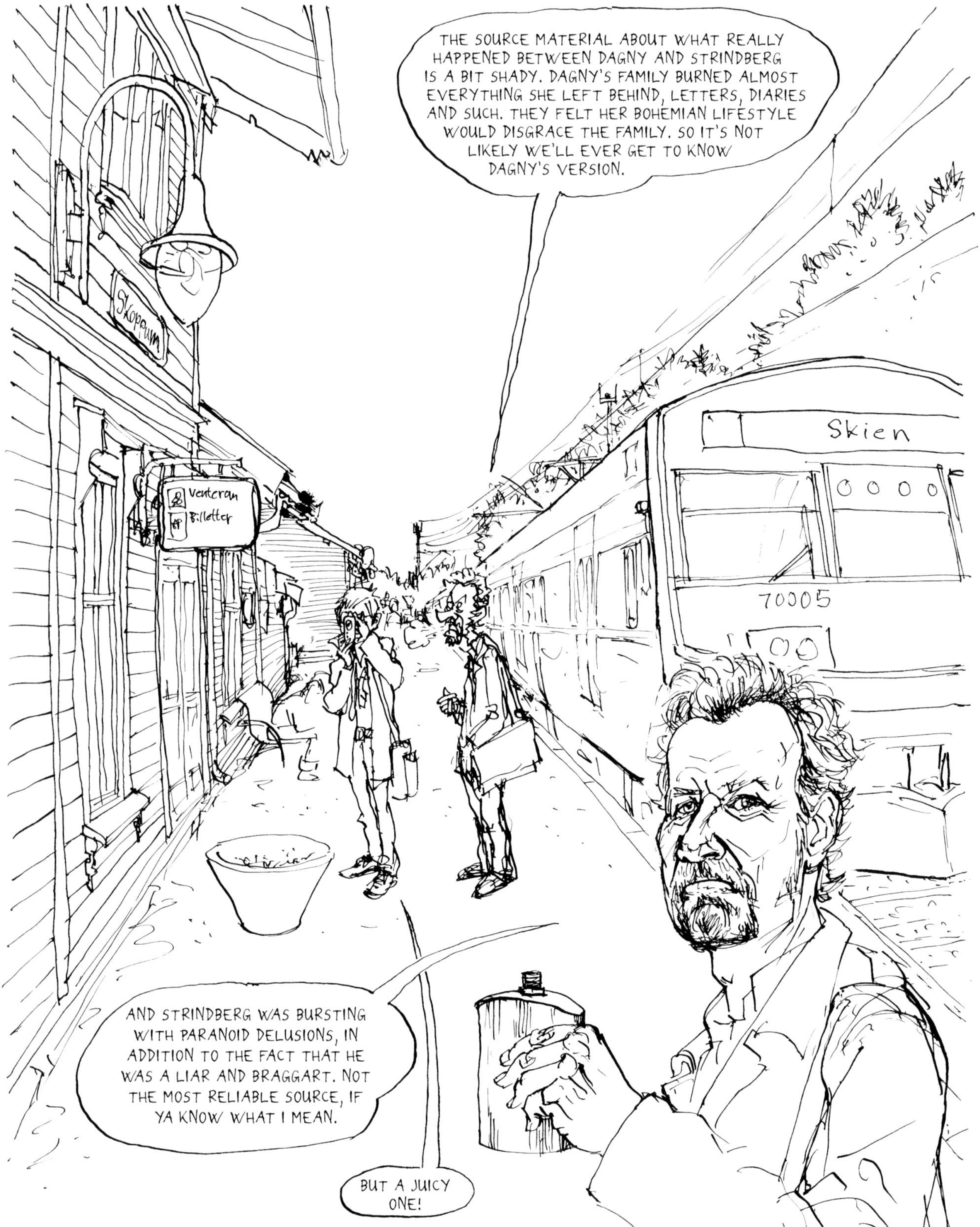

ABSOLUTELY. IN OLOF LAGERCRANTZ'S* STRINDBERG BIOGRAPHY, IT SAYS:

"HE CLAIMS THAT SHE THREW HERSELF AT HIM WITHOUT 'THE ANTICIPATED COYNESS' AND THAT HE WAS SEIZED BY AN AVERSION TO HER BODY."

AND FURTHER:

"...THAT DAGNY JUEL WAS HIS LOVER FOR THREE WEEKS AND THEREAFTER, UNDER UNCOUTH AND HUMILIATING CIRCUMSTANCES, HE HANDED HER OVER TO SCHLEICH, ALTERNATIVELY LIDFORSS."

TYPICAL STRINDBERG.

YEAH, BUT HE OBVIOUSLY COULDN'T GET HER OUT OF HIS HEAD; CHECK OUT WHAT HIS FIANCÉE FRIDA WROTE:

* OLOF LAGERCRANTZ (1911-2002), SWEDISH AUTHOR.

FRIDA STRINDBERG:
WE WERE HAVING A SIESTA IN HIS ROOM AT THE LINDEN HOTEL. HE HAD MADE TEA AND WAS NOW PREPARING SANDWICHES IN THE SWEDISH MANNER, A PLEASED AND PROUD HOST.

ALL AT ONCE, FOOTSTEPS COULD BE HEARD, AND THE DOOR WAS OPENED ABRUPTLY BY AN INVISIBLE HAND.

AND NOW I AM REMINDED OF STRINDBERG'S WORDS... "THE MOST MODERN TYPE, DELICATE AND REFINED, MORE SPIRITUALLY SEDUCTIVE THAN PHYSICALLY. A VAMPIRE OF THE SOUL WITH A YEARNING FOR SOMETHING NOBLER."

HE SMILED AND TURNED AROUND –

DO YOU KNOW WHO THAT WAS?

NOW I HAVE NO DOUBT! WHAT DID ASPASIA WANT?

TO SEE YOU. TO SEE STRINDBERG'S FIANCÉE! NOW THAT SHE HAS SEEN YOU, SHE WILL HAVE REVENGE!

BUT SHE LOOKED COMPLETELY INDIFFERENT.

SHE IS NOT INDIFFERENT. THAT IS PRECISELY THE PROBLEM. THE SERPENT ALSO REMAINS COLD. THAT DOESN'T CHANGE THE FACT THAT ITS BITE IS LETHAL!

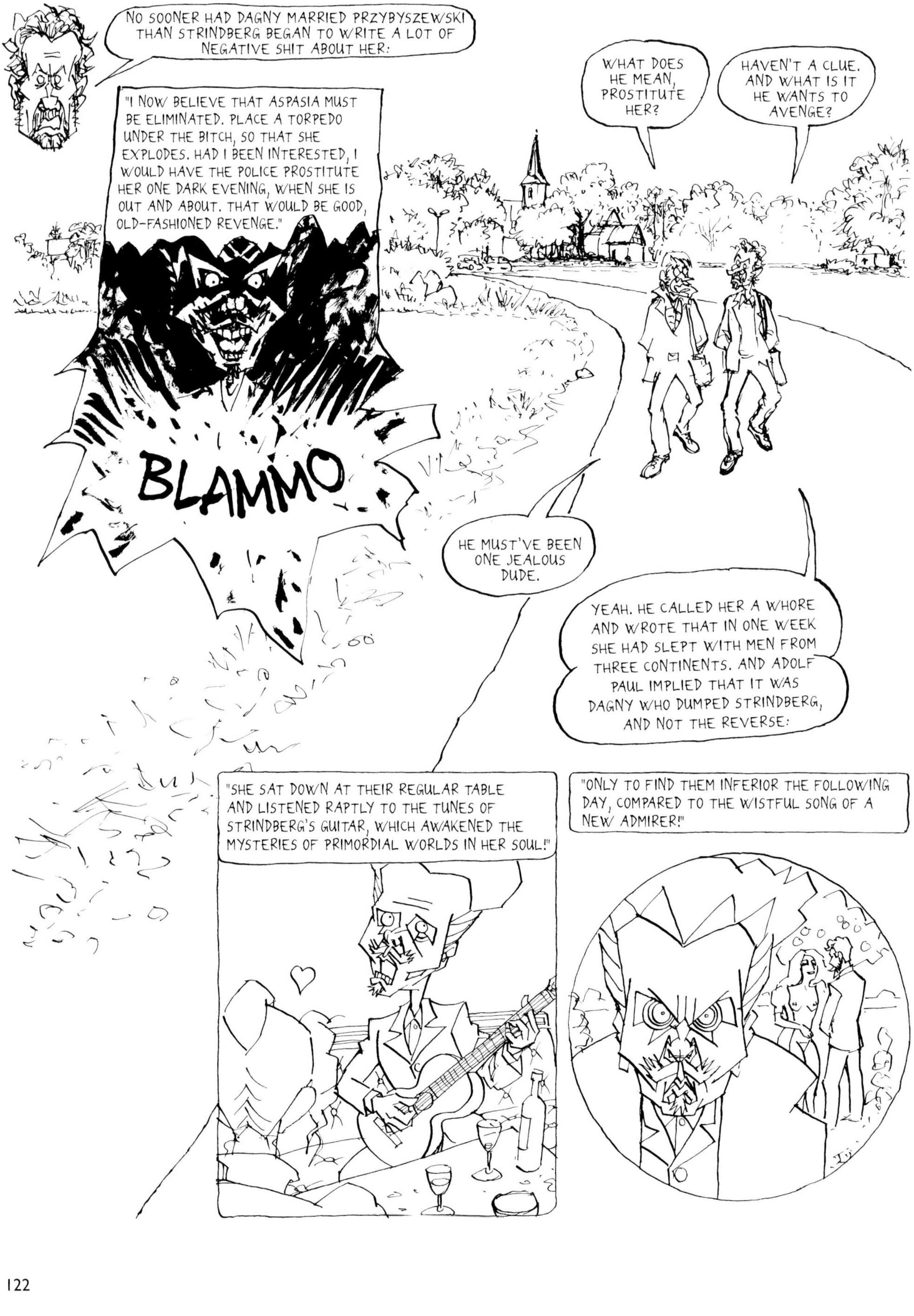
NO SOONER HAD DAGNY MARRIED PRZYBYSZEWSKI THAN STRINDBERG BEGAN TO WRITE A LOT OF NEGATIVE SHIT ABOUT HER:
"I NOW BELIEVE THAT ASPASIA MUST BE ELIMINATED. PLACE A TORPEDO UNDER THE BITCH, SO THAT SHE EXPLODES. HAD I BEEN INTERESTED, I WOULD HAVE THE POLICE PROSTITUTE HER ONE DARK EVENING, WHEN SHE IS OUT AND ABOUT. THAT WOULD BE GOOD, OLD-FASHIONED REVENGE."
BLAMMO
WHAT DOES HE MEAN, PROSTITUTE HER?
HAVEN'T A CLUE. AND WHAT IS IT HE WANTS TO AVENGE?
HE MUST'VE BEEN ONE JEALOUS DUDE.
YEAH. HE CALLED HER A WHORE AND WROTE THAT IN ONE WEEK SHE HAD SLEPT WITH MEN FROM THREE CONTINENTS. AND ADOLF PAUL IMPLIED THAT IT WAS DAGNY WHO DUMPED STRINDBERG, AND NOT THE REVERSE:
"SHE SAT DOWN AT THEIR REGULAR TABLE AND LISTENED RAPTLY TO THE TUNES OF STRINDBERG'S GUITAR, WHICH AWAKENED THE MYSTERIES OF PRIMORDIAL WORLDS IN HER SOUL!"
"ONLY TO FIND THEM INFERIOR THE FOLLOWING DAY, COMPARED TO THE WISTFUL SONG OF A NEW ADMIRER!"

OLOF LAGERCRANTZ:
"ACCORDING TO A NORWEGIAN RUMOUR, SHE SPURNED HIM, SAYING THAT HE WAS TOO OLD FOR HER AND MAKING FUN OF HIS CORPULENCE."

I HAVEN'T HEARD THAT GOSSIP BEFORE!

ME NEITHER. BUT WHY THE HELL WAS STRINDBERG SO JEALOUS? HE WAS NEWLY MARRIED AT THAT TIME!

EVEN THOUGH STRINDBERG WAS HAPPILY MARRIED, HE WAS NEVER COMPLETELY HAPPY UNTIL HE HAD DESTROYED THE LIFE OF HIS EX.

APROPOS NEWLY MARRIED, FRIDA WROTE ABOUT THEIR WEDDING AND THEIR WEDDING NIGHT:

2 MAY 1893, HELGOLAND:
AUGUST STRINDBERG AND I WERE BOTH MOVED AND NERVOUS.

DO YOU SWEAR THAT YOU ARE NOT CARRYING ANY CHILD CONCEIVED BY ANOTHER BENEATH YOUR HEART?

WITH INCREDIBLE DIGNITY, AUGUST STRINDBERG RESPONDED TO THE QUESTION, WHICH COULD ONLY APPLY TO ME, SOLEMNLY AND TRUTHFULLY IN GRAMMATICALLY INCORRECT GERMAN:

I SWEAR THAT I AM NOT CARRYING ANY CHILD CONCEIVED BY ANOTHER BENEATH MY HEART!

TEE-HEE!

I SLEPT DISPROPORTIONATELY LATE THE MORNING AFTER OUR WEDDING, IT HAD BEEN AN UNEASY NIGHT. FOR HE HAD AWAKENED SUDDENLY FROM A DREAM AT DAWN,

AND COULD NOT IMMEDIATELY RECALL THAT HE NOW HAD THE LEGITIMATE RIGHT TO BE INTIMATE WITH HIS YOUNG WIFE, AND IN HIS INITIAL CONFUSION SOUGHT TO STRANGLE THE INTRUDER HE MISTOOK ME FOR.

HE MIGHT NEARLY HAVE SUCCEEDED —

WHEN A FAMILIAR NOTE IN MY PROTESTING VOICE BROUGHT HIM TO HIS SENSES.

ALTHOUGH HE SOUGHT TO REASSURE ME BY TELLING ME THAT THE ATTACK DID NOT CONCERN ME BUT, PRESUMABLY OUT OF HABIT, HIS FIRST WIFE,

I COULD NOT FALL ASLEEP AGAIN FOR A WHILE. I WRESTLED WITH DISTURBING THOUGHTS.

DURING THIS PERIOD, MUNCH ALSO MET THE NORWEGIAN SCULPTOR GUSTAV VIGELAND IN BERLIN. THEY LIVED TOGETHER FOR A WHILE IN A LOFT.

WE WERE BOTH POOR AND SHARED EVERYTHING, EVEN A GIRLFRIEND.

ONE EVENING I TOOK HER OUT, ALTHOUGH IT WAS ACTUALLY VIGELAND'S TURN.

WHEN I CAME HOME AND WAS ON MY WAY UPSTAIRS, VIGELAND STOOD ON TOP OF THE LANDING.

WHEN HE SAW ME, HE RAN INTO HIS ROOM TO FETCH A BUST OF ME THAT HE HAD JUST FINISHED.

HE THREW IT AT ME.

IT BARELY MISSED.

I BECAME SO FRIGHTENED THAT I RAN OUT AND JUMPED ONTO A TRAIN.

I DON'T THINK MUCH OF VIGELAND'S ART. FIRST HE STOLE FROM RODIN, THEN FROM MAILLOL AND ME, BUT THAT BUST HE THREW AT ME WAS GOOD. PERHAPS THE BEST THING HE EVER MADE.

DAMN FEMININE INTRIGUE.

JENS THIIS: WE RECEIVED AN INVITATION FROM RICHARD DEHMEL, WHO HAD A VILLA IN PANKOW, A RURAL SUBURB OF BERLIN, AT THE TIME.

IT BECAME A FIRST-CLASS "ARTISTS EVENING" THAT LASTED 24 HOURS AT LEAST, I BELIEVE LONGER.

MUNCH SPOKE EXTEMPORANEOUSLY WITH HIS DISJOINTED AND STIRRING PARADOXES.

OBSTFELDER, WHO OFTEN CARRIED HIS VIOLIN WITH HIM, PLAYED GRIEG, SVENDSEN AND BACH.

VIGELAND PRESENTED PHOTOGRAPHS OF HIS WORKS, "HELL" AND THE FIRST PASSIONATE GROUPS OF LOVERS, WHICH AROUSED THE GREATEST INTEREST.

IT WAS A DELIGHTFUL EVENING. BUT MADAME DEHMEL WAS A STRICT LADY WHO BELIEVED THAT ALL THINGS SHOULD COME TO AN END.

WE DID NOT THINK SO, AND THE SYMPOSIUM WAS MOVED TO STACHU AND DUCHA'S PLACE.

HERE THE HOST DISAPPEARED FROM OUR MIDST, AND WHEN WE LOOKED FOR HIM, WE FOUND HIM NOT IN HIS BED, BUT OUT IN THE WOODSHED, SITTING STARK NAKED ATOP A STACKED PILE OF BIRCH.

HE SAT THERE ALL BY HIMSELF IMPERSONATING SATAN, THE MADMAN! VIGELAND'S "HELL" HAD IMPRESSED HIM TO THAT EXTENT.

STRANGELY ENOUGH HE DID NOT CATCH PNEUMONIA, FOR IT WAS THE 10TH OF FEBRUARY AND BITTER COLD.

130

Dear Aunt!

I have good faith that the cash situation will soon improve – I have several good friends down here, so I always manage – I spend a considerable amount of time with a promising Polish writer, Przybyszewski, who last year married a daughter of Dr Juell from Kongsvinger – With greetings to everyone

Your devoted Edv. Munch.

Dear Edvard!

I have received your postcard and I thank you for that – it is so good to hear from you. We are living as usual here, are well. Andreas came by on Sunday – Laura has been to church, but Inger and I have stayed at home – I hope that you are well.

Greetings from all of us
Your devoted Karen Bjølstad.

EDVARD MUNCH'S SURVIVING FAMILY

PETER ANDREAS MUNCH, BROTHER

LAURA MUNCH, SISTER

KAREN BJØLSTAD, HIS MOTHER'S SISTER

INGER MARIE MUNCH, SISTER

THE NEXT CHAPTER OF THIS MUNCH BOOK HAS BEEN DIFFICULT TO DO. SORTA LIKE SCRAPING AWAY THE SCABS ON OLD SORES. MUNCH'S FAMILY DIED LIKE FLIES AROUND HIM, JUST LIKE MINE. I'M THE ONLY ONE LEFT NOW, SO IT MAKES SENSE THAT I IDENTIFIED WITH IT A LITTLE.

SOMETIMES IT ALMOST FEELS LIKE MAKING A VICARIOUS AUTOBIOGRAPHY.

EVERY TIME I START DRAWING MUNCH AS A YOUNG MAN, I "SEE" MY BROTHER, TORE. THEY DON'T REALLY RESEMBLE EACH OTHER, ONLY IN MY DRAWN VERSION OF THEM. THERE'S SOMETHING ABOUT THE HAIRSTYLE AND THE NOSE...

I DID DRAWINGS OF TORE IN "SLYNGEL"* AND IN "SLIK HAR DE DET DER"**. HE DIED IN 2000.

① WHAT IF THERE'S A FIRE?

PHOOEY! THERE'RE STONES AROUND THE WHOLE THING!

②

* ① FROM "SLYNGEL" (SCOUNDRELS), 2002. ② FROM "SLIK HAR DE DET DER" (THAT'S HOW THEY'RE LIVING THERE), 1995.

132

* GUDLABADNET: FAVOURITE CHILD (DIALECT).

Dear Aunt,
Thank you for the money orders, which are very welcome
— although I guess I will soon be able to return the loan —
With greetings to everyone, your devoted E. Munch.

Dear Edvard!
You are absolutely too kind to send us money; many
thanks from all of us.
Everyone sends their greetings. Your devoted K. Bjølstad.

Dear Aunt!
You would not believe how the studio looked when I came home — the worst pigsty I have ever seen, I could barely stand to be there —

but after 3 days of contemplation I came upon a splendid idea —

I got hold of a broom — and it helped a lot —

It's quite nice now — I have made a comfortable divan out of a paint crate and a couple of blankets.

Your devoted E. Munch.

Dear Edvard!
I wish that I could clean your room; it is good that it is swept, but it should be washed thoroughly — it is very strange to think that you should be doing that kind of work. The little girls send their warmest greetings!

Your devoted K. Bjølstad.

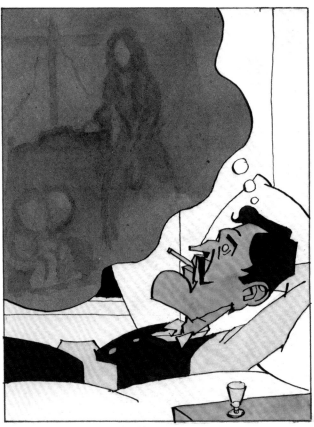

EDVARD MUNCH:
AT THE BOTTOM OF THE LARGE DOUBLE BED THEY SAT PRESSED TOGETHER ON TWO SMALL CHILDREN'S CHAIRS; THE TALL FIGURE OF A WOMAN STOOD NEXT TO THEM, BIG AND DARK AGAINST THE WINDOW.

SHE SAID SHE WOULD BE LEAVING THEM, WAS FORCED TO LEAVE THEM – AND ASKED IF THEY WOULD BE GRIEVED WHEN SHE WAS GONE – AND THEY HAD TO PROMISE HER TO KEEP CLOSE TO JESUS, THEN THEY WOULD MEET HER AGAIN IN HEAVEN.

THEY DID NOT REALLY UNDERSTAND – BUT THOUGHT IT WAS
UNBEARABLY SAD AND THEN THEY BOTH STARTED TO CRY – TO SOB –

BEFORE LAURA CATHRINE MUNCH DIED, AT ONLY 30 YEARS OLD, SHE HAD GIVEN BIRTH TO FIVE CHILDREN DURING HER SEVEN-YEAR
MARRIAGE. WHEN SHE DIED, INGER WAS 11 MONTHS OLD, LAURA 2 YEARS, PETER ANDREAS 3, EDVARD 5 AND SOPHIE 6. THE TWO
ELDEST, EDVARD AND SOPHIE, WERE CLOSELY TIED TO EACH OTHER AND EXPERIENCED THEIR MOTHER'S DEATH TOGETHER.

EDVARD MUNCH: WE WERE AWAKENED IN THE MIDDLE OF THE NIGHT

WE HAD TO GO AWAY
WE UNDERSTOOD AT ONCE
WE GOT DRESSED WITH SLEEP IN OUR EYES

THEN WE HAD TO GO ONE BY ONE OVER TO THE BED AND SHE GAZED AT US TENDERLY AND KISSED US.

THEN WE LEFT AND THE MAID BROUGHT US TO SOME STRANGERS.

THEY WERE ALL SO KIND TO US AND WE WERE GIVEN AS MANY CAKES AND TOYS AS WE DESIRED.

"THE DEAD MOTHER/DEATH AND SPRING", PAINTING, OIL ON CANVAS, 1893.

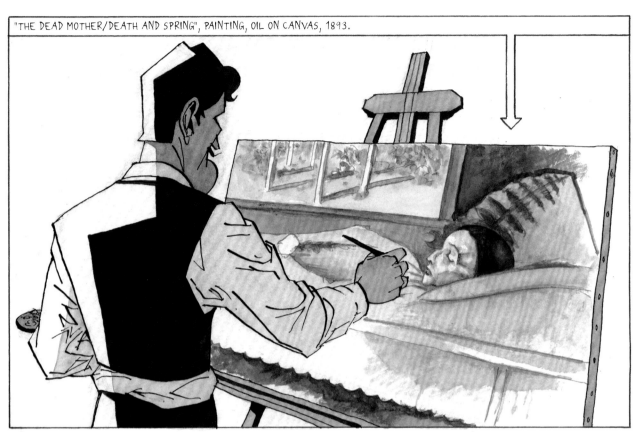

"THE DEAD MOTHER AND CHILD", INTAGLIO PRINT, LINE ETCHING, OPEN BITE AND AQUATINT ON ZINC PLATE, 1901.

A YEAR AFTER LAURA MUNCH DIED, HER YOUNGEST SISTER, KAREN BJØLSTAD, TOOK OVER THE HOUSEHOLD. IT WAS SHE WHOM EDVARD BECAME ATTACHED TO.

MUNCH'S FATHER, CHRISTIAN, WAS A PHYSICIAN. BEFORE, HE HAD READ STORIES FOR THE CHILDREN. NOW HE HAD BECOME A DISHEARTENED RELIGIOUS ZEALOT WHO PREFERRED TO READ THE BIBLE.

EDVARD MUNCH:
DISEASE AND INSANITY AND DEATH WERE THE BLACK ANGELS THAT STOOD BY MY CRADLE. A MOTHER WHO DIED EARLY – GAVE ME THE SEED OF CONSUMPTION – A DISTRAUGHT FATHER – PIOUSLY RELIGIOUS, VERGING ON MADNESS – GAVE ME THE SEEDS OF INSANITY –

CHRISTMAS DAY, 1875, THORVALD MEYERS
STREET 48, GRÜNERLØKKA*, KRISTIANIA:
HE CARESSED MY HEAD –

BUT HE WAS AFRAID – HE FELT THE BLOOD CHURNING IN HIS BREAST – WHEN HE
BREATHED, IT FELT AS THOUGH HIS ENTIRE CHEST HAD COME LOOSE – AS THOUGH ALL OF
HIS BLOOD WOULD SPURT OUT OF HIS MOUTH –

DO NOT BE
AFRAID, MY SON...

PAPA, I AM DYING – I
CANNOT DIE – I AM AFRAID
– JESUS CHRIST –

LORD, COME TO HIS AID IF IT IS
YOUR WILL – DO NOT LET HIM
DIE – I BESEECH YOU, OH LORD –

HE WAS INTERRUPTED BY A NEW FIT OF
COUGHING – A NEW HANDKERCHIEF –

THE BLOOD DISCOLOURED NEARLY THE
ENTIRE HANDKERCHIEF –

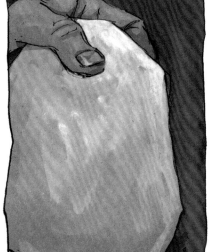

* CENTRAL NEIGHBOURHOOD IN OSLO.

140

BERTA {MUNCH'S OLDER SISTER SOPHIE} LAY EXTENDED ON THE BED NEXT TO HIM AND PRAYED OUT LOUD WHILE WEEPING, AND AROUND THE BED ALL OF THE OTHERS, SOME RED IN THE FACE FROM WEEPING, OTHERS WHITE —

JESUS, HELP ME, I AM DYING.

I MUST NOT DIE NOW.

15 NOVEMBER 1877, FOSSVEIEN 7, GRÜNERLØKKA:

MY BELOVED MAJA {SOPHIE} — I MUST TELL YOU — THE LORD WILL SOON CALL YOU TO HIM —

DO YOU WISH TO LIVE —

YES, I DO —

IS SHE REALLY GOING TO DIE – IN THE LAST HALF HOUR, SHE SEEMED TO FEEL LIGHTER THAN BEFORE – THE PAIN HAD DISAPPEARED –
SHE TRIED TO SIT UP – POINTED TO THE ARMCHAIR BY THE BED –

HOW STRANGELY SHE FELT – THE ROOM HAD CHANGED – AS THOUGH SEEN THROUGH
A VEIL –

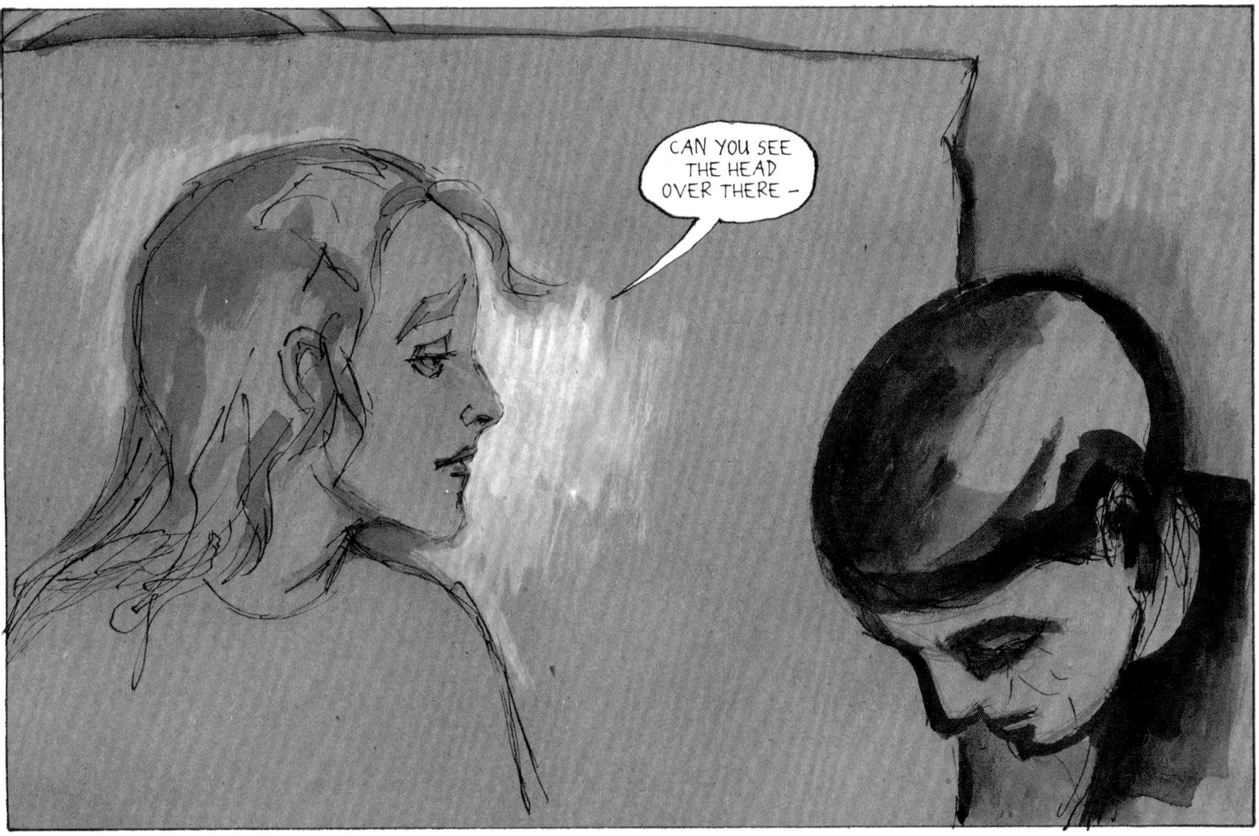
CAN YOU SEE THE HEAD OVER THERE –

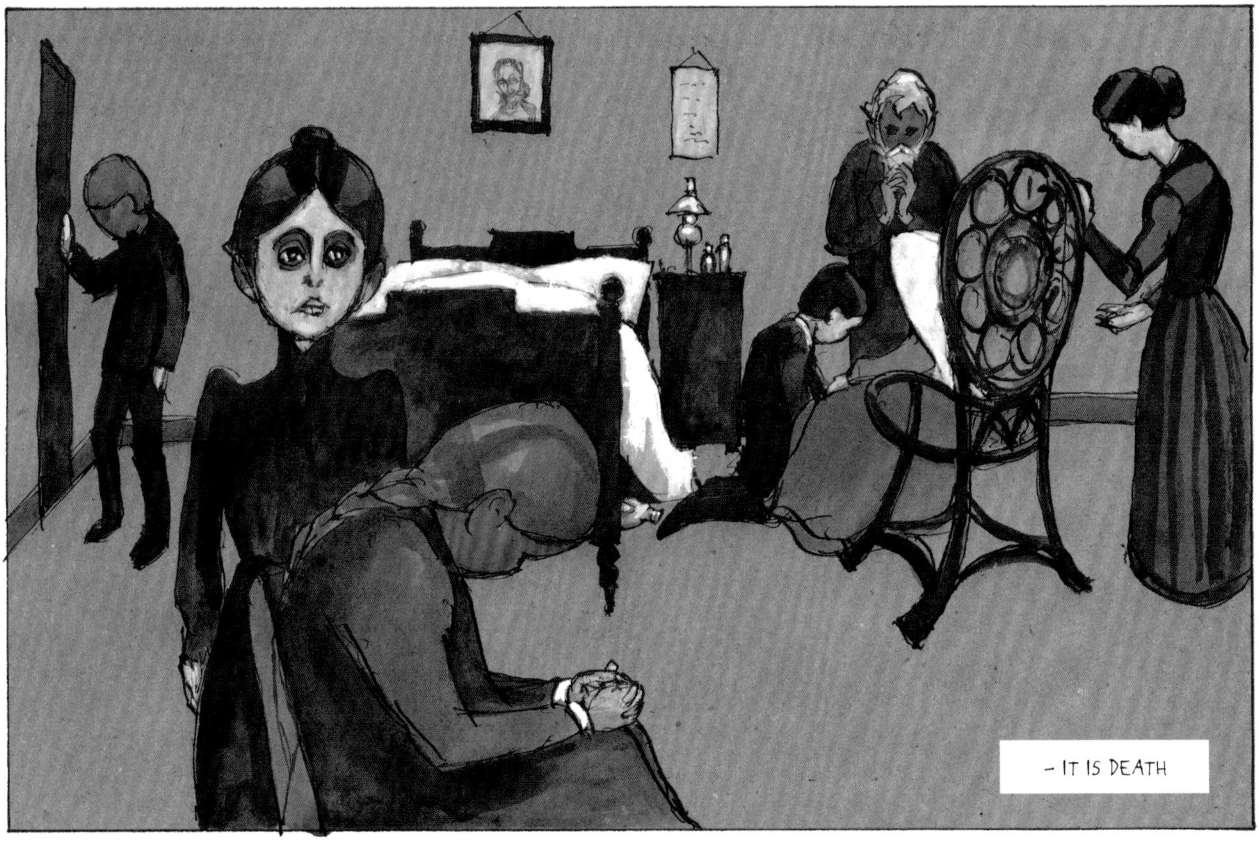
– IT IS DEATH

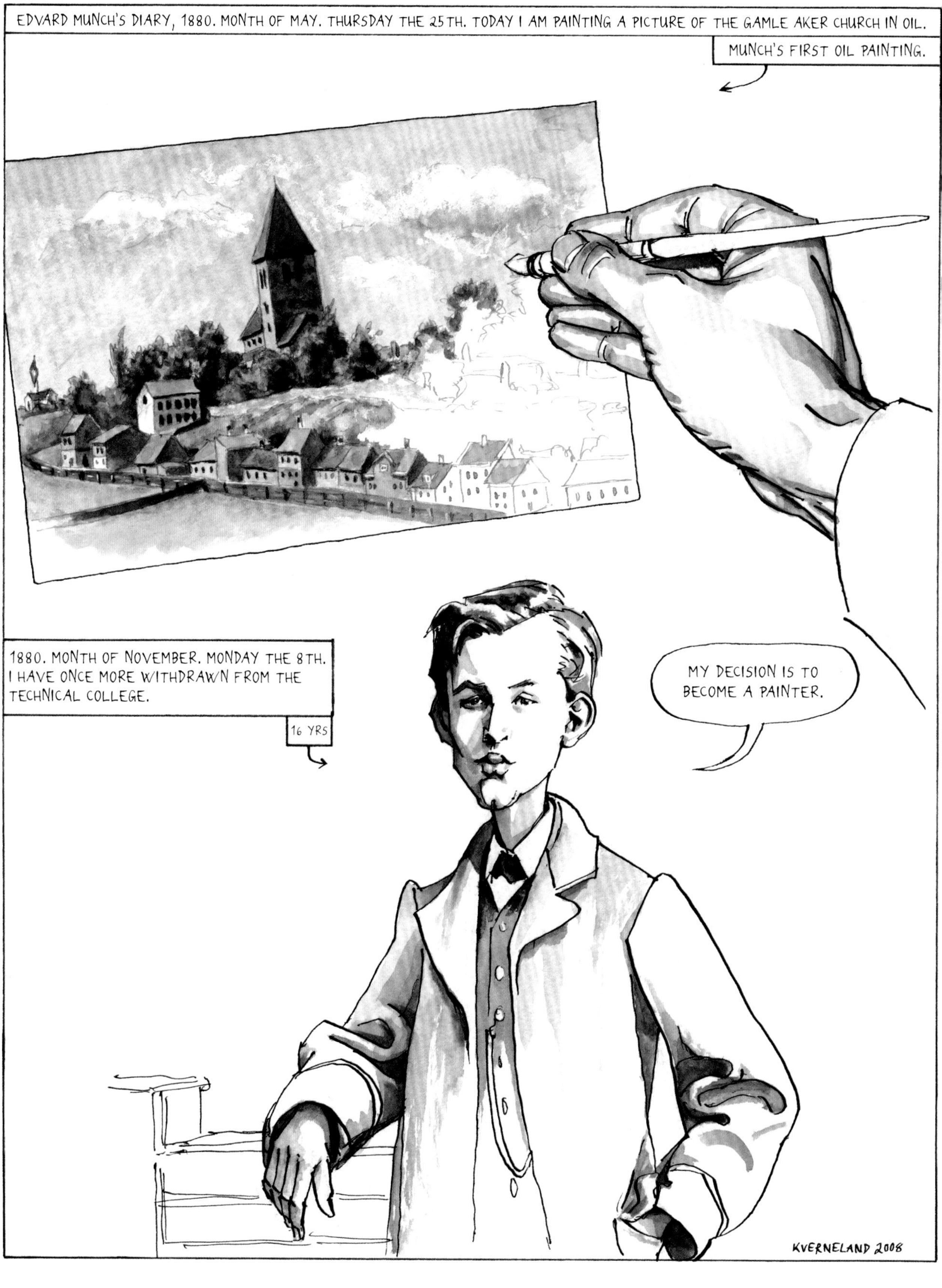
EDVARD MUNCH'S DIARY, 1880. MONTH OF MAY. THURSDAY THE 25TH. TODAY I AM PAINTING A PICTURE OF THE GAMLE AKER CHURCH IN OIL.
MUNCH'S FIRST OIL PAINTING.
1880. MONTH OF NOVEMBER. MONDAY THE 8TH. I HAVE ONCE MORE WITHDRAWN FROM THE TECHNICAL COLLEGE.
16 YRS
MY DECISION IS TO BECOME A PAINTER.
KVERNELAND 2008

HE MET THE RADICAL NATURALISTS IN 1882, AT THE AGE OF 19. IT MUST HAVE BEEN QUITE A SHOCK FOR THE RATHER YOUNG MUNCH, WHO CAME FROM A PURITANICAL, SEMI-IMPOVERISHED AND DEEPLY RELIGIOUS HOME, TO MEET THIS GROUP OF REBELS. TOGETHER WITH SEVERAL LIKE-MINDED YOUNG PAINTERS, HE RENTED A STUDIO DIRECTLY ACROSS FROM THE STORTING* ("PULTOSTEN"), WHERE THE THIRTY-YEAR-OLD KROHG GAVE CRITIQUE TO THE PAINTERS WHO WERE TEN YEARS YOUNGER.

* PARLIAMENT.

145

JENS THIIS: MUNCH WISHED TO PAINT SINGDAHLSEN'S* PORTRAIT. THE PORTRAIT WAS BEGUN AND KROHG ARRIVED, SWAGGERING AND IMPOSING ON HIS FIRST VISIT.

WHAT IS THIS MEANT TO BE?

A PORTRAIT OF MY FRIEND SINGDAHLSEN.

THAT IS A MISCONCEPTION. LET ME SEE YOUR PALETTE!

* ANDREAS SINGDAHLSEN, NORWEGIAN PAINTER.

MUNCH RELUCTANTLY PROFFERED A CIGAR BOX LID OR THE LIKE, SMEARED ON BOTH SIDES WITH THICK LAYERS OF PAINT.

GIVE ME A PROPER PALETTE, EXCLAIMED "THE PROFESSOR", WHO THEN MADE A FEW CORRECTIVE BRUSHSTROKES ON MUNCH'S PICTURE.

THE NEXT TIME I COME, I DEMAND THAT YOU HAVE A PROPER PALETTE AND THAT YOU WIPE IT CLEAN OF ANY SPILLED PAINT WITH SPIRITS.

THEN WE CAN BEGIN TO PAINT.

THE FOOL!! NOW HE HAS DESTROYED EVERYTHING FOR ME.

ON THE REVERSE SIDE OF THE PAINTING IS THE INSCRIPTION: "PORTRAIT OF A. SINGDAHLSEN PAINTED BY EDV. MUNCH AND CHRISTIAN KROHG – 1883."

MUNCH LATER CLAIMED, TO KROGH'S INDIGNATION, THAT HE HAD CONTRIBUTED IN DETERMINING THE COLOUR SCHEME OF KROHG'S MAJOR WORK "ALBERTINE TO SEE THE POLICE SURGEON" (1886-87), WHICH KROHG WAS WORKING ON AT THE TIME. MUNCH HAD SUPPOSEDLY MADE THE FIRST APPLICATIONS OF COLOUR ON THE WHITE CANVAS AND PAINTED ONE OF THE WOMEN DOWN TO THE WAIST.

VIA ARTIST FRIENDS AND KROHG, MUNCH EVENTUALLY JOINED THE BOHEMIAN CIRCLE, WHERE HE MADE MANY CLOSE FRIENDS, WHOSE FLUCTUATING FATES HE BECAME INVOLVED IN.

MILLY IHLEN/ THAULOW/BERGH	JØRGEN ENGELHART	GUNNAR HEIBERG	HANS JÆGER	ODA LASSON/ ENGELHART/KROHG	JAPPE NILSSEN	CHRISTIAN KROHG	EDVARD MUNCH

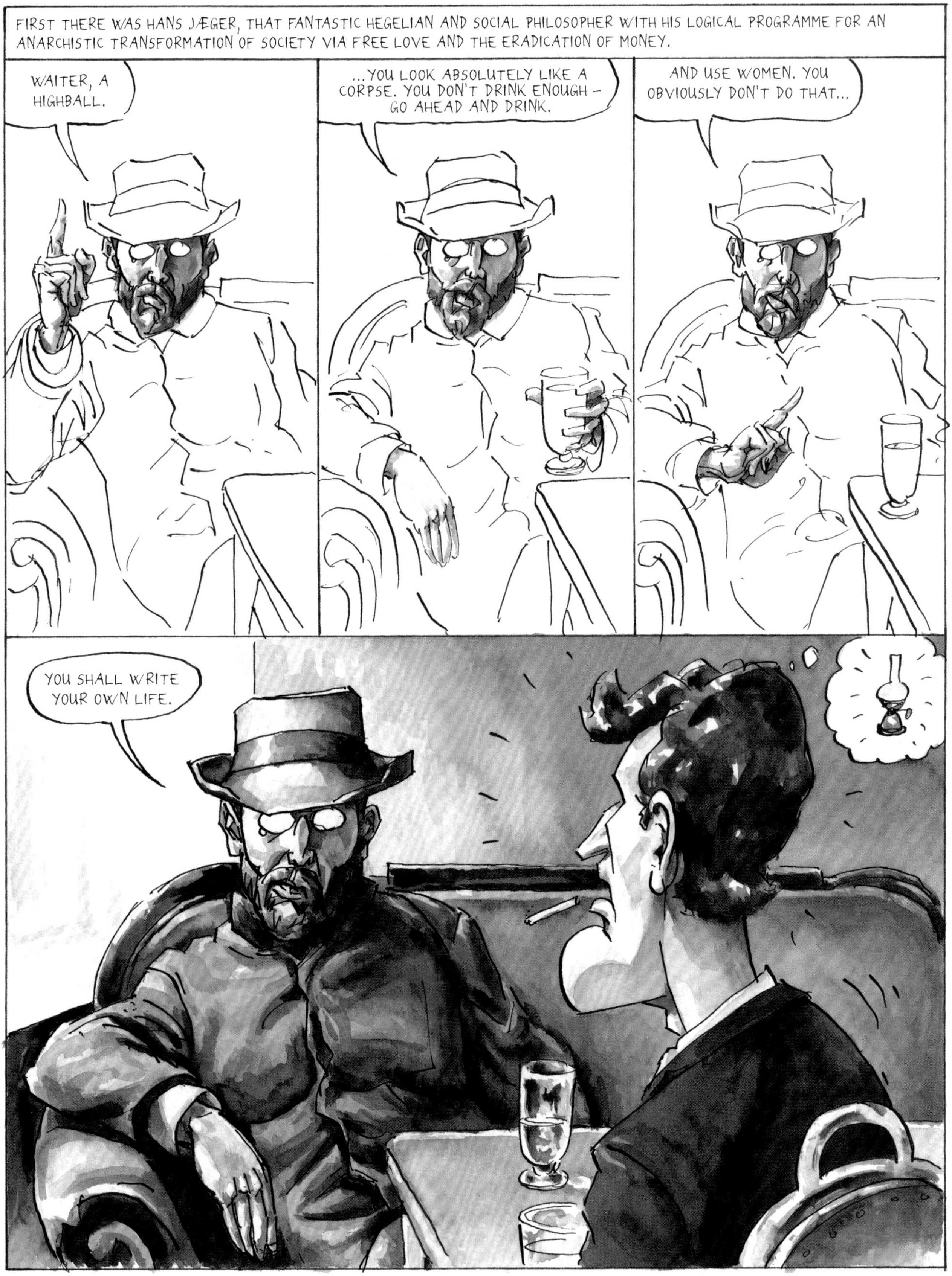
FIRST THERE WAS HANS JÆGER, THAT FANTASTIC HEGELIAN AND SOCIAL PHILOSOPHER WITH HIS LOGICAL PROGRAMME FOR AN ANARCHISTIC TRANSFORMATION OF SOCIETY VIA FREE LOVE AND THE ERADICATION OF MONEY.
WAITER, A HIGHBALL.
...YOU LOOK ABSOLUTELY LIKE A CORPSE. YOU DON'T DRINK ENOUGH - GO AHEAD AND DRINK.
AND USE WOMEN. YOU OBVIOUSLY DON'T DO THAT...
YOU SHALL WRITE YOUR OWN LIFE.

FROM THE VERY BEGINNING, MUNCH FOUND A SIGNIFICANT SUPPLY OF MOTIFS IN HIS CLOSE SURROUNDINGS. FAMILY, FRIENDS AND PERSONAL EXPERIENCES BECAME THE MOST IMPORTANT SOURCES FOR HIS MOTIFS.

FROM THE TIME HE BEGAN TO EXHIBIT, LIKE NO OTHER NORWEGIAN ARTIST, HE WAS MET WITH ENTHUSIASM AND PRAISE FROM THOSE WHO HAD THE LEAST IDEA OF WHAT IT WAS ALL ABOUT.

① FRITS THAULOW, ② ERIK WERENSKIOLD, ③ KALLE LØCHEN, ④ CHRISTIAN KROHG, ⑤ EILIF PETERSSEN.

CHRISTIAN KROHG:

HE PAINTS — THAT IS, SEES — DIFFERENTLY THAN THE OTHER ARTISTS.

HE SEES ONLY THE ESSENCE AND OF COURSE PAINTS ONLY THAT.

THAT IS WHY MUNCH'S PICTURES ARE AS A RULE "UNFINISHED", WHICH PEOPLE ARE SO THRILLED TO DISCOVER.

MUNCH HAS MANY ADMIRERS AMONG THE YOUNG, BUT ONE THING IS COMICAL,

EVEN AMONG THEM, NO ONE VIEWS A NEW PICTURE BY MUNCH WITHOUT HAVING TO SHAKE THEIR HEAD AND SMILE, AND ONLY THEN DO THEY EXCLAIM:

YES, GOD KNOWS — IT IS GOOD.

"SELF-PORTRAIT", OIL ON CARDBOARD, 1882-83.

KRISTIANIA, 18 OCTOBER 1886, THE ARTISTS' FIFTH AUTUMN EXHIBITION OPENS IN THE SCULPTURE MUSEUM*.

"SUCH RUBBISH!"

"IT IS A SCANDAL THAT THE LIKES OF THIS SHALL BE ALLOWED TO HANG HERE!"

"IT IS NOTHING BUT SALMON MOUSSE IN LOBSTER SAUCE!"

* THE MIDSECTION OF TODAY'S NATIONAL GALLERY.

No other painting has aroused such indignation in Norway.

When I entered the hall where it hung on the opening day, people stood crowded together in front of the picture – shouting and laughter could be heard –

When I went out into the street again, the young naturalist painters stood together with their leader Wentzel {Gustav Wentzel (1859–1927), Norwegian painter}.

Ptui! Humbug painter! I never thought you would begin painting that kind of drivel!

No, maybe not, but not everyone can be a nail and twig painter, either!*

* Wentzel painted with great realism and detail.

153

HANS JÆGER INTRODUCED MUNCH'S SENSATIONAL "STUDY" IN A NEWSPAPER ARTICLE WRITTEN AS A FICTITIOUS CONVERSATION BETWEEN HIMSELF AND AN ANONYMOUS "EMACIATED ART CHAP":

WHAT ARE THOSE STRANGE STRIPES* DOWN THERE ON THE BOTTOM OF MUNCH'S PICTURE?

IT IS THE GENIUS, RUNNING IN LARGE STREAKS DOWN THE PAINTING.

* DRIPPED PAINT, WHICH MUNCH LATER PAINTED OVER.

THE MAN LAUGHED DERISIVELY.

HA, HA, HA!

WHAT MUNCH HAS PRODUCED IN HIS SKETCH, THAT IS SOMETHING NO ONE CAN LEARN TO DO; WHAT HE HAS NOT DONE, THAT IS AT ANY RATE SOMETHING THAT CAN BE LEARNED.

WHEN I SAW THE SICK CHILD FOR THE FIRST TIME — THE PALE HEAD WITH THE VIBRANT RED HAIR AGAINST THE WHITE CUSHION — IT MADE AN IMPRESSION THAT DISAPPEARED AS I WORKED ON IT.

I PAINTED THE PICTURE* NUMEROUS TIMES IN THE COURSE OF A YEAR — SCRAPED IT — DISSOLVED IT IN GENEROUS AMOUNTS OF SOLVENT — AND ENDEAVOURED AGAIN AND AGAIN TO ATTAIN THE FIRST IMPRESSION —

THE TRANSLUCENT — PALE COMPLEXION AGAINST THE CANVAS —

THE QUIVERING MOUTH —

THE TREMBLING HANDS.

* THE PICTURE WAS PAINTED AT SCHOUS PLASS 1 IN 1885–86. MUNCH'S AUNT KAREN AND THE FAMILY'S HOUSEMAID BETZY NIELSEN SAT AS MODELS.

155

I HAD OVERDONE THE CHAIR AND THE GLASS; IT DISTRACTED FROM THE HEAD — SHOULD I REMOVE IT COMPLETELY?

NO, IT CONTRIBUTED TO DEEPEN AND ACCENTUATE THE HEAD — I SCRAPED AWAY THE SURROUNDINGS PARTWAY AND ALLOWED THEM TO REMAIN AS MASSES —

I DISCOVERED FURTHERMORE THAT MY OWN EYELASHES HAD CONTRIBUTED TO THE VISUAL IMPRESSION.

HENCE I INCLUDED A HINT OF THEM AS SHADOWS ON THE SURFACE OF THE PICTURE — THE HEAD BECAME THE PICTURE IN A WAY.

I FINALLY CEASED, EXHAUSTED — I HAD ACHIEVED A GREAT DEAL OF THE FIRST IMPRESSION, THE QUIVERING MOUTH — THE TRANSLUCENT COMPLEXION — THE WEARY EYES —

IT WAS A BREAKTHROUGH IN MY ART — MOST OF WHAT I HAVE DONE SINCE HAD ITS GENESIS IN THIS PICTURE.

"STUDY/THE SICK CHILD", OIL ON CANVAS, 1885-86.

IN THE SAME CHAIR THAT I PAINTED THE SICK CHILD, I AND ALL OF MY DEAR ONES HAVE SAT YEARNING FOR THE SUN.

"WITH MUNCH'S PICTURES, THE LEVEL OF THE PRESENT AUTUMN EXHIBITION HAS GREATLY DETERIORATED, AND BY ACCEPTING THEM THE JURY HAS DONE THEIR FELLOW ARTISTS A DISSERVICE."*

* JONAS RASCH IN *AFTENPOSTEN*.

"MUNCH DOES HAVE GENIUS. BUT THERE IS ALSO A DANGER THAT IT WILL GO TO THE DOGS. FOR MUNCH'S OWN SAKE, I WOULD HAVE HOPED THAT HIS "SICK CHILD" HAD BEEN REFUSED. THE WAY THIS "STUDY" (!) NOW APPEARS, IT IS SIMPLY A DISCARDED, HALF SCRATCHED-OUT SKETCH. IT IS AN ABORTION."*

IT IS BETTER TO PAINT A GOOD UNFINISHED PICTURE THAN A POOR FINISHED ONE!

* ANDREAS AUBERT IN *MORGENBLADET*.

THE CRITICS' AND THE PUBLIC'S ATTITUDE TOWARDS MUNCH WAS ONE THING; THE OPINION OF THE ARTISTS WAS ANOTHER. THE ESSENTIAL FACT WAS THAT THE JURY HAD ACCEPTED HIS PICTURES AND PLACED "THE SICK CHILD" IN A PLACE OF HONOUR IN THE EXHIBITION.

IN ANY CASE, KROHG'S UNCONDITIONAL ENTHUSIASM FOR "THE SICK CHILD" HAD SUCH AN EFFECT ON MUNCH THAT HE GAVE IT TO KROHG IN GRATITUDE.

IT WAS IN THE DAYS WHEN LITTLE GIRLS FROM GOOD FAMILIES, WHISPERING AND SMIRKING, WALKED IN A LARGE CIRCLE AROUND HANS JÆGER WHEN HE "DARED" TO SHOW HIMSELF ON KARL JOHAN STREET. AND MANY OF THE CITY'S INHABITANTS GLARED ANGRILY AT EDVARD MUNCH AS HE WALKED ERECT AND DEFIANT OR IN PASSIONATE AND GESTICULATING CONVERSATION DOWN THE PROMENADE THAT HE LOVED.

HANS JÆGER'S FIRST GREAT LITERARY WORK, "FROM THE KRISTIANIA BOHEMIA", WAS IMMEDIATELY CONFISCATED AND, AFTER A LONG AND HUMILIATING PROSECUTION, THE AUTHOR WAS SENTENCED TO PRISON AND A LARGE FINE.

HE WAS LATER DISCHARGED AS A STENOGRAPHER AT THE STORTING AND DISMISSED FROM THE UNIVERSITY.

159

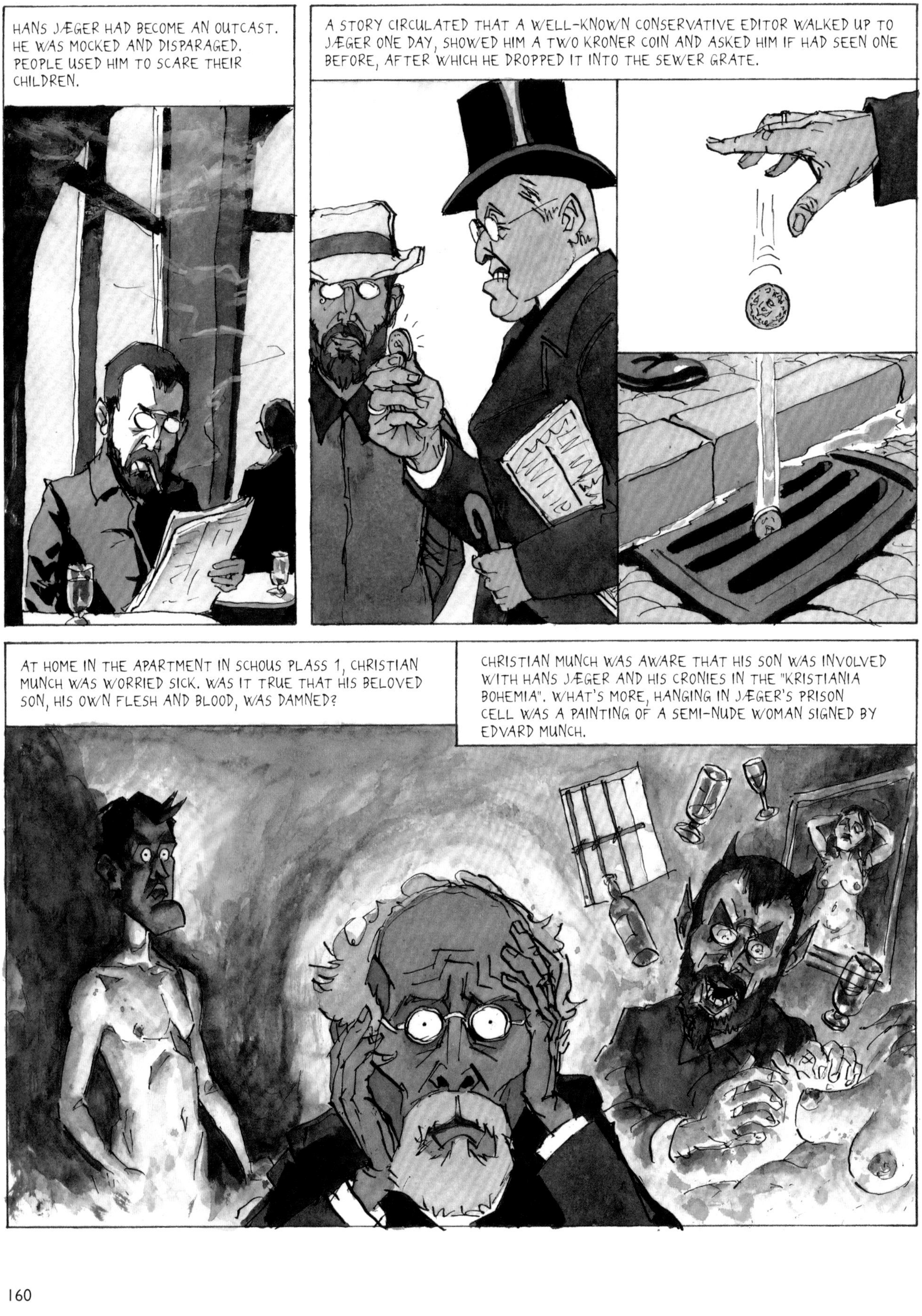
HANS JÆGER HAD BECOME AN OUTCAST. HE WAS MOCKED AND DISPARAGED. PEOPLE USED HIM TO SCARE THEIR CHILDREN.
A STORY CIRCULATED THAT A WELL-KNOWN CONSERVATIVE EDITOR WALKED UP TO JÆGER ONE DAY, SHOWED HIM A TWO KRONER COIN AND ASKED HIM IF HAD SEEN ONE BEFORE, AFTER WHICH HE DROPPED IT INTO THE SEWER GRATE.
AT HOME IN THE APARTMENT IN SCHOUS PLASS 1, CHRISTIAN MUNCH WAS WORRIED SICK. WAS IT TRUE THAT HIS BELOVED SON, HIS OWN FLESH AND BLOOD, WAS DAMNED?
CHRISTIAN MUNCH WAS AWARE THAT HIS SON WAS INVOLVED WITH HANS JÆGER AND HIS CRONIES IN THE "KRISTIANIA BOHEMIA". WHAT'S MORE, HANGING IN JÆGER'S PRISON CELL WAS A PAINTING OF A SEMI-NUDE WOMAN SIGNED BY EDVARD MUNCH.

ONE EVENING, EDVARD GOT INTO AN ARGUMENT WITH HIS FATHER ABOUT HOW LONG NON-BELIEVERS HAD TO SUFFER THE TORMENTS OF HELL. EDVARD BELIEVED THAT NO SIN WAS SO GREAT THAT GOD WOULD ALLOW HIM TO SUFFER MORE THAN A THOUSAND YEARS.

HIS FATHER, ON THE OTHER HAND, BELIEVED THEY WOULD BE TORMENTED FOR A THOUSAND TIMES A THOUSAND YEARS.

EDVARD WOULD NOT GIVE IN, AND FINALLY SLAMMED THE DOOR AND ESCAPED OUT INTO THE STREETS.

EDVARD MUNCH:
HOW STRANGE OF JÆGER TO SAY THAT THERE IS NO LIFE AFTER DEATH.

ONE CAN JUST AS WELL CLAIM THAT SOMETHING EXISTS THAT DOES NOT EXIST — ONE KNOWS NOTHING.

IT IS ODD JUST THE SAME THAT WHEN ONE IS ON ONE'S DEATHBED THE FEAR ALWAYS COMES —

IT IS AS IF ONE FEELS INSTINCTIVELY THAT SOMETHING WILL COME AFTER — AND THAT QUESTION OF GOD THAT EVERYONE STRUGGLES WITH.

IT IS TERRIBLE, HOW LONG THIS {INFLUENCE} FROM THE BIBLE HANGS ON.

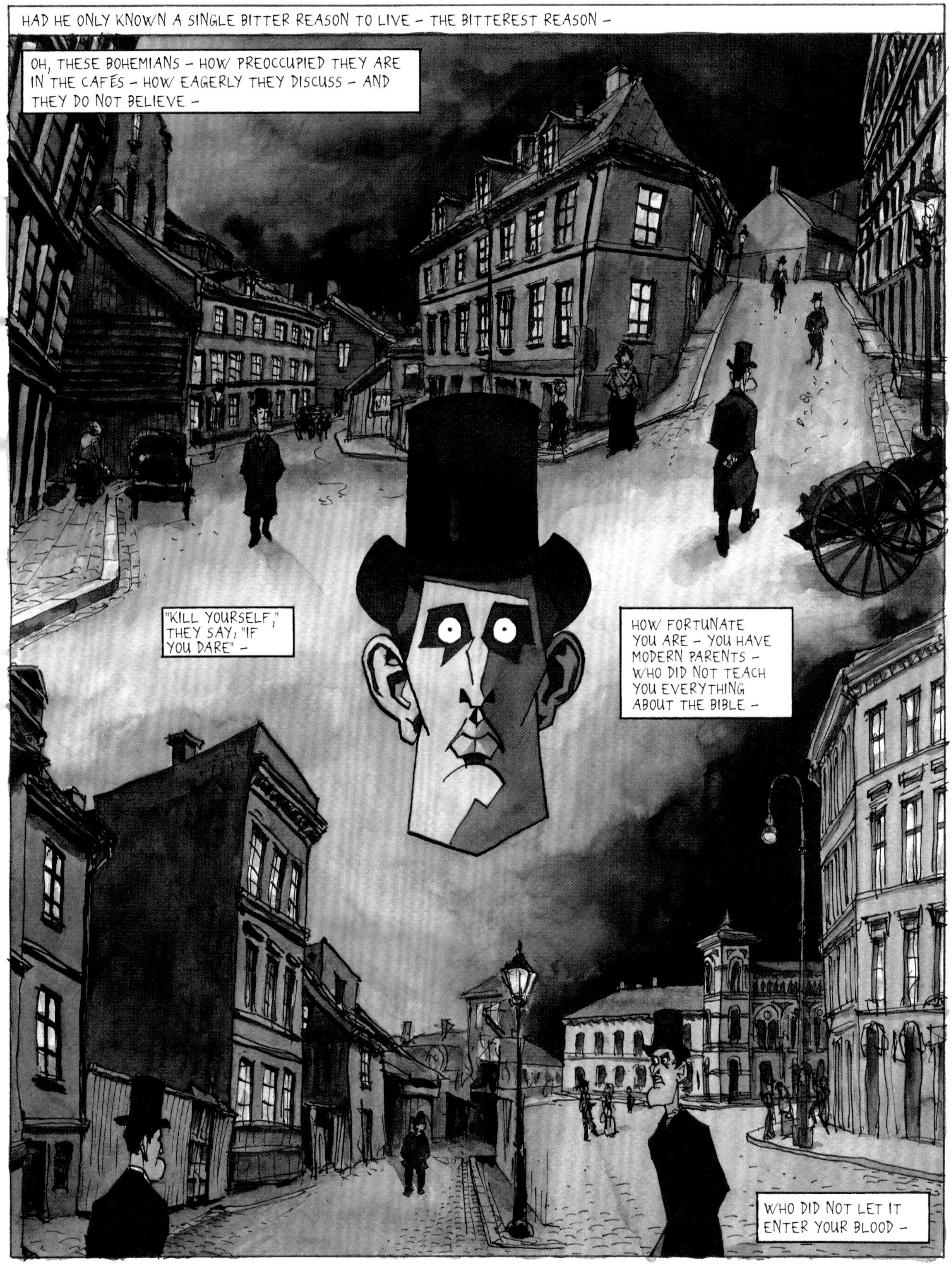
HAD HE ONLY KNOWN A SINGLE BITTER REASON TO LIVE – THE BITTEREST REASON –
OH, THESE BOHEMIANS – HOW PREOCCUPIED THEY ARE IN THE CAFÉS – HOW EAGERLY THEY DISCUSS – AND THEY DO NOT BELIEVE –
"KILL YOURSELF," THEY SAY, "IF YOU DARE" –
HOW FORTUNATE YOU ARE – YOU HAVE MODERN PARENTS – WHO DID NOT TEACH YOU EVERYTHING ABOUT THE BIBLE –
WHO DID NOT LET IT ENTER YOUR BLOOD –

OH, THESE BEAUTIFUL DREAMS – THE ONES ABOUT JOY AND LIFE AFTER DEATH – YOU HAVE NOT HAD THIS GREAT DISAPPOINTMENT WHEN YOU SEE THAT THERE IS NOTHING

AND I HAD ACQUIRED THE HABIT OF IT – THE BELIEF IN SOMETHING GLORIOUS – SOMETHING GRAND THAT WOULD COME – AND WHEN I NO LONGER BELIEVED IN THE BIBLE, IT WAS STILL IN MY BLOOD – LATER, THE REJOICING WILL COME LATER –

AND I WORKED AND WORKED WITH MY LIFE'S BLOOD TO CREATE SOMETHING GREAT –

HOW TERRIBLY CLEAR I NOW SEE THE DARK VOID, SO TERRIBLY CLEAR

"SPRING", SIGNED "E. MUNCH 1889", IS A DISPLAY OF PAINTERLY, TECHNICAL AND COMPOSITIONAL SKILL — TOTALLY DIFFERENT FROM "STUDY" FROM THREE YEARS BEFORE.

"SPRING" WAS THE TERMINALLY ILL CHILD'S YEARNING FOR LIGHT AND WARMTH FOR LIFE.

BETZY NIELSEN (THE MODEL FOR BOTH "SPRING" AND "STUDY/THE SICK CHILD"): I CAN REMEMBER THAT HE WORE A SHABBY JACKET THAT WAS TOO SHORT. HE STOOD THE ENTIRE TIME NERVOUSLY PULLING AT IT WHILE HE PAINTED.

TEE HEE!

EDVARD WAS NOW OVER TWENTY-FIVE AND WAS STILL ONLY KNOWN AS BEING TALENTED.

HE HAD TO GET AWAY FROM PROVINCIAL KRISTIANIA. A GRANT APPLICATION WAS UNDER CONSIDERATION AT THE MINISTRY.

HE HAD RENTED THE STUDENT UNION'S LITTLE HALL AND SURPRISED EVERYONE WHEN HE OPENED THE DOORS TO HIS FIRST SOLO EXHIBITION ON 20 APRIL 1889.

AT THE TIME, GROUP EXHIBITIONS WERE THE NORM IN THE NORWEGIAN CAPITAL. ONE-MAN SHOWS WERE VERY RARE – AND IT WAS UNHEARD OF FOR A YOUNG ARTIST TO HAVE ONE.

IT WAS BOUND TO CAUSE A STIR, AND WITH THE "RIGHT" PICTURES THE CHANCES OF GETTING A STATE TRAVEL GRANT WOULD INCREASE. "SPRING" MIGHT SATISFY THE CONSERVATIVES; WHILE A PORTRAIT OF HANS JÆGER, WHICH HE PAINTED HASTILY IN THE RENTED ROOMS OF A FRIEND, MIGHT PLEASE THE MORE RADICAL JUDGES.

AS A PORTRAIT, IT IS MUNCH'S BEST.

JENS THIIS

HIS APPLICATION WOULD BE CONSIDERED IN THE AUTUMN.

THAT SUMMER, HE RENTED A HOUSE IN ÅSGÅRDSTRAND FOR THE FIRST TIME, THE VILLAGE THAT WOULD BECOME HIS REGULAR "SUMMER RETREAT" FOR A DOZEN YEARS.

IT WOULD INFLUENCE HIS NOTION OF LANDSCAPE, ALLOW HIM TO EXPERIENCE THE MYSTERY OF WHITE NIGHTS AND OFFER HIM THE SOFT UNDULATING SHORELINE, WHICH IN HIS OWN WORDS WOULD WEAVE THROUGH "THE FRIEZE OF LIFE" AND BIND IT TOGETHER.

EDVARD MUNCH: DOWN HERE BY THE SHORE I FEEL THAT I FIND AN IMAGE OF MYSELF — OF MY LIFE.

IS IT BECAUSE WE WALKED ALONG THE SHORE TOGETHER IN BYGONE DAYS?

THAT PECULIAR SCENT OF SEAWEED REMINDS ME OF HER — THE STRANGE BOULDERS THAT MYSTERIOUSLY PROTRUDE FROM THE WATER AND TAKE ON THE SHAPES OF FANTASTIC CREATURES WHICH RESEMBLED TROLLS THE OTHER NIGHT.

IN THE MURKY GREEN WATER I SEE THE COLOUR OF HER EYES.

FAR – FAR IN THE DISTANCE – THAT SOFT LINE WHERE THE AIR MEETS THE OCEAN – IT IS INCOMPREHENSIBLE – LIKE EXISTENCE – INCOMPREHENSIBLE LIKE DEATH – AS UNENDING AS LONGING.

AND LIFE IS LIKE THIS CALM SURFACE – IT REFLECTS THE LIGHT OF THE ATMOSPHERE – PURE COLOURS – IT CONCEALS THE DEPTHS WITH ITS SLIME – ITS VERMIN – LIKE DEATH.

MY SISTER AND I ARE HAVING A PERFECTLY DELIGHTFUL TIME HERE. THE BACHELOR'S LIFE IS AND WILL REMAIN MOST DESIRABLE.

"SUMMER NIGHT/INGER ON THE SHORE", OIL ON CANVAS, 1889.

IT SEEMS I WILL BE TRAVELLING TO PARIS THIS AUTUMN AS I EVIDENTLY HAVE BEEN AWARDED THE GRANT.

171

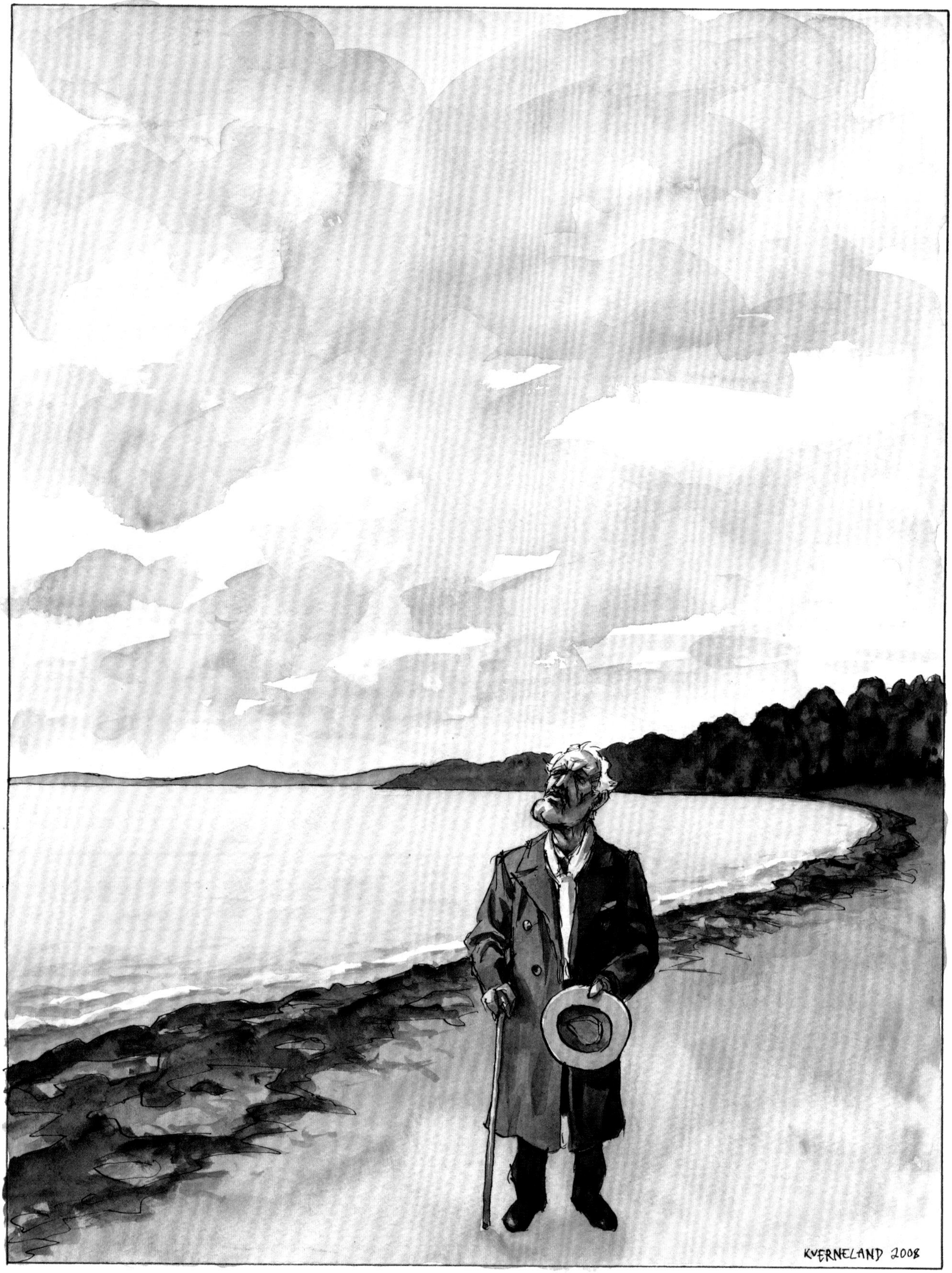
KVERNELAND 2008

ÅSGÅRDSTRAND

① "MELANCHOLY", OIL PAINTING, 1892. ② "MELANCHOLY III", WOODCUT, 1902–06. ③ "MELANCHOLY", OIL PAINTING, 1891–94.

THE FRIEZE IS INTENDED AS
A SEQUENCE OF DECORATIVE
PICTURES, WHICH TOGETHER WOULD
REPRESENT AN IMAGE OF LIFE.
THE SINUOUS SHORELINE WEAVES
THROUGH THEM ALL. BEYOND IT, IN
PERPETUAL MOTION, IS THE OCEAN,
AND BENEATH THE TREETOPS
MULTIFARIOUS LIFE UNFOLDS WITH
ALL OF ITS JOYS AND SORROWS.

I CONSIDER THE PICTURE SERIES TO
BE ONE OF MY MOST SIGNIFICANT
WORKS, IF NOT THE MOST
SIGNIFICANT.

"THE THREE STAGES OF WOMAN/
SPHINX", OIL, 1894.

TO WALK IN ÅSGÅRDSTRAND IS TO WALK AMIDST
MY PICTURES — I HAVE SUCH A DESIRE TO PAINT
WHEN I AM IN ÅSGÅRDSTRAND

HE WAS ALWAYS IN ÅSGÅRDSTRAND IN THE SUMMERS. IT WAS UP HERE IN THE WOODS THAT HE LOST HIS VIRGINITY TO MILLIE THAULOW IN '85, AND HE FOUND THE MOTIFS FOR MANY OF HIS FAMOUS PAINTINGS HERE.

TRY TO LOOK SEXY AND SEDUCTIVE, BE MILLIE THAULOW!

YEAH, YEAH.

TAKE A PICTURE! DO I LOOK LIKE I JUST GOT LAID?

"SUMMER NIGHT/ THE VOICE", OIL, 1896.

"SUMMER NIGHT/ INGER ON THE BEACH", OIL, 1889.

I SHOULD HAVE BROUGHT A WHITE SUMMER DRESS.

"ASHES", OIL, 1895.

"THE GIRLS ON THE BRIDGE", OIL, 1901.

THIS ISN'T A BRIDGE, IT'S A JETTY.

WE AREN'T GIRLS.

ONE SUMMER AFTERNOON IN 1938, A STOCKBROKER {ROLF E. STENERSEN} DROVE MUNCH TO ÅSGÅRDSTRAND.

I WONDER IF THE OLD WOMAN IS HERE.

THE ONE WHO THOUGHT I STOLE HER EGGS.

SHE CLAIMED THAT I SCATTERED GRAIN FROM HER HOUSE TO MY GARDEN.

THEN THE CHICKENS WOULD FOLLOW THE GRAIN AND LAY THEIR EGGS IN MY POT.

WHEN KARSTEN* HEARD OF IT, HE BOUGHT GRAIN AND SCATTERED IT.

WE DIDN'T GET ANY EGGS, BUT HE PAINTED THE CHICKENS.

SHE CAME RUNNING THEN.

!!

THEY LOOKED SO SHABBY. I THOUGHT I'D FRESHEN THEM UP A BIT.

IT'S A GIFT. NORMALLY I TAKE FIFTY KRONER.

KARSTEN WAS TERRIBLE.

CAN YOU BELIEVE HE TRIED HIS TRICKS ON ME, TOO?

WE WERE SITTING IN MY COTTAGE HERE IN ÅSGÅRDSTRAND, DRINKING.

* LUDVIG KARSTEN (1876–1926), NORWEGIAN PAINTER.

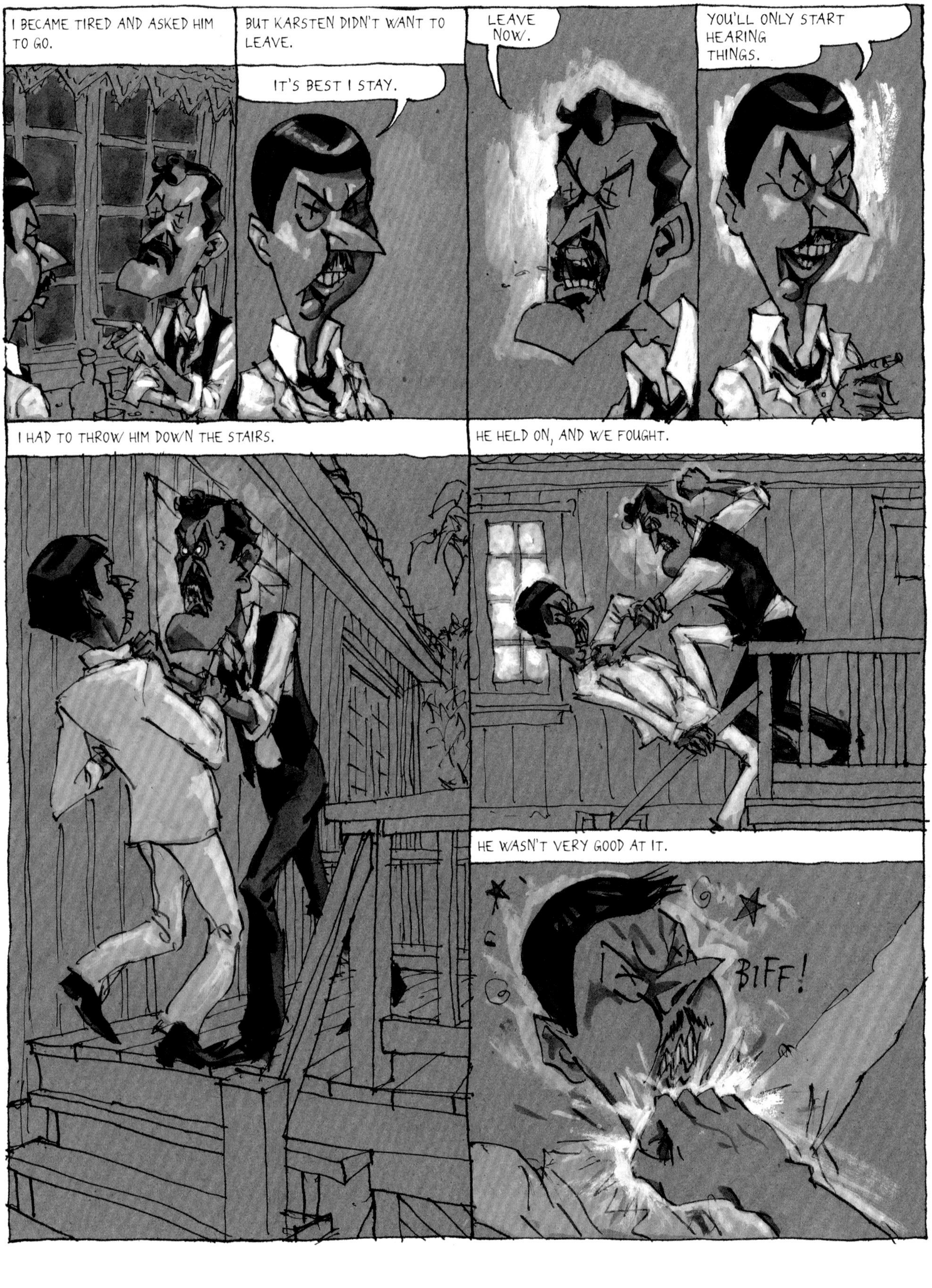

I BECAME TIRED AND ASKED HIM TO GO.
BUT KARSTEN DIDN'T WANT TO LEAVE.
IT'S BEST I STAY.
LEAVE NOW.
YOU'LL ONLY START HEARING THINGS.
I HAD TO THROW HIM DOWN THE STAIRS.
HE HELD ON, AND WE FOUGHT.
HE WASN'T VERY GOOD AT IT.
BIFF!

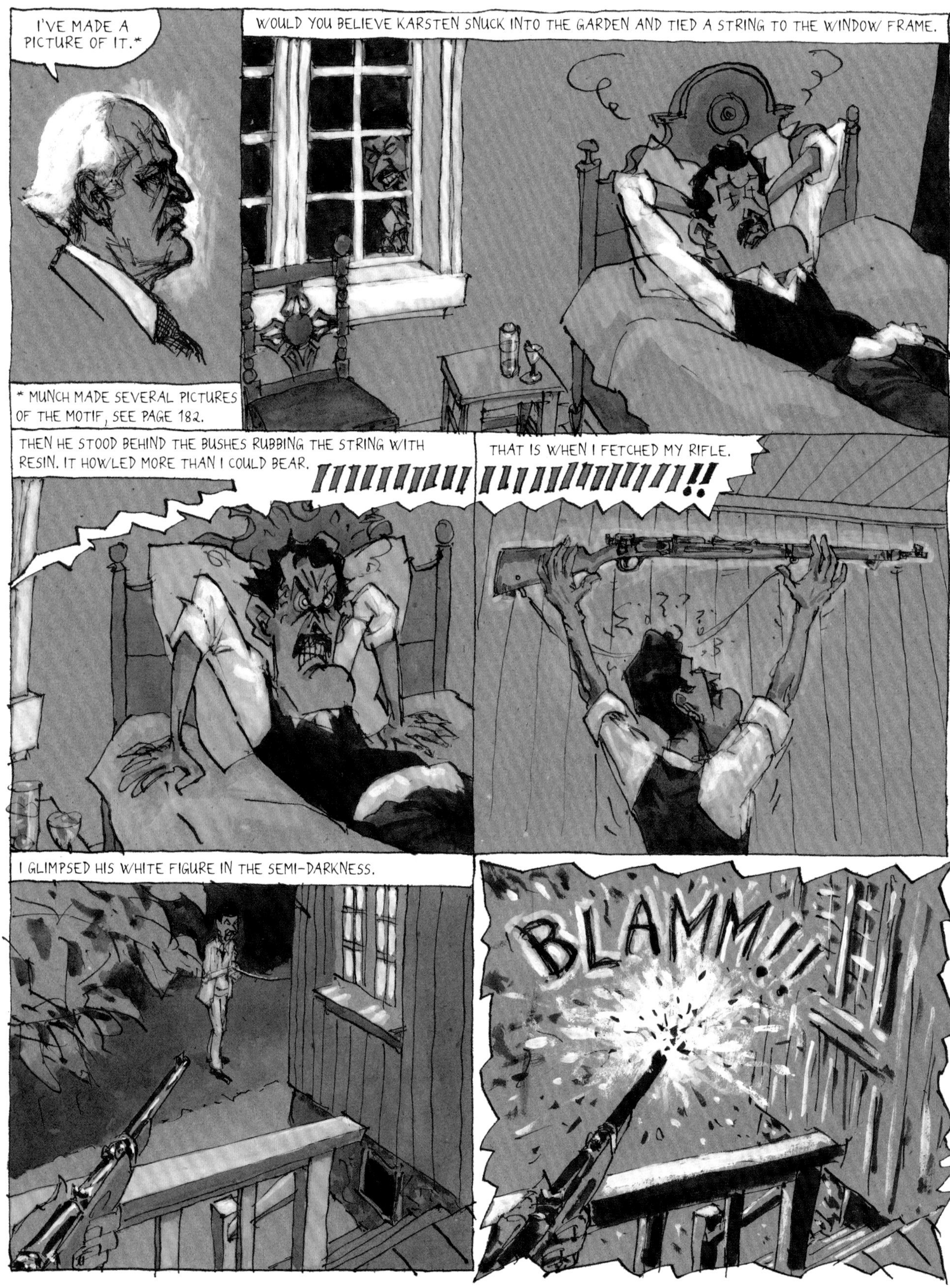

I'VE MADE A PICTURE OF IT.*
WOULD YOU BELIEVE KARSTEN SNUCK INTO THE GARDEN AND TIED A STRING TO THE WINDOW FRAME.
* MUNCH MADE SEVERAL PICTURES OF THE MOTIF, SEE PAGE 182.
THEN HE STOOD BEHIND THE BUSHES RUBBING THE STRING WITH RESIN. IT HOWLED MORE THAN I COULD BEAR.
THAT IS WHEN I FETCHED MY RIFLE.
I GLIMPSED HIS WHITE FIGURE IN THE SEMI-DARKNESS.
BLAMM!!

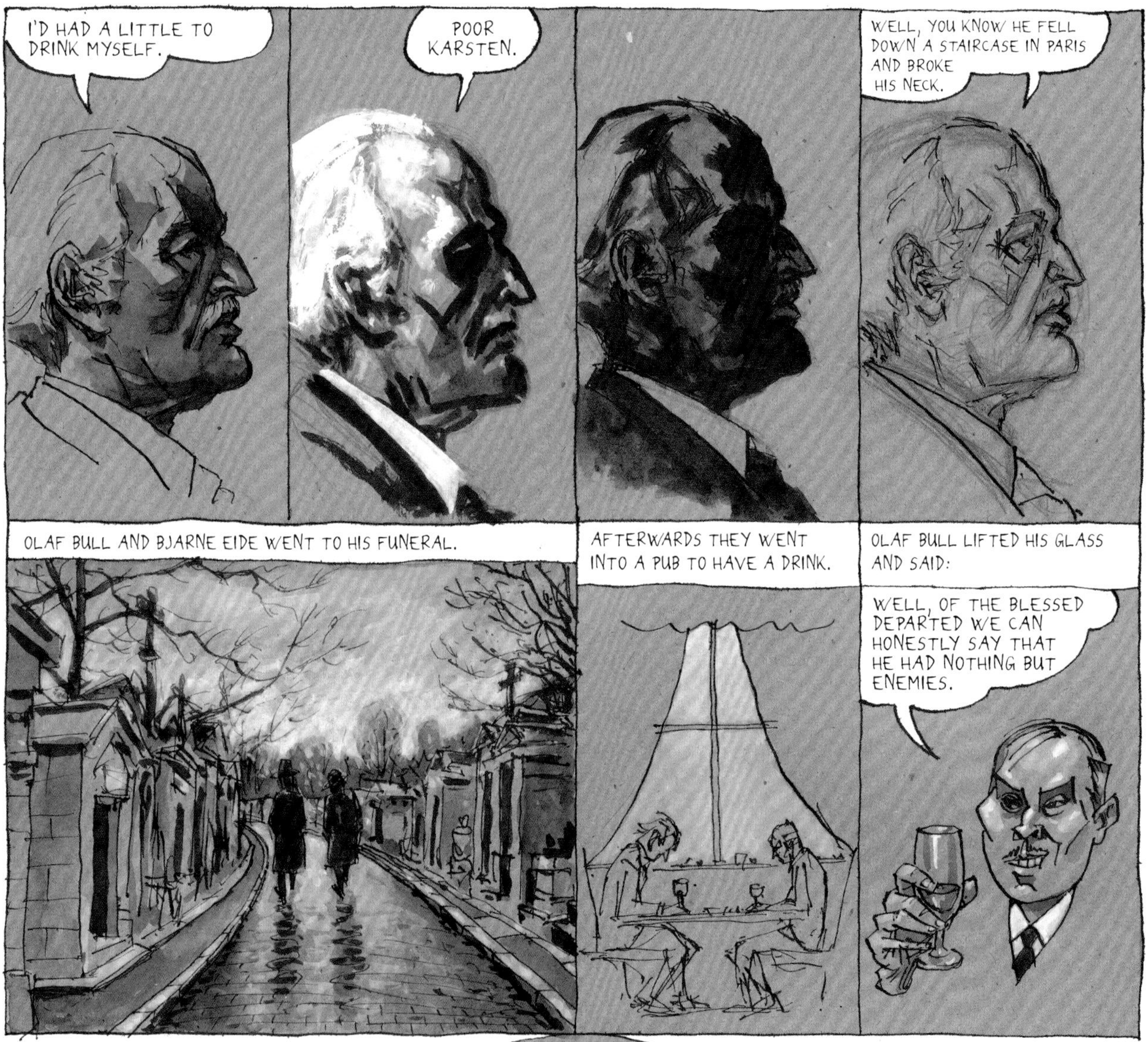
I'D HAD A LITTLE TO DRINK MYSELF.
POOR KARSTEN.
WELL, YOU KNOW HE FELL DOWN A STAIRCASE IN PARIS AND BROKE HIS NECK.
OLAF BULL AND BJARNE EIDE WENT TO HIS FUNERAL.
AFTERWARDS THEY WENT INTO A PUB TO HAVE A DRINK.
OLAF BULL LIFTED HIS GLASS AND SAID:
WELL, OF THE BLESSED DEPARTED WE CAN HONESTLY SAY THAT HE HAD NOTHING BUT ENEMIES.

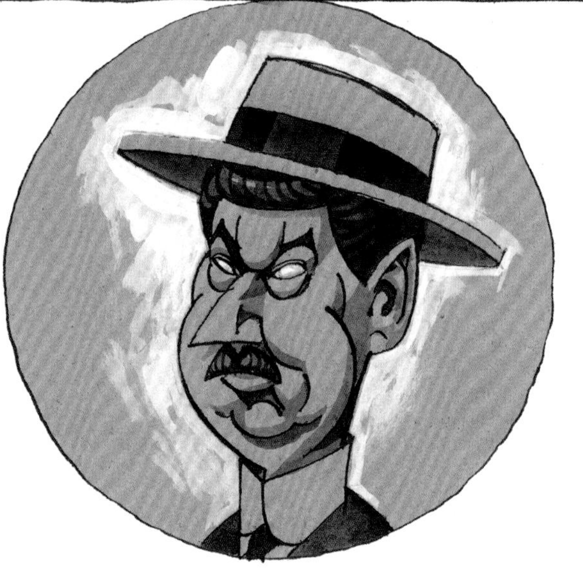

SHIT, THERE IT IS! MUNCH'S SUMMERHOUSE! THE HOLY GRAIL!

IT'S LIKE AN AMUSEMENT PARK. MUNCHLAND!

I SHOT MY WAD!

THERE ARE THE STAIRS! MUNCH MADE LOTS OF PICTURES OF THE FIGHT, AMONG THEM THIS ONE, WHICH OF COURSE IS CALLED "THE FIGHT":

MUNCH MUST'VE GOT THAT FIGHT STUCK IN HIS BRAIN. WE SAW A BUNCH OF OIL PAINTINGS OF IT THE LAST TIME WE WERE AT THE MUNCH MUSEUM.

YEAH, SOMEONE GAVE ME A BOOK WITH THIS SELF-PORTRAIT:

THE BRAWL HAPPENED IN 1905, BUT THE PICTURES WERE PAINTED LATER.

THAT RIFLE PICTURE MUST BE A STUDY OR SOMETHING FOR THE PICTURE I THINK IS CALLED "UNINVITED GUEST" THAT WE SAW ANOTHER TIME.

YEAH, AND THIS IS CALLED "UNINVITED GUESTS". BUT WHO'S THAT OTHER GEEZER OUTSIDE THE WINDOW?

KARSTEN PROBABLY DRAGGED ALONG ALL KINDS OF SCUMBAGS WHEN HE STOPPED BY FOR A VISIT. AN UNINVITED GUEST WITH AN UNINVITED STRANGER.

IN THE STENERSEN ANECDOTE, KARSTEN IS ALONE. BUT THEN STENERSEN USED A LOT OF POETIC LICENSE WHEN HE WROTE. CONDENSED, DELETED AND SIMPLIFIED.

LIV* AND I SAW A GOOSE THIS SUMMER THAT LOOKED A HELL OF A LOT LIKE LUDVIG KARSTEN.

MUNCH DID, TOO, FOR SURE.

WOW! ALL THAT'S MISSING IS THE MOUSTACHE AND THE CORNY HAIRDO.

* LIV BRAATHEN, THE NARRATOR'S WIFE.

183

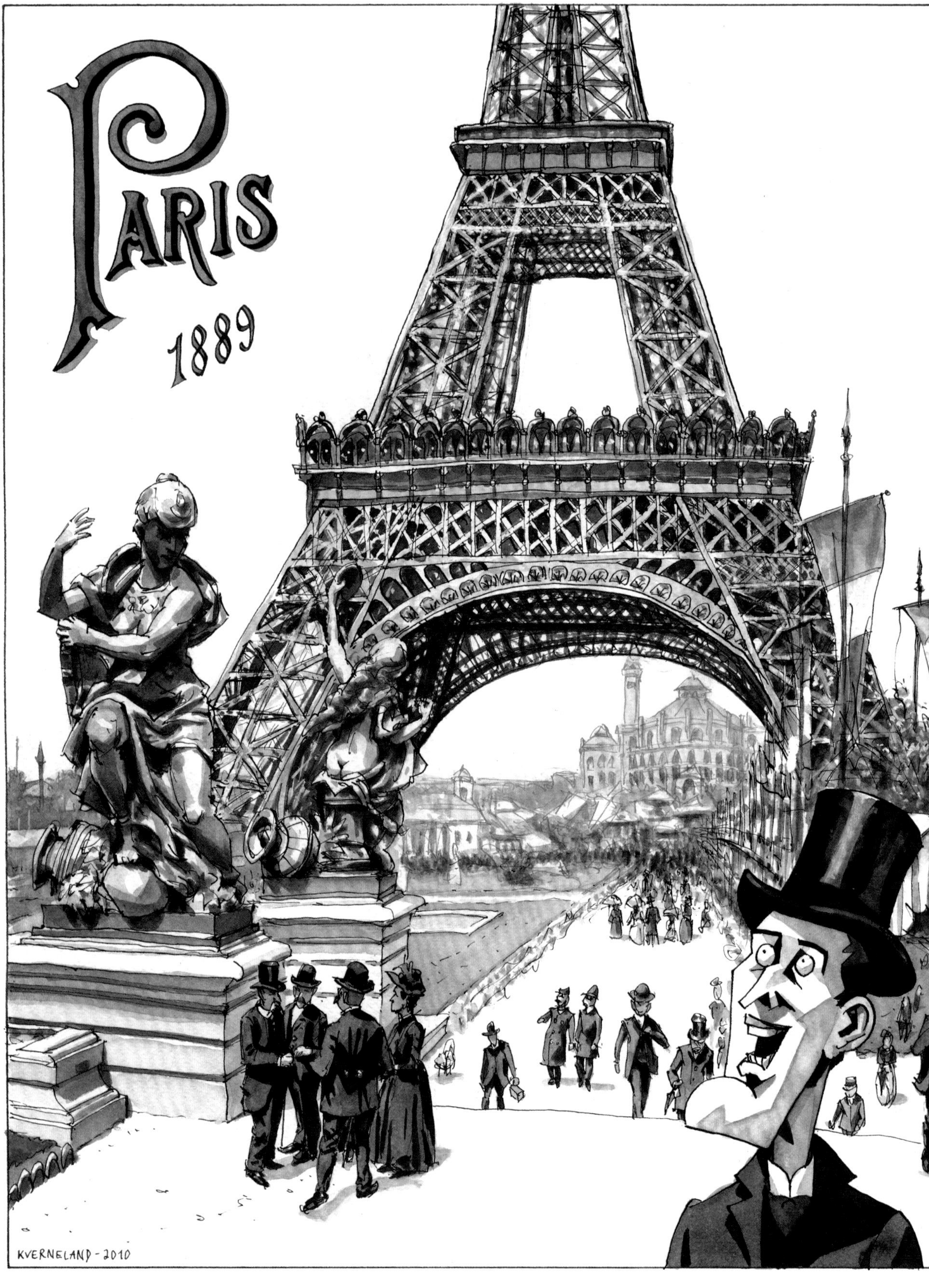
PARIS
1889
KVERNELAND - 2010

I WORK AT THE STUDIO {LEON BONNAT'S SCHOOL} IN THE MORNING — EXTEND MY ARM AND MEASURE WITH MY PENCIL THE PROPORTIONS OF THE BODY OF THE NAKED MODEL STANDING IN THE MIDDLE OF THE STUDIO.

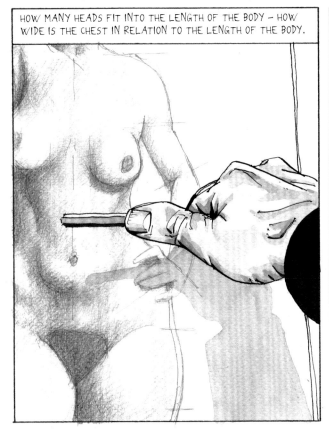

HOW MANY HEADS FIT INTO THE LENGTH OF THE BODY — HOW WIDE IS THE CHEST IN RELATION TO THE LENGTH OF THE BODY.

IT BORES AND TIRES ME — MAKES ME APATHETIC.

On Sunday, I went to see Bilbao Bill*. Bilbao Bill has fought in many battles against the Indians.

Among them, a great battle against a famous Indian chief.

It became a duel between the two, and Bill killed the Indian chief with a knife and took his scalp.

The knife and the scalp are on display in his tent.

* WILLIAM FREDERICH "BUFFALO BILL" CODY (1846–1917) TOURED EUROPE WITH HIS "WILD WEST SHOW" IN 1887–89.

186

Dear Edvard!
Thank you for your letter; praise the Lord that you are well.

I unfortunately neglected to send you your hymnal, but will make sure to have Wang bring it to you; for one cannot live entirely without the word of God.

It must have been amusing to see the Indians, yet I am a bit doubtful whether Mr Bill really is an old trapper and about the authenticity of the knife and the scalp.
Your devoted Kr. Munch.

187

* VALENTIN KIELLAND (1866–1944), NORWEGIAN SCULPTOR AND PAINTER, FRIEND OF MUNCH IN PARIS.

My dearest Edvard!

It seems like a dream, almost impossible to take it all in – and yet it is true. Papa has joined Mamma and Sophie and is able to sense how utterly profound our grief is and to see into our despondent and heavy hearts.

I HAD TO GET OUT.

I GAVE A START — I SAW AN OLD MAN FAR OFF — HOW HE RESEMBLED MY FATHER.

CLOSE UP HE NO LONGER LOOKED LIKE HIM.

I WENT INTO A RESTAURANT AND READ THE LETTER OVER AND OVER AGAIN.

I PULLED MY HAT DOWN OVER MY EYES. HOW DISMAL AND LARGE THE RESTAURANT WAS — IT WAS EMPTY BUT FOR A COUPLE OF WAITERS AND MYSELF — OVER TO THE SIDE WERE TWO HUGE GAPING BILLIARD TABLES.

THERE WERE SO MANY LITTLE THINGS THAT CAME TO MIND — SMALL INCIDENCES THAT NAGGED ME. WORDS THAT HAD CAUSED DISTRESS. MY EYES FILLED WITH TEARS.

IT HAD SOMETHING TO DO WITH HER.

WHY HAD I NOT TOLD HIM EVERYTHING — THEN HE WOULD HAVE UNDERSTOOD WHY I WAS SO IMPETUOUS —

SO NERVOUS — SO OFTEN UNYIELDING AND CALLOUS —

WHY HAD I NOT REMAINED AT HOME WHEN HE ASKED ME TO.

WHY HAD I SO OFTEN COME HOME LATE AT NIGHT –

I HAD TO GET OUT – OUT – IN ORDER TO RUN AWAY FROM MY THOUGHTS.

I HAD TO GET OUT IN ORDER TO FORGET HER AND IN ORDER TO SEEK HER OUT – THE PLACES WHERE SHE HAD BEEN.

I WAS NO LONGER ALONE IN MYSELF. SHE WAS IN ME – SHE WAS IN MY BLOOD.

HOW I HAD WISHED THAT A TIME WOULD COME WHEN WE MIGHT CONVERSE AMICABLY – THAT I MIGHT HOLD THAT GREY HEAD CLOSE TO ME.

THERE IS A CITY WITHIN THE CITY, THE CHURCHYARD OF THE DEAD. IT HAS WIDE STREETS — ALLEYS AND BOULEVARDS.

THE GRAVES LIE THERE SIDE BY SIDE — SOME HIGH, OTHERS LOW.

CRYPTS AND PALACES — QUIET PEOPLE LIVE THERE — THE DEAD.

THEIR BONES DISINTEGRATE AND MAKE WAY FOR NEW ONES.

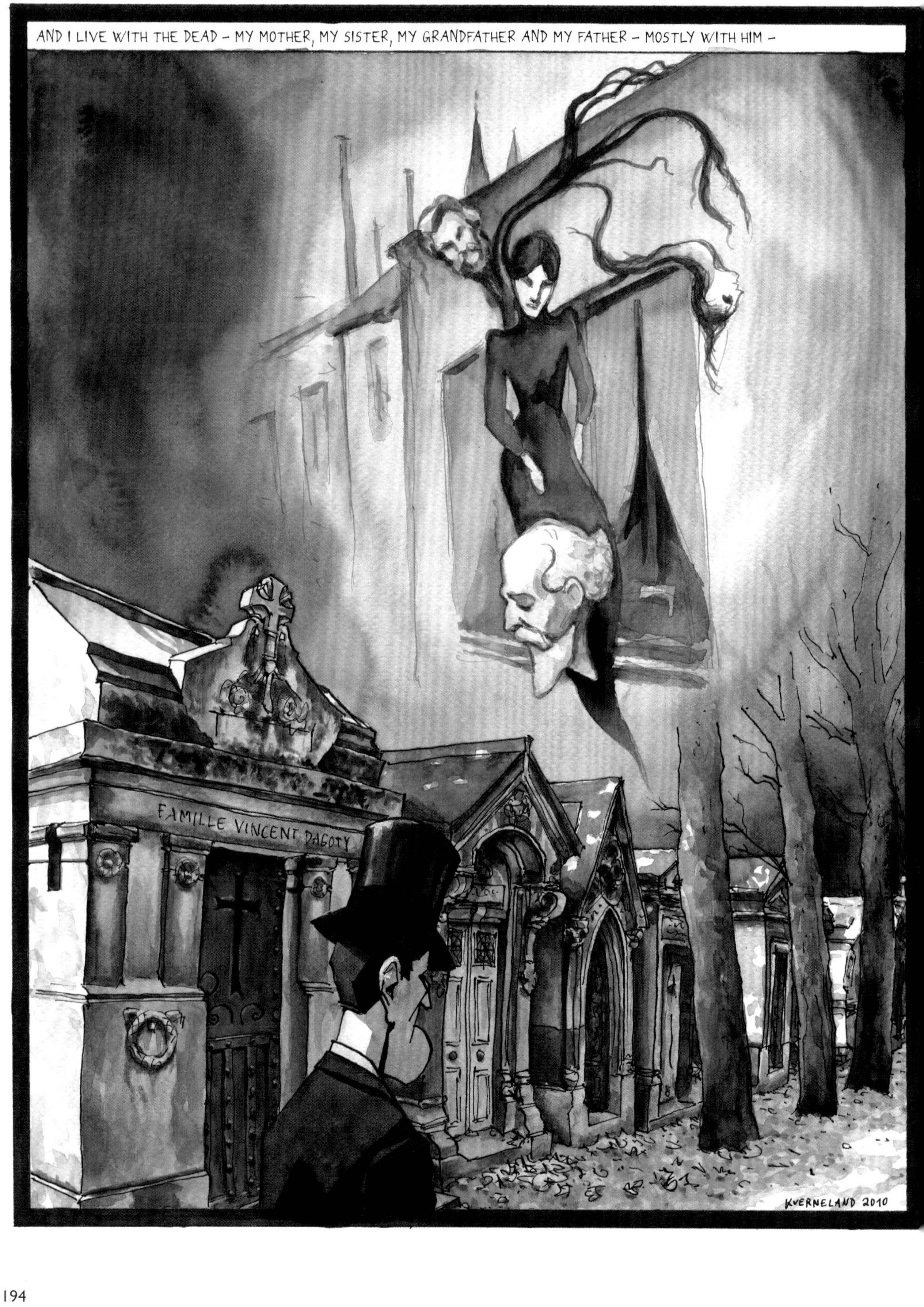
AND I LIVE WITH THE DEAD – MY MOTHER, MY SISTER, MY GRANDFATHER AND MY FATHER – MOSTLY WITH HIM –
FAMILLE VINCENT DAGOTY
KVERNELAND 2010

I WAS VISITING GOLDSTEIN {EMANUEL GOLDSTEIN, DANISH WRITER}.

YES, IT IS ALWAYS PAINFUL WHEN THERE HAS BEEN CONFLICT.

BUT WE WERE ALSO VERY FOND OF EACH OTHER – HE WAS SO GENTLE, YOU SEE, LIKE A LAMB.

IS YOUR FATHER STILL ALIVE?

YES.

I ENVIED HIM THAT.

THAT JÆGER – HE WAS A TOUGH ONE – DO YOU KNOW WHAT HE SAID –

KILL HIM.

MY OWN FATHER – WHO HAD SUCH A GOOD HEART. I DIDN'T UNDERSTAND JÆGER. I COULD LOVE HIM – BUT I ALSO HATED HIM.

THAT WAS THE WORST, FOR MY FATHER – MY RELATIONSHIP WITH JÆGER.

SO MANY STRANGE THINGS COME TO MIND AND WHAT'S WORSE – SMALL INCIDENTS – THAT HE UNDOUBTEDLY SOON FORGOT ABOUT.

HE RETURNED HOME FROM HELGELANDSMOEN – HAD BEEN AWAY FOR A LONG WHILE – HE BROUGHT OUT A BOTTLE OF WINE –

HERE, THIS IS FOR YOU – LET US DRINK IT TOGETHER.

IT WAS CHEAP CHAMPAGNE – I RESPONDED COOLLY –

I'M NOT SURE I LIKE IT.

HE WAS DISAPPOINTED.

WHEN I THINK OF IT NOW – WHY DIDN'T I EMBRACE HIM – GAZE AT LENGTH INTO THOSE KINDLY AGED FEATURES – IF ONLY I HAD THE CHANCE NOW.

I SHOOK THEM ALL BY THE HAND. WE WERE A LITTLE SELF-CONSCIOUS – I WAS RELUCTANT TO SHOW EXCESSIVE EMOTION –

BE SURE TO TAKE CARE IN PARIS – YOU KNOW THE CLIMATE IS DAMP – SO YOU COULD EASILY GET ARTHRITIS –

STAY AT HOME – I HAVE HEARD THERE WILL BE BAD WEATHER –

THAT IS OUT OF THE QUESTION. I COULD NOT BEAR TO STAY ONE MORE DAY HERE IN TOWN.

VERY WELL THEN.

WE SHOULD HAVE ACCOMPANIED YOU DOWN THERE — BUT I DO NOT HAVE THE TIME.

OH, THAT'S NOT NECESSARY.

I WISH HE HAD DONE IT ANYWAY.

DOWN BY THE STEAMBOAT THE DECK WAS FULL OF MY FRIENDS — AND WAAGE STANG AND HORNEMAN WERE ALREADY DRUNK — THEY HAD BROUGHT BOTTLES ALONG.

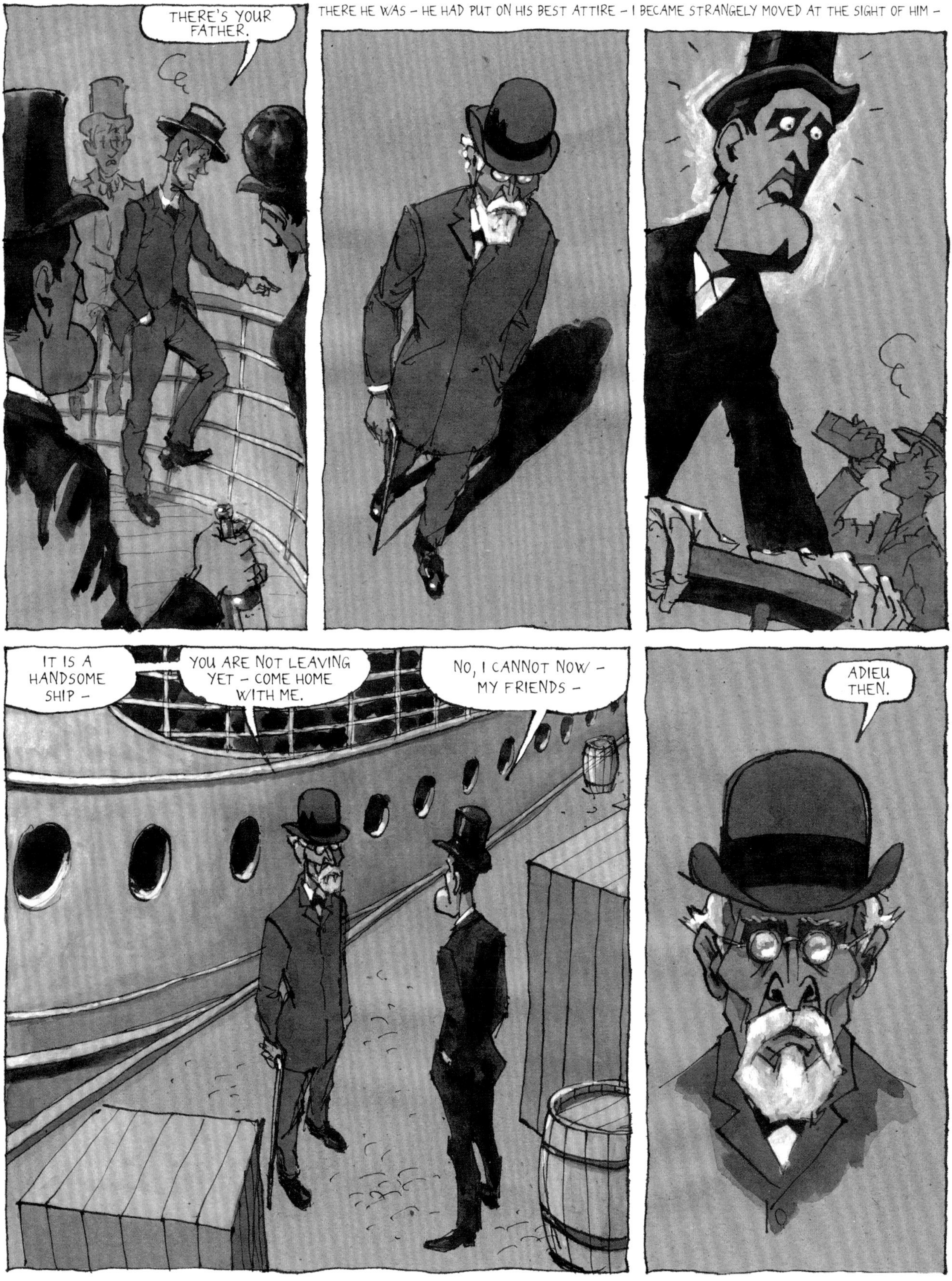
THERE'S YOUR FATHER.
THERE HE WAS – HE HAD PUT ON HIS BEST ATTIRE – I BECAME STRANGELY MOVED AT THE SIGHT OF HIM –
IT IS A HANDSOME SHIP –
YOU ARE NOT LEAVING YET – COME HOME WITH ME.
NO, I CANNOT NOW – MY FRIENDS –
ADIEU THEN.

BY PAINTING THOSE COLOURS AND LINES AND SHAPES I HAD SEEN IN AN EMOTIONAL STATE — I WISHED AS WITH A PHONOGRAPH TO MAKE THE EMOTIONAL STATE VIBRATE ONCE AGAIN —

TOP: "DEATH IN THE SICK ROOM", 1893. "STUDY/THE SICK CHILD", 1885–86. CENTRE: "BY THE DEATHBED", 1895. "THE DEAD MOTHER AND THE CHILD", 1899. BOTTOM: "THE SMELL OF DEATH", 1895.

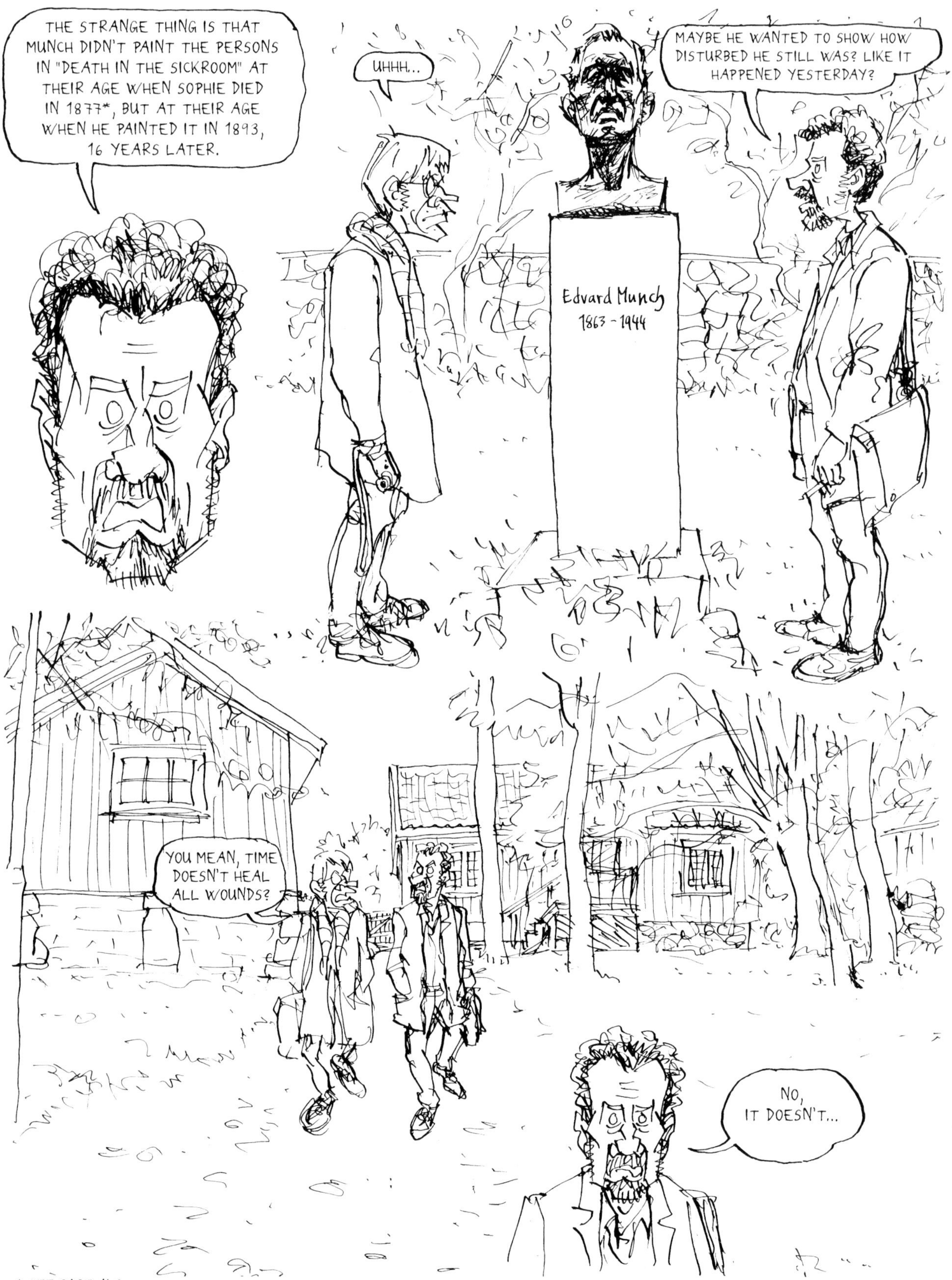
THE STRANGE THING IS THAT MUNCH DIDN'T PAINT THE PERSONS IN "DEATH IN THE SICKROOM" AT THEIR AGE WHEN SOPHIE DIED IN 1877*, BUT AT THEIR AGE WHEN HE PAINTED IT IN 1893, 16 YEARS LATER.
UHHH...
Edvard Munch 1863 - 1944
MAYBE HE WANTED TO SHOW HOW DISTURBED HE STILL WAS? LIKE IT HAPPENED YESTERDAY?
YOU MEAN, TIME DOESN'T HEAL ALL WOUNDS?
NO, IT DOESN'T...

* SEE PAGE 143.

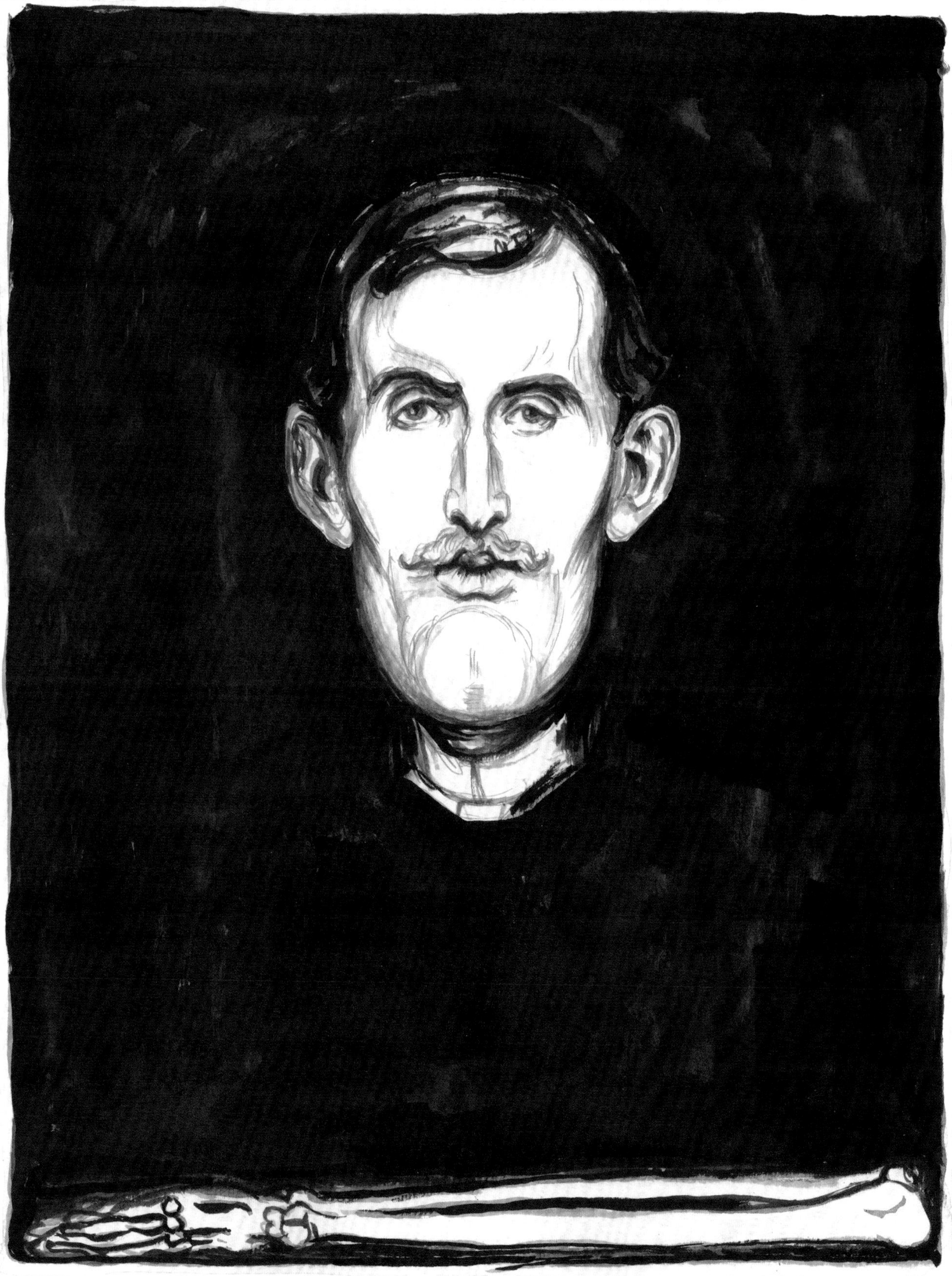

ANGST HAS RAGED IN ME FROM THE DAY I BECAME CONSCIOUS – JUST AS ILLNESS HAS SINCE THE DAY I WAS BORN – BOTH INHERITED. IT HAS BEEN LIKE AN UNJUST CURSE THAT HAS FOLLOWED ME.

YET I OFTEN HAVE THE FEELING THAT I MUST HAVE THE ANGST – IT IS NECESSARY TO ME – AND THAT I WOULD NOT WANT TO BE WITHOUT IT.

IN PERIODS WITHOUT ANGST OR ILLNESS I HAVE FELT LIKE A SHIP SAILING IN A STRONG WIND WITHOUT A RUDDER – AND HAVE ASKED MYSELF: WHITHER? WHERE WILL I GO AGROUND?

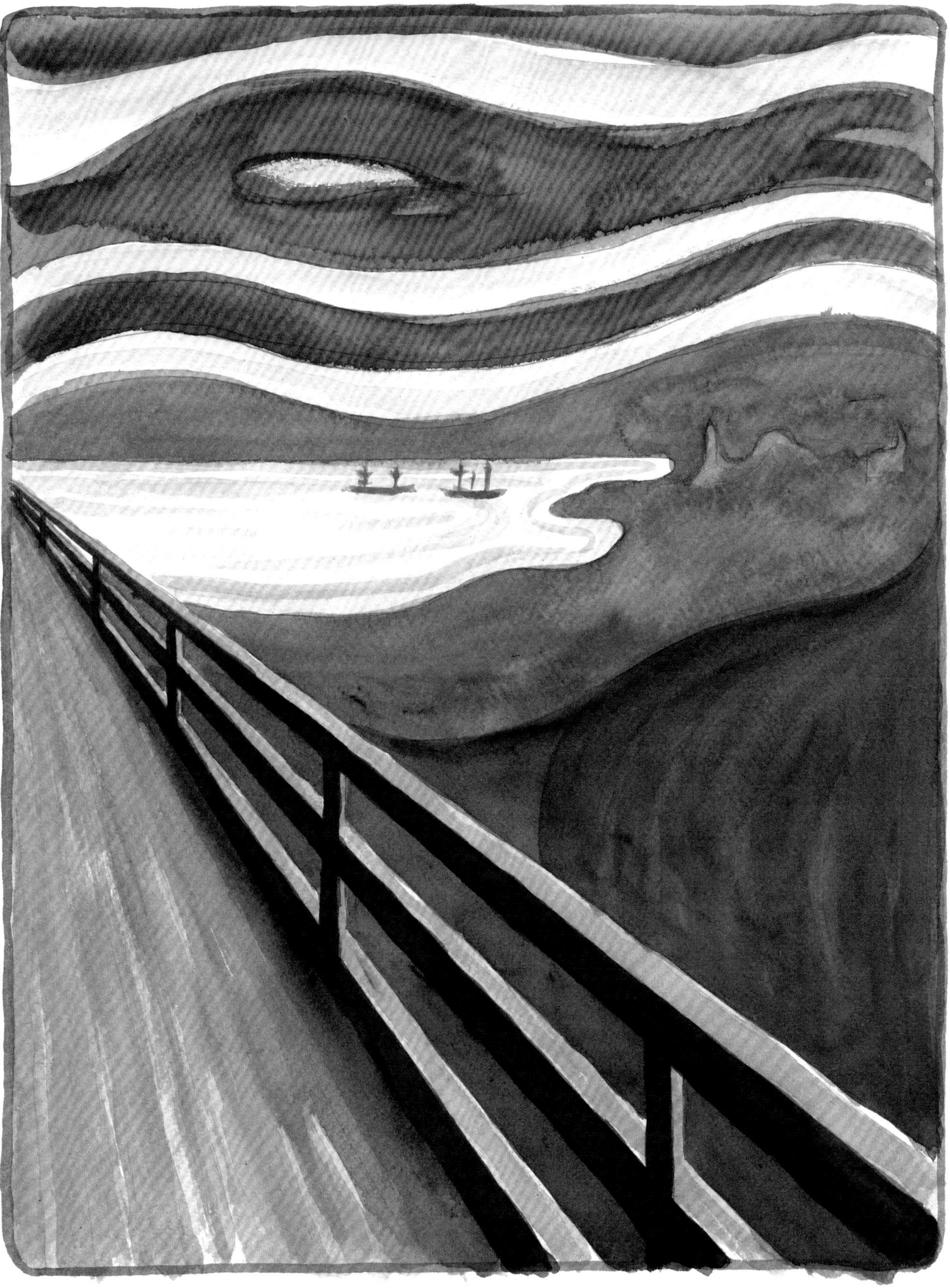

KRAKATOA, INDONESIA, 27 AUGUST 1883:

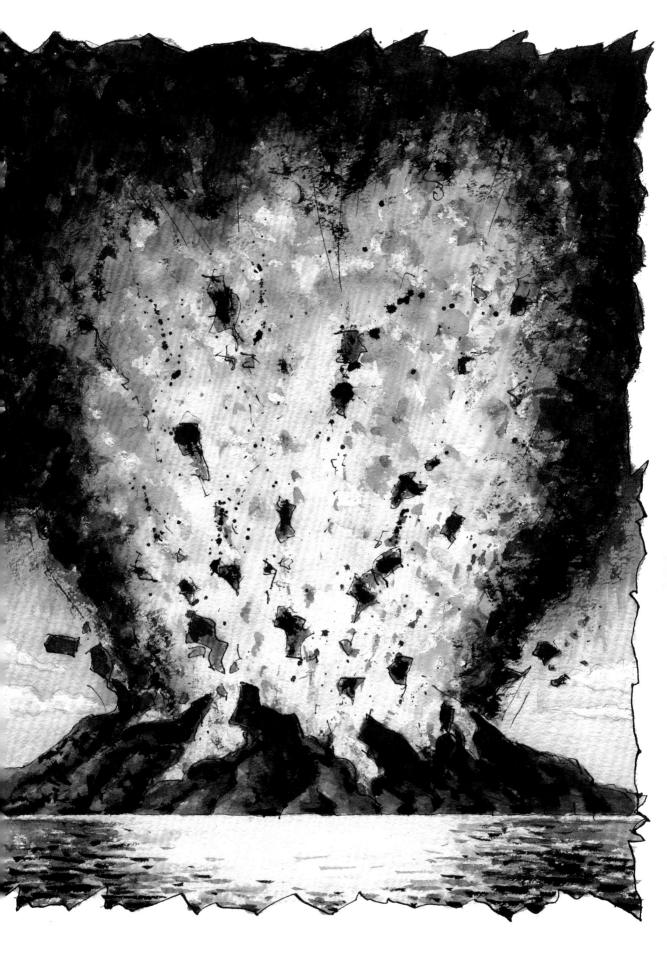

AN IMAGINED MEETING BETWEEN TWO FRIENDS IN KRISTIANIA, 1891:

"THE RED CLOUDS ON THE HORIZON RISE SWIFTLY AND MUTELY INTO THE ATMOSPHERE,"

"BEHIND THEM, A BLUISH GLOW AND FLICKERS OF YELLOW:"

"AS THOUGH BLISTERED RED SKIN SPREADS ACROSS THE HEAVENLY VAULT,"

VILHELM KRAG (1871–1933), NORWEGIAN POET AND FRIEND OF MUNCH.

"AND ITS VAST PULSE THROBS WITH MALIGNANT BLOOD."

"I JUMP UP IN UNSPEAKABLE ANGST,"

"CLASP MY HANDS TO MY TEMPLES AND SCREAM OUT ACROSS THE TWILIGHT EXPANSE."*

* EXCERPT FROM KRAG'S "NIGHT. POEMS IN PROSE", 1892.

209

AUTUMN 1891, KRISTIANIA, EAST STATION:

IT PAINS ME GREATLY TO LEAVE BEKKELAGET – THE WEATHER WAS SO LOVELY TODAY. BUT I AM ILL, I MUST GET TO NIZZA*.
KOFF–KOFF!

* NICE.

CHRISTIAN SKREDSVIG**:
HE LOOKED EVEN LEANER AND MORE WRETCHED IN HIS GRANDFATHER'S VOLUMINOUS PASSÉ TRAVELLING COAT. IN HIS ARMS, HE CARRIED ALL OF THE ACCOUTREMENTS OF HIS TRADE.

SKREDSVIG.

HE INSISTED ON HAVING IT ALL WITH HIM IN THE COMPARTMENT.

** NORWEGIAN PAINTER (1854–1945).

FROM HAMBURG VIA FRANKFURT AND ALL THE WAY TO BASEL, WE ALTERNATED BETWEEN LYING, SITTING AND STANDING IN 4TH CLASS.

MUNCH CURSED AND ENGAGED IN HEATED ARGUMENTS WITH GREY, GROWLING WORKERS – DUE TO THE CROWDED SPACE.

WE COULD HAVE TRAVELLED 3RD CLASS.

MUNCH RESPONDED BY CURSING THE GOVERNMENT FOR GRANTING SUCH PALTRY STIPENDS.

NICE: IT'S PLEASANT ENOUGH HERE, BUT I HARDLY SLEPT LAST NIGHT, I COULDN'T STOP THINKING ABOUT THE HORRIBLE INCIDENT I EXPERIENCED LAST YEAR OVER THERE IN THE OLD TOWN. KOFF–KOFF!

211

I CHECKED INTO A FILTHY, DREADFUL HOTEL THERE. THE PROPRIETORS REEKED OF ONION, GLISTENED WITH COOKING OIL AND SPOKE PIEMONTESE.

I WAS STILL FEVERISH AND SPENT MOST OF THE DAY IN MY ROOM.

KOFF-KOFF!

THEN MY INKPOT SPILLED ALL OVER THE WHITE COVERLET. IT WAS A TERRIBLE SIGHT – IT RESEMBLED AN ENORMOUS MAP OF RUSSIA.

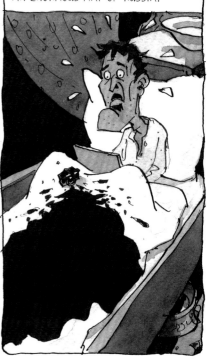

FORTUNATELY I HAD SEVERAL LARGE TUBES OF WHITE IN MY PAINTBOX. AROUND DUSK THE NEXT AFTERNOON THERE WAS NOTHING LEFT OF RUSSIA.

THEN I COLLECTED MY THINGS, LOCKED THE DOOR, BUT KEPT THE KEY, PAID AND WALKED TO THE OTHER SIDE OF TOWN, WHERE I FOUND A ROOM.

AT FIRST I DIDN'T DARE GO OUTSIDE TO PAINT.

I SAT ON THE ROOFTOP TERRACES IN THE EVENING PAINTING THE MOONLIGHT. THE GALLERY BOUGHT ONE OF THEM*.

* "NIGHT IN NICE", 1891, THE NATIONAL GALLERY'S FIRST MUNCH ACQUISITION.

I WAS SAVED IN A WAY – BUT I KEPT IMAGINING I SAW THE SWARTHY, ONION-REEKING LANDLORD LEADING HIS BAND OF CUTTHROATS THROUGH TOWN IN PURSUIT OF ME.

HE SCRIMPED AND SAVED IN ORDER TO REMAIN IN THE RIVIERA OVER THE WINTER.

OH, THOSE BRUTES, HAMMERING IT INTO OUR TORMENTED HEADS THAT ARTISTS MUST SUFFER.

WHAT A CONTEMPTIBLE, ROMANTIC LIE!

JUST BECAUSE MILLET* SUFFERED HUNGER AND COLD AND YET PAINTED MAGNIFICENT PICTURES, DOES THAT MEAN COROT*, WITH HIS WEALTH AND HIS INTEREST RATES, IS ANY LESS TALENTED?

* FRENCH PAINTERS.

HE WHO HAS SHALL RECEIVE MORE, AND HE WHO HAD NOTHING, HE SHALL YET BE DEPRIVED.

KOFF–KOFF!

LISTEN! ISN'T OUR GREAT B.B.** AT THIS VERY MOMENT MEDDLING IN THE MEAGRE BONE THAT HAS BEEN TOSSED TO ME, MY STIPEND, CLAIMING THAT IT IS TOO GOOD FOR ME?

BUT JUST YOU WAIT – I SHALL REPORT HIM MYSELF.

** BJØRNSTJERNE BJØRNSON (PROMINENT NORWEGIAN WRITER) PROTESTED AGAINST RENEWING MUNCH'S GRANT BECAUSE HE HAD BEEN ILL (AND THUS UNABLE TO WORK).

EDVARD MUNCH, 14 JANUARY 1892:

YOU WILL CREATE GREAT WORKS – IMMORTAL MASTERPIECES WILL ISSUE FROM YOUR HAND.

YES – I KNOW – BUT CAN THEY DISPEL THIS SERPENT THAT DIGS AT THE VERY ROOTS OF MY HEART ?

NO – THEY CAN NEVER DO THAT.

CHRISTIAN SKREDSVIG:

FOR THE LONGEST TIME HE WANTED TO PAINT THE MEMORY OF A SUNSET. IT WAS AS RED AS BLOOD. NO, IT WAS BLOOD, CLOTTED BLOOD.

BUT NO ONE ELSE WOULD HAVE FELT AS HE DID. EVERYONE WOULD THINK OF CLOUDS.

AS HE SPOKE, HE BECAME MELANCHOLY ABOUT THIS THING THAT HAD SEIZED HIM WITH SUCH TERROR.

MELANCHOLY BECAUSE THE INADEQUATE MEANS OF PAINTING WOULD NEVER SUFFICE TO CAPTURE IT.

WHEN THE CLOUDS IN A SUNSET APPEARED TO ONE WHILE IN A STATE OF ANGST, AS A BLOODY COVER — THERE IS NO POINT IN PAINTING SOME ORDINARY CLOUDS —

ONE MUST TAKE THE DIRECT ROUTE — AND PAINT THE IMMEDIATE IMPRESSION — THE IMAGE — PAINT THE BLOOD OF THE CLOUDS.

THE EFFECT OF A WORK OF ART DEPENDS ON WHAT IT CONVEYS — BUT WHAT IS EXPECTED IS AN EXTRACT OF NATURE — THE SQUARE ROOT OF NATURE.

"HE CRAVES THE IMPOSSIBLE AND HAS MADE DESPAIR HIS RELIGION," I THOUGHT, BUT I ADVISED HIM TO PAINT IT.

I was walking along the road with two friends

— when the sun went down

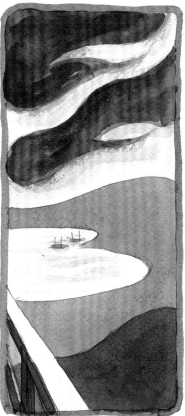

The sky suddenly turned blood-red

— and I felt a wave of sadness — a tugging ache beneath my heart —

I paused, leaned against the railing tired to death

– above the blue-black fjord and city, blood hovered in flaming tongues

My friends walked on and stayed behind quaking with angst –

and I felt as though a vast endless scream passed through nature

"SICK MOOD AT SUNSET/DESPAIR", OIL ON CANVAS, 1892.

THE PAINTING "DESPAIR" ATTRACTED ENORMOUS ATTENTION WHEN IT WAS FIRST EXHIBITED IN KRISTIANIA* AND THEN IN BERLIN IN AUTUMN 1892 UNDER THE TITLE "SICK MOOD AT SUNSET".

* EDVARD MUNCH'S PAINTING EXHIBITION IN THE TOSTRUPGÅRDEN (SEE PAGE 12).

"THESE ARE NOT CLOUDS AGAINST A RUSSET SUNSET, NOR THE GLOW OF A DAY THAT HAS WANED:"

"HERE ARE LICKING FLAMES AND TRICKLING BLOOD, BLAZING SWORDS AND A RIVER OF FIERY RED,"

"HERE ARE DOOMSDAY ANGST AND THE TORMENTS OF DEATH, A SCRIPTURE ABLAZE IN THE NOCTURNAL VAULT OF THE HEAVENS..."

"THE INSCRUTABLE TERROR OF ALL LIFE."**

** EXCERPT OF VILHELM KRAG'S POEM DEDICATED TO "SICK MOOD AT SUNSET" IN *DAGBLADET*, 1892.

"THE SCREAM", PASTEL ON CARDBOARD, 74 X 56CM, 1893.

UNFINISHED PAINTING ON THE REVERSE OF "THE SCREAM", 1893.

223

"THE SCREAM", TEMPERA AND PASTEL ON CARDBOARD, 91 X 73.5CM, 1893. THE NATIONAL GALLERY.

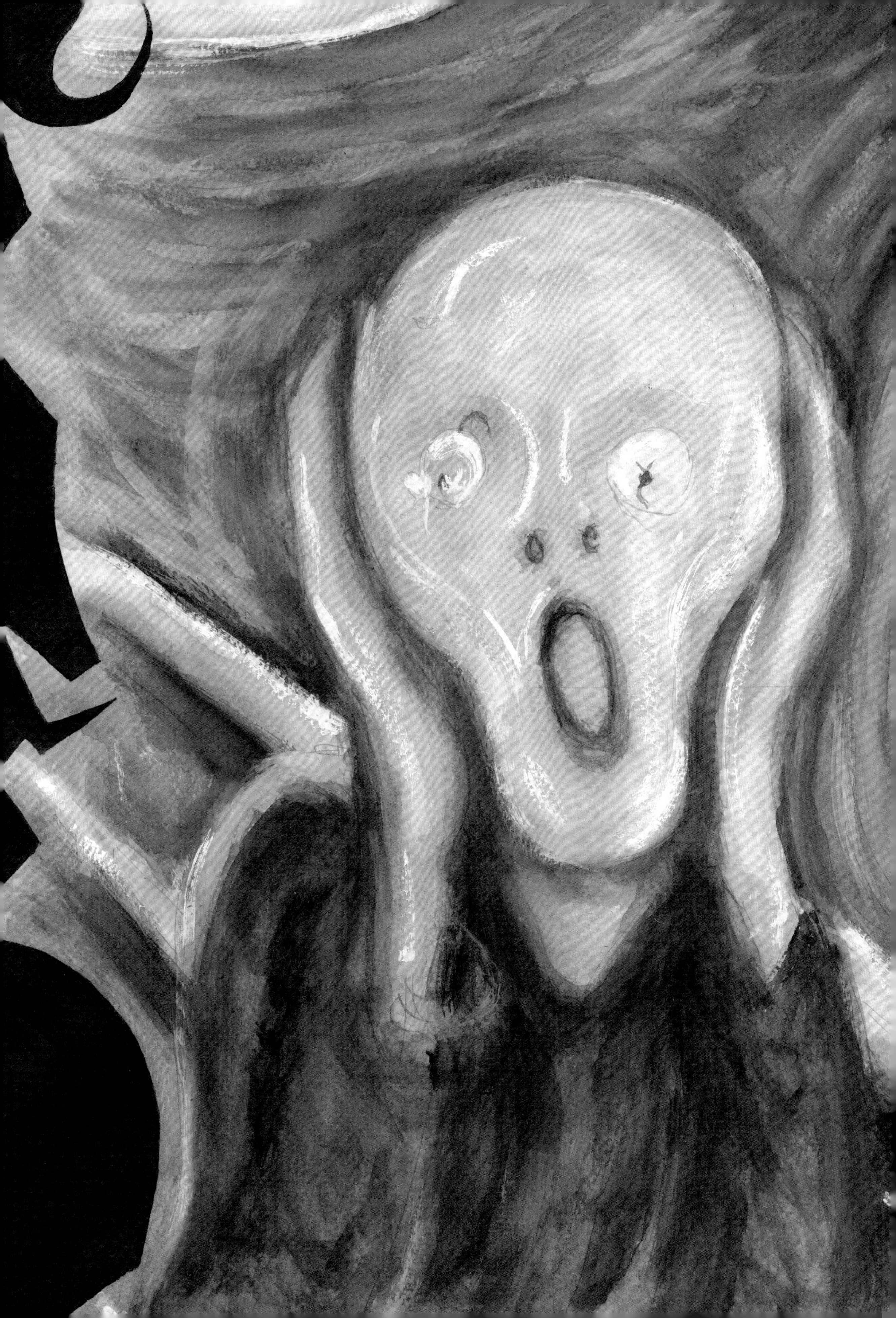

"THE SCREAM" IS KINDA LIKE A MENTAL SELF-PORTRAIT. MUNCH DISTILLED THE RAW ANGST HE FELT ON THE HILLSIDE OVER THERE INTO A BALD EMBRYO DUDE.

IT'S THE SICKEST SELF-PORTRAIT EVER. LIKE BEN KINGSLEY WITH PLANETS FOR EYES.

IN THE UPPER LEFT SECTION OF THE PAINTING, ON THE BRIGHT RED CLOUDS, SOME TAGGER HAS SCRIBBLED IN PENCIL "COULD ONLY HAVE BEEN PAINTED BY AN INSANE MAN".

GEEZ! WHO DID IT?

NO ONE KNOWS, BUT IT WAS ALREADY THERE IN 1904.

HEH HEH, PROBABLY ONE OF KARSTEN'S ANTICS.

* A HILL OVERLOOKING THE OSLO HARBOUR.

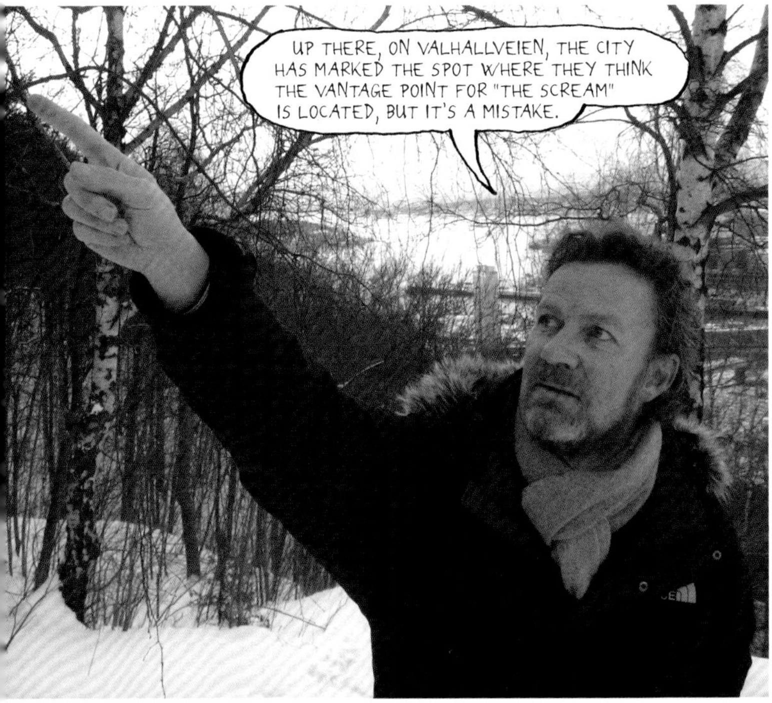
UP THERE, ON VALHALLVEIEN, THE CITY HAS MARKED THE SPOT WHERE THEY THINK THE VANTAGE POINT FOR "THE SCREAM" IS LOCATED, BUT IT'S A MISTAKE.

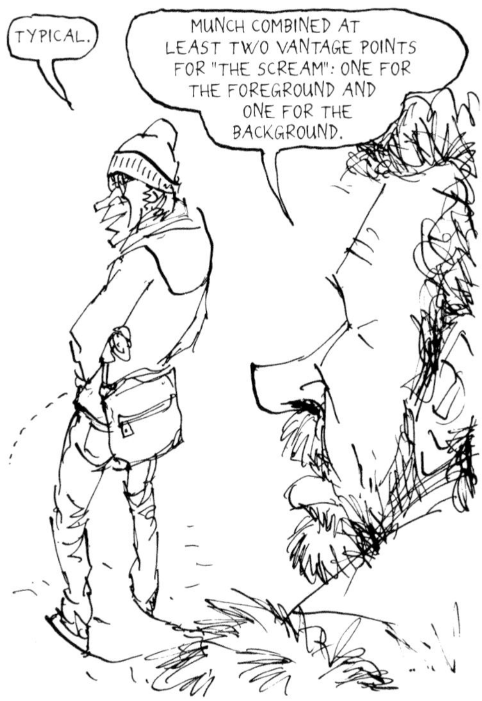
TYPICAL.
MUNCH COMBINED AT LEAST TWO VANTAGE POINTS FOR "THE SCREAM": ONE FOR THE FOREGROUND AND ONE FOR THE BACKGROUND.

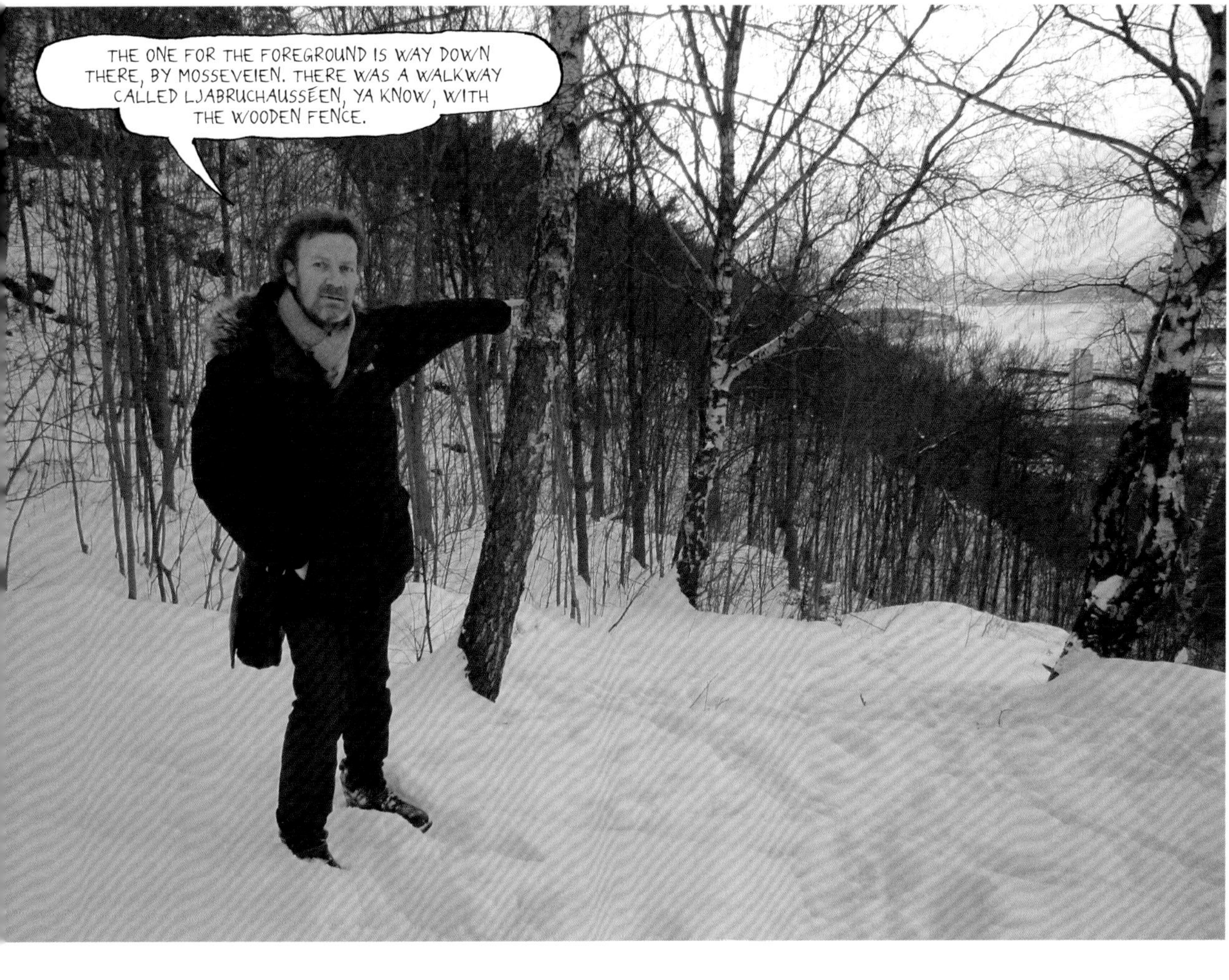
THE ONE FOR THE FOREGROUND IS WAY DOWN THERE, BY MOSSEVEIEN. THERE WAS A WALKWAY CALLED LJABRUCHAUSSÉEN, YA KNOW, WITH THE WOODEN FENCE.

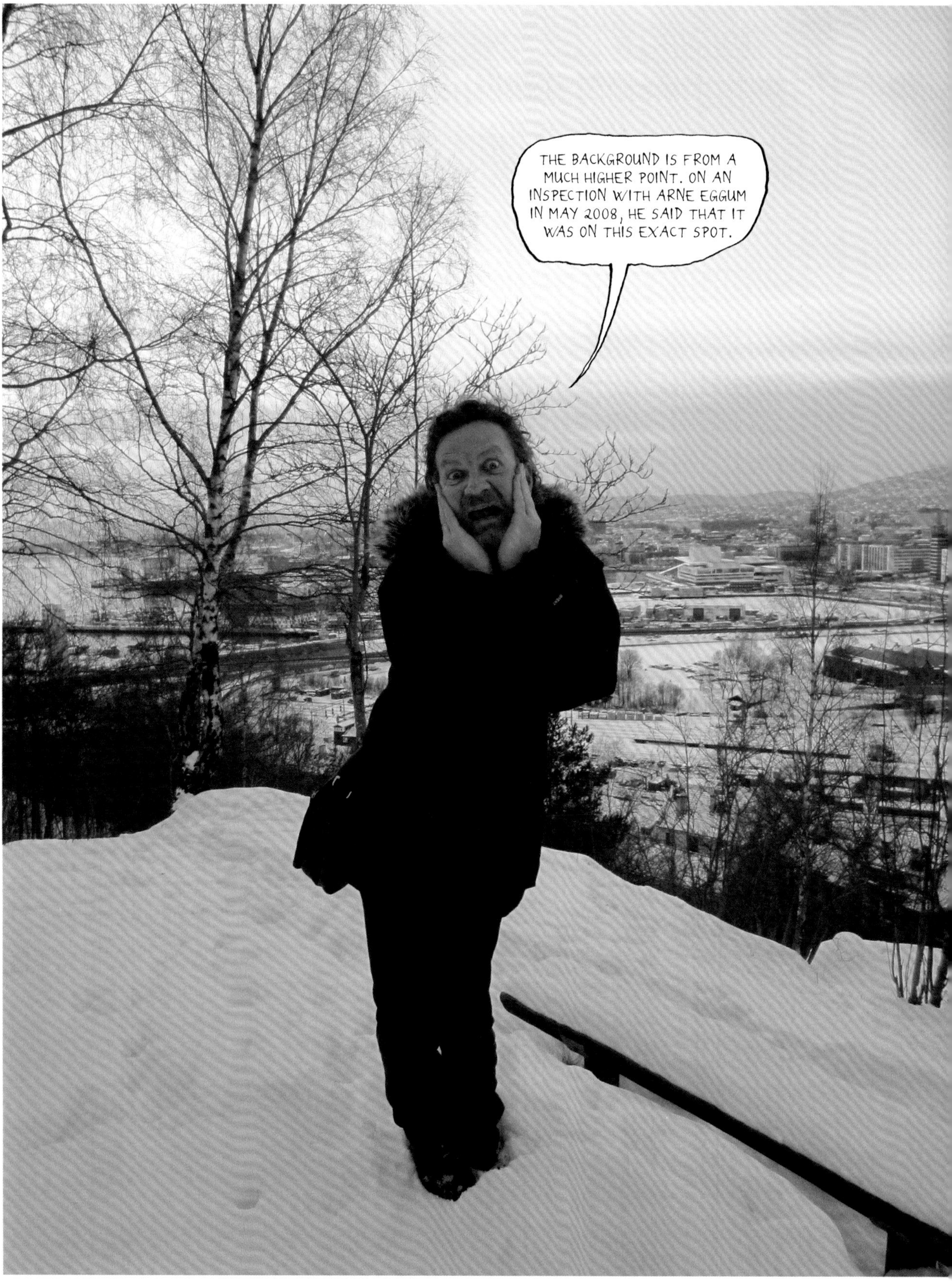
THE BACKGROUND IS FROM A MUCH HIGHER POINT. ON AN INSPECTION WITH ARNE EGGUM IN MAY 2008, HE SAID THAT IT WAS ON THIS EXACT SPOT.

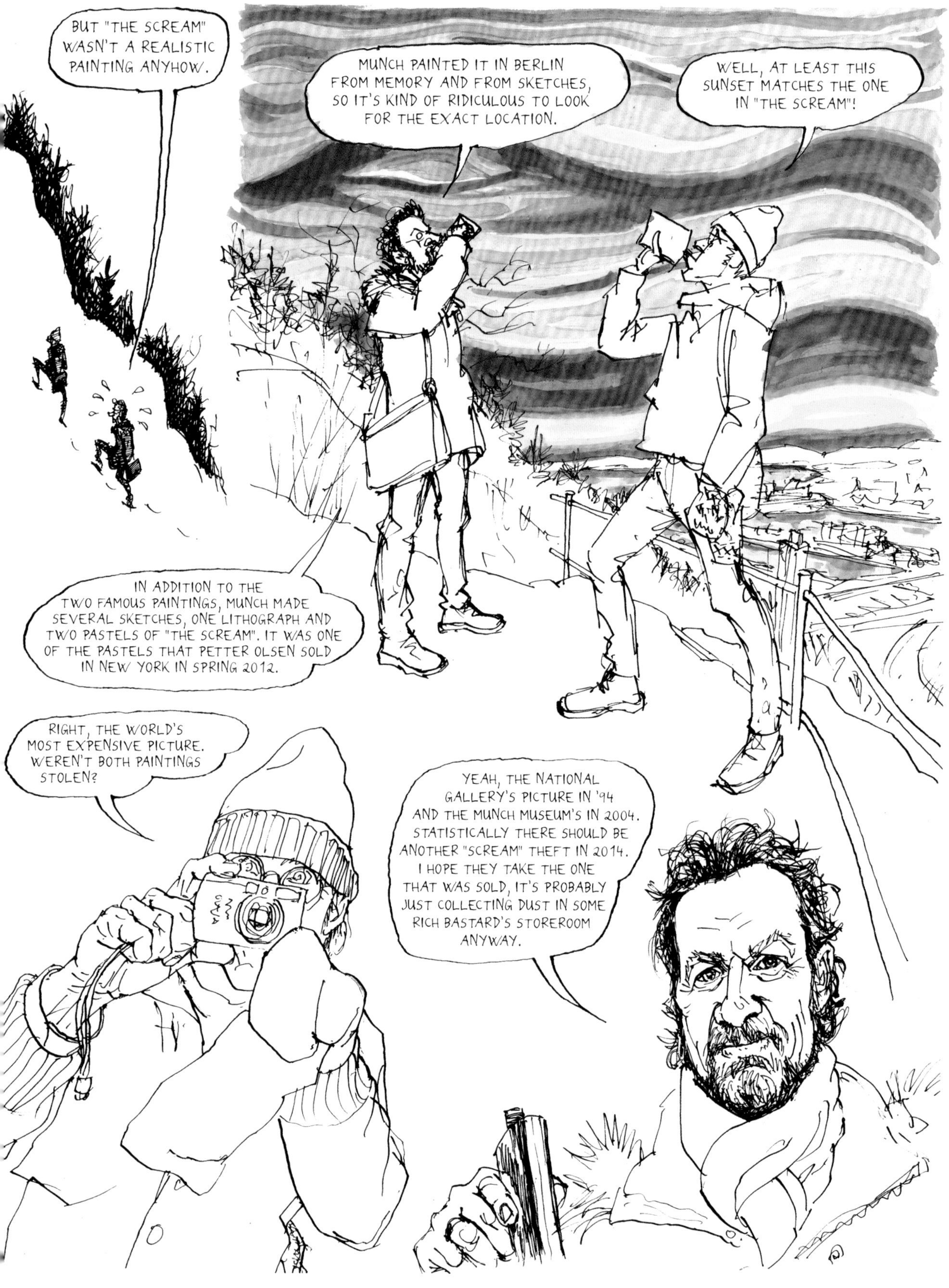
BUT "THE SCREAM" WASN'T A REALISTIC PAINTING ANYHOW.
MUNCH PAINTED IT IN BERLIN FROM MEMORY AND FROM SKETCHES, SO IT'S KIND OF RIDICULOUS TO LOOK FOR THE EXACT LOCATION.
WELL, AT LEAST THIS SUNSET MATCHES THE ONE IN "THE SCREAM"!
IN ADDITION TO THE TWO FAMOUS PAINTINGS, MUNCH MADE SEVERAL SKETCHES, ONE LITHOGRAPH AND TWO PASTELS OF "THE SCREAM". IT WAS ONE OF THE PASTELS THAT PETTER OLSEN SOLD IN NEW YORK IN SPRING 2012.
RIGHT, THE WORLD'S MOST EXPENSIVE PICTURE. WEREN'T BOTH PAINTINGS STOLEN?
YEAH, THE NATIONAL GALLERY'S PICTURE IN '94 AND THE MUNCH MUSEUM'S IN 2004. STATISTICALLY THERE SHOULD BE ANOTHER "SCREAM" THEFT IN 2014. I HOPE THEY TAKE THE ONE THAT WAS SOLD, IT'S PROBABLY JUST COLLECTING DUST IN SOME RICH BASTARD'S STOREROOM ANYWAY.

THE MUNCH MUSEUM, 22 AUGUST 2004:

IT WAS REALLY BIZARRE, MAN. THE VILLAINS JUST WALKED RIGHT IN AND TOOK "THE SCREAM" AND "MADONNA".

REALLY WEIRD. AND DURING THE '80S ANOTHER SCOUNDREL WENT IN AND TOOK "VAMPIRE".

1988:

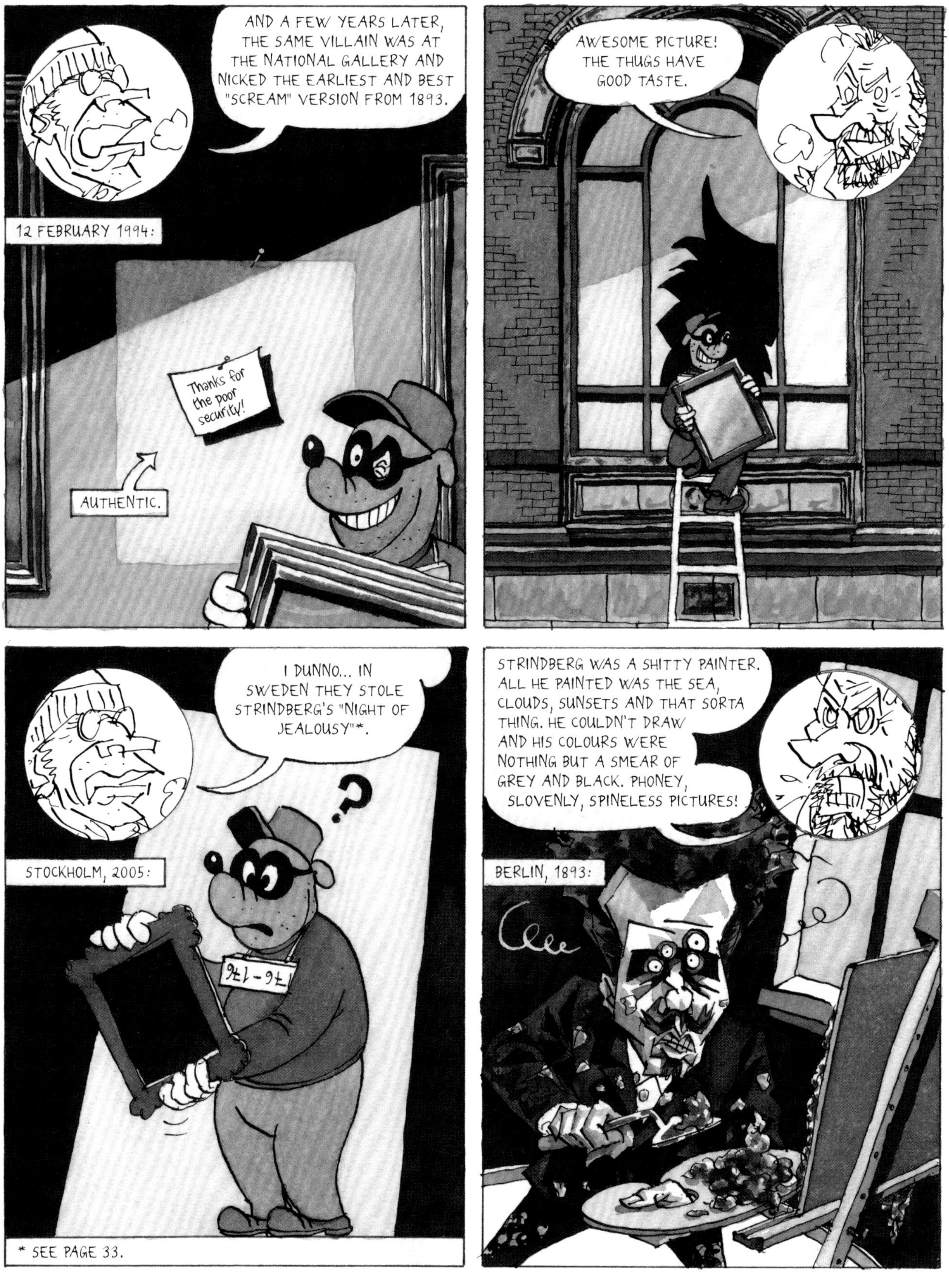
AND A FEW YEARS LATER, THE SAME VILLAIN WAS AT THE NATIONAL GALLERY AND NICKED THE EARLIEST AND BEST "SCREAM" VERSION FROM 1893.
12 FEBRUARY 1994:
Thanks for the poor security!
AUTHENTIC.
AWESOME PICTURE! THE THUGS HAVE GOOD TASTE.
I DUNNO... IN SWEDEN THEY STOLE STRINDBERG'S "NIGHT OF JEALOUSY"*.
?
STOCKHOLM, 2005:
STRINDBERG WAS A SHITTY PAINTER. ALL HE PAINTED WAS THE SEA, CLOUDS, SUNSETS AND THAT SORTA THING. HE COULDN'T DRAW AND HIS COLOURS WERE NOTHING BUT A SMEAR OF GREY AND BLACK. PHONEY, SLOVENLY, SPINELESS PICTURES!
BERLIN, 1893:
* SEE PAGE 33.

HE PAINTED LIKE A NINCOMPOOP. BUT IT WAS RADICAL! HE WAS SO CONCEITED THAT IT'S ALMOST FUNNY HE HAD TO FAKE IT.

THE NERVE OF THEM TO STEAL "THE SCREAM" AND "MADONNA" JUST TO DISTRACT FROM AN ORDINARY CASH BURGLARY.

AS THOUGH MUNCH HAS ANYTHING TO DO WITH MONEY*!

* 1,000 KRONER NOTE WITH MUNCH'S PICTURE ON IT.

WHAT A SCANDAL! THE BURGLARS HAVE NO RESPECT FOR ART. WE WOULD HAVE MADE BETTER ART THIEVES!

"NIGHT OF JEALOUSY"

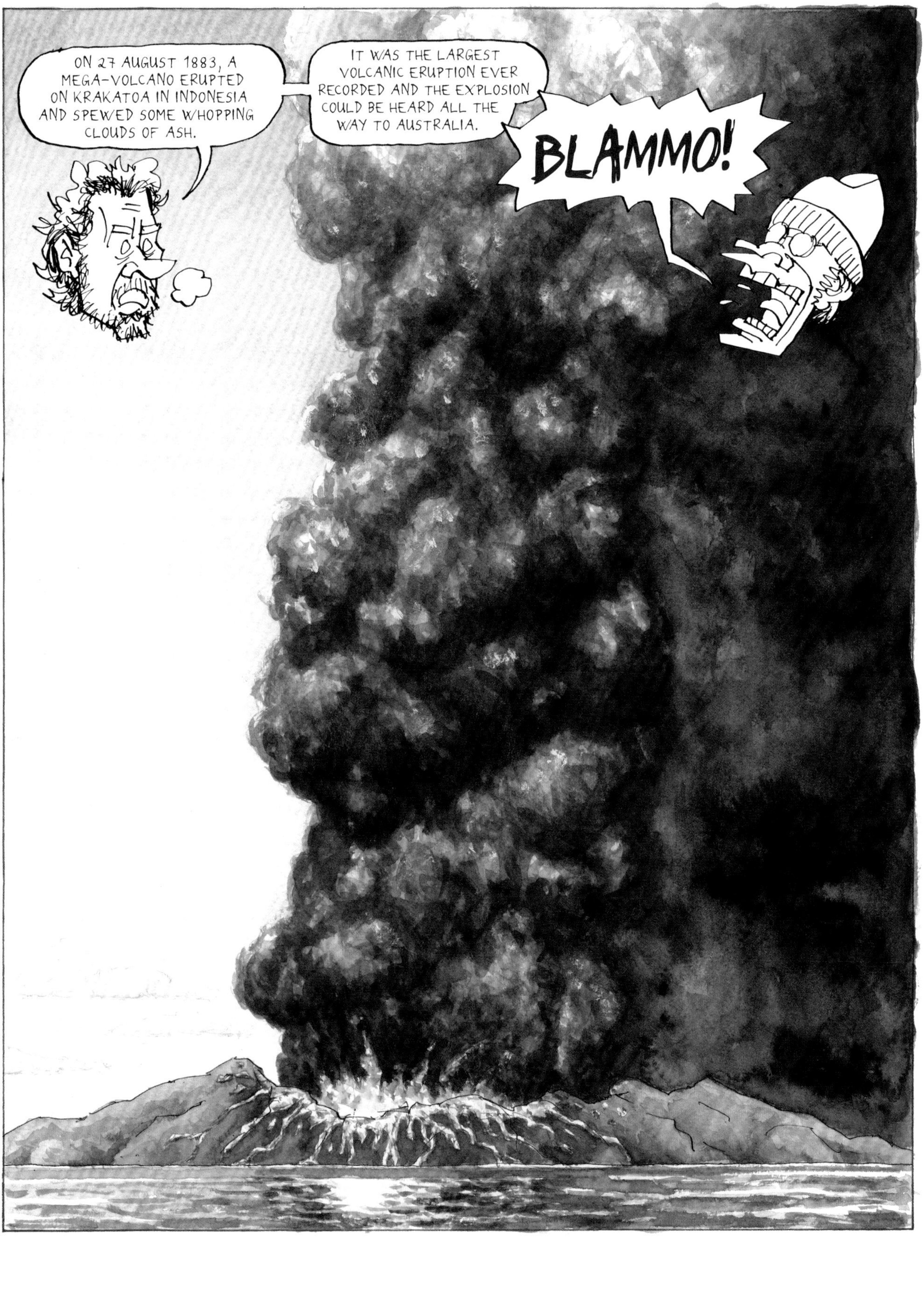
ON 27 AUGUST 1883, A MEGA-VOLCANO ERUPTED ON KRAKATOA IN INDONESIA AND SPEWED SOME WHOPPING CLOUDS OF ASH.
IT WAS THE LARGEST VOLCANIC ERUPTION EVER RECORDED AND THE EXPLOSION COULD BE HEARD ALL THE WAY TO AUSTRALIA.
BLAMMO!

THE CLOUDS OF ASH DRIFTED ALL THE WAY TO EUROPE AND NORWAY, COLOURING THE SUNSETS A BRIGHT RED. PEOPLE WERE FREAKED OUT AND SCREAMED ABOUT BLOODY SKIES AND ARMAGEDDON.

 I HAVE A THEORY: THESE BOHEMIANS WERE SUPPOSED TO BE SO DAMNED SENSITIVE AND SPOKE INCESSANTLY ABOUT NERVES AND ANGST. AT THE SAME TIME, THEY WERE ALWAYS OUT PARTYING AND DRINKING...

ERGO THEY MUST HAVE BEEN CHRONICALLY HUNGOVER...

SO IT MAKES SENSE THAT A HYPERSENSITIVE MUNCH WITH THE HEEBIE-JEEBIES WOULD FREAK OUT WHEN THE SKY SUDDENLY TURNED BRIGHT RED.

BLOOD!

EDVARD MUNCH: IT WAS IN 1895.

— I HAD AN EXHIBITION AT BLOMQVIST IN THE AUTUMN.

— THERE WAS A HEATED CONTROVERSY ABOUT THE PICTURES.

— THERE WERE CALLS TO BOYCOTT THE VENUES — THE POLICE.

- ONE DAY I MET IBSEN DOWN THERE – HE WALKED OVER TO ME.

I FIND IT EXTREMELY INTERESTING.

- I HAD TO ACCOMPANY HIM AND VIEW EVERY PICTURE.

- A GREAT PART OF "THE FRIEZE OF LIFE" WAS DISPLAYED.

HE WAS PARTICULARLY INTERESTED IN THE STAGES OF WOMAN. I HAD TO EXPLAIN IT TO HIM.

THE IDEALISTIC WOMAN – THE WOMAN WITH A LUST FOR LIFE – WOMAN AS A NUN – THE PALE ONE AMONG THE TREES.

– THEN HE WAS AMUSED BY MY PORTRAITS – HOW I HAD EMPHASISED A CERTAIN CHARACTERISTIC – SO THAT IT BORDERED ON CARICATURE.

BELIEVE ME – YOU WILL HAVE THE SAME FATE AS I – THE MORE ENEMIES, THE MORE FRIENDS.

THE WRITER OBSTFELDER, WHO WAS GREETED WITH APPLAUSE, CLIMBED THE PODIUM, GAVE HIS LECTURE ON "MUNCH'S ART" (TO BEGIN WITH RATHER HALTINGLY AND FUMBLINGLY — INTERRUPTED BY LAUGHTER — EVENTUALLY MORE COHERENTLY).

CAN WE NOT THEREFORE FIND IT IN US TO UNDERSTAND AND TO TAKE OUR HATS OFF TO MUNCH?

(THUNDERING APPLAUSE)

SCHARFFENBERG* THEN ASKED TO SPEAK.

AHEM!

IN MUNCH'S ART, THERE HAVE BEEN VARIOUS STAGES – MORE GENERALLY COMPREHENSIBLE IN EARLIER PERIODS – BUT LATER MORE AND MORE "PECULIAR".

ONE MIGHT QUESTION WHETHER THERE IS CAUSE FOR BEING SO "PECULIAR" AND "ODD".

IN THE SPEAKER'S OPINION, IT MIGHT RATHER BE A QUESTION OF MUNCH'S MENTAL STATE.

* JOHAN SCHARFFENBERG (1869–1965), NORWEGIAN PSYCHIATRIST AND TEETOTALLER.

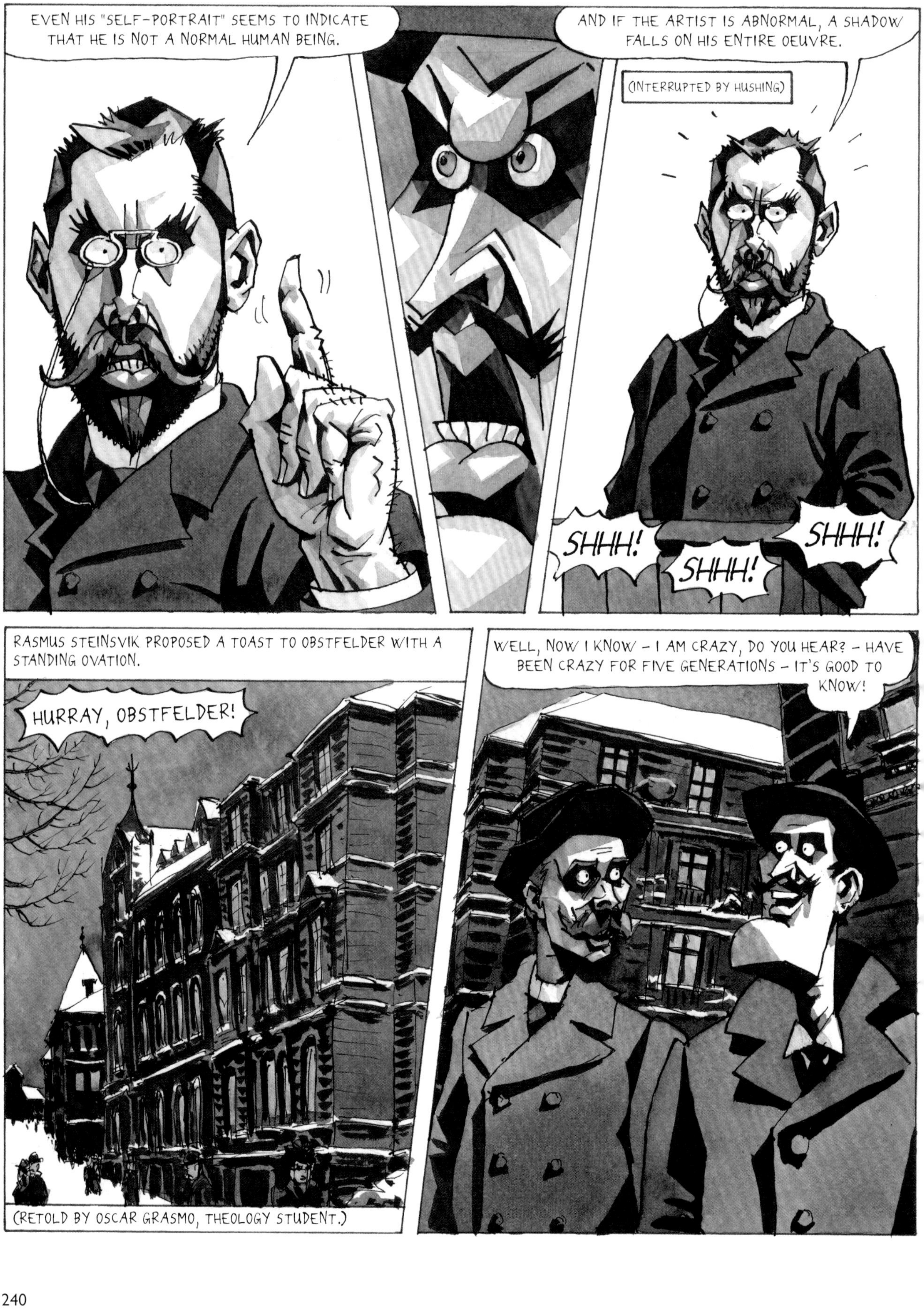
EVEN HIS "SELF-PORTRAIT" SEEMS TO INDICATE THAT HE IS NOT A NORMAL HUMAN BEING.
AND IF THE ARTIST IS ABNORMAL, A SHADOW FALLS ON HIS ENTIRE OEUVRE.
(INTERRUPTED BY HUSHING)
SHHH!
SHHH!
SHHH!
RASMUS STEINSVIK PROPOSED A TOAST TO OBSTFELDER WITH A STANDING OVATION.
HURRAY, OBSTFELDER!
(RETOLD BY OSCAR GRASMO, THEOLOGY STUDENT.)
WELL, NOW I KNOW – I AM CRAZY, DO YOU HEAR? – HAVE BEEN CRAZY FOR FIVE GENERATIONS – IT'S GOOD TO KNOW!

I DON'T REMEMBER ANYTHING OF PARIS.

I REMEMBER WE HAD A FEW DRAMS BEFORE BREAKFAST IN ORDER TO SOBER UP, AND LATER WE DRANK TO BECOME INEBRIATED.

PAUL HERRMANN* WAS PRESENT WHEN THE LITHOGRAPH "THE SICK CHILD" (1896) WAS PRINTED: THE LITHOGRAPHIC STONES OF THE LARGE HEAD LAY SIDE BY SIDE IN A ROW, READY TO BE PRINTED.

MUNCH ARRIVES, STANDS IN FRONT OF THE ROW, CLOSES HIS EYES AND WITHOUT LOOKING WAVES HIS FINGER IN THE AIR, SAYING:

PRINT... GREY, GREEN, BLUE, BROWN.

* PAUL HERRMANN: GERMAN PAINTER AND PRINTMAKER.

LET'S GO HAVE A SCHNAPPS...

SO THE PRINTER PROCEEDED WITH HIS WORK UNTIL MUNCH RETURNED AND ONCE AGAIN WITHOUT LOOKING COMMANDED:

YELLOW, PINK, RED.

AND SO ON A FEW MORE TIMES.

JENS THIIS: WHEN I MET MUNCH THAT SPRING AND ATE WITH HIM AT A LITTLE SIDEWALK RESTAURANT ON HIS STREET, HE WOULD DWELL OBSESSIVELY ON STRINDBERG AND HIS FATE.

PENNILESS, DISTRAUGHT AND DISCOURAGED, STRINDBERG HAD BARRICADED HIMSELF IN HIS HOTEL BEHIND THE LUXEMBOURG GARDENS AND WOULD NOT SEE ANYONE. HE WAS MENTALLY ILL, VERY ILL.

AT THAT TIME, STRINDBERG WAS A PROFOUNDLY UNHAPPY MAN. RECENTLY DIVORCED FROM HIS SECOND WIFE, THE AUSTRIAN, HE FELT PERSECUTED FROM ALL SIDES. AND AS FOR HIM, HE WAS POSSESSED WITH A DIABOLICAL DESIRE FOR VENGEANCE TOWARDS HIS CIRCLE OF FRIENDS IN BERLIN. "THE POLE" AND HIS "ASPASIA" WERE HIS MAIN TARGETS.

MUNCH, HIS FRIEND FROM BERLIN, TRIED TO APPROACH HIM, BUT HE TOO WAS REBUFFED:

AND THEN HE RETURNED TO HIS FLASKS AND RETORTS, TO HIS "GOLD PRODUCTION".

YOU TOO ARE CONSPIRING WITH MY ENEMIES, WITH THAT CURSED POLE AND THE OTHERS THAT PERSECUTE ME FROM AFAR WITH THEIR EVIL RAYS, BUT I SHALL FIND A WAY TO DEFEND MYSELF!

THE RELATIONSHIP BETWEEN MUNCH AND STRINDBERG MUST HAVE IMPROVED LATER THAT YEAR, BECAUSE IT WAS IN '96 IN PARIS THAT MUNCH DREW HIS STRIKING LITHOGRAPHIC PORTRAIT OF THE PLAYWRIGHT.

THE LAST TIME I SAW YOU, I THOUGHT YOU LOOKED LIKE AN ASSASSIN — OR AT LEAST A HENCHMAN.

(LITHOGRAPHS ARE INVERTED IN THE PRINTING PROCESS)

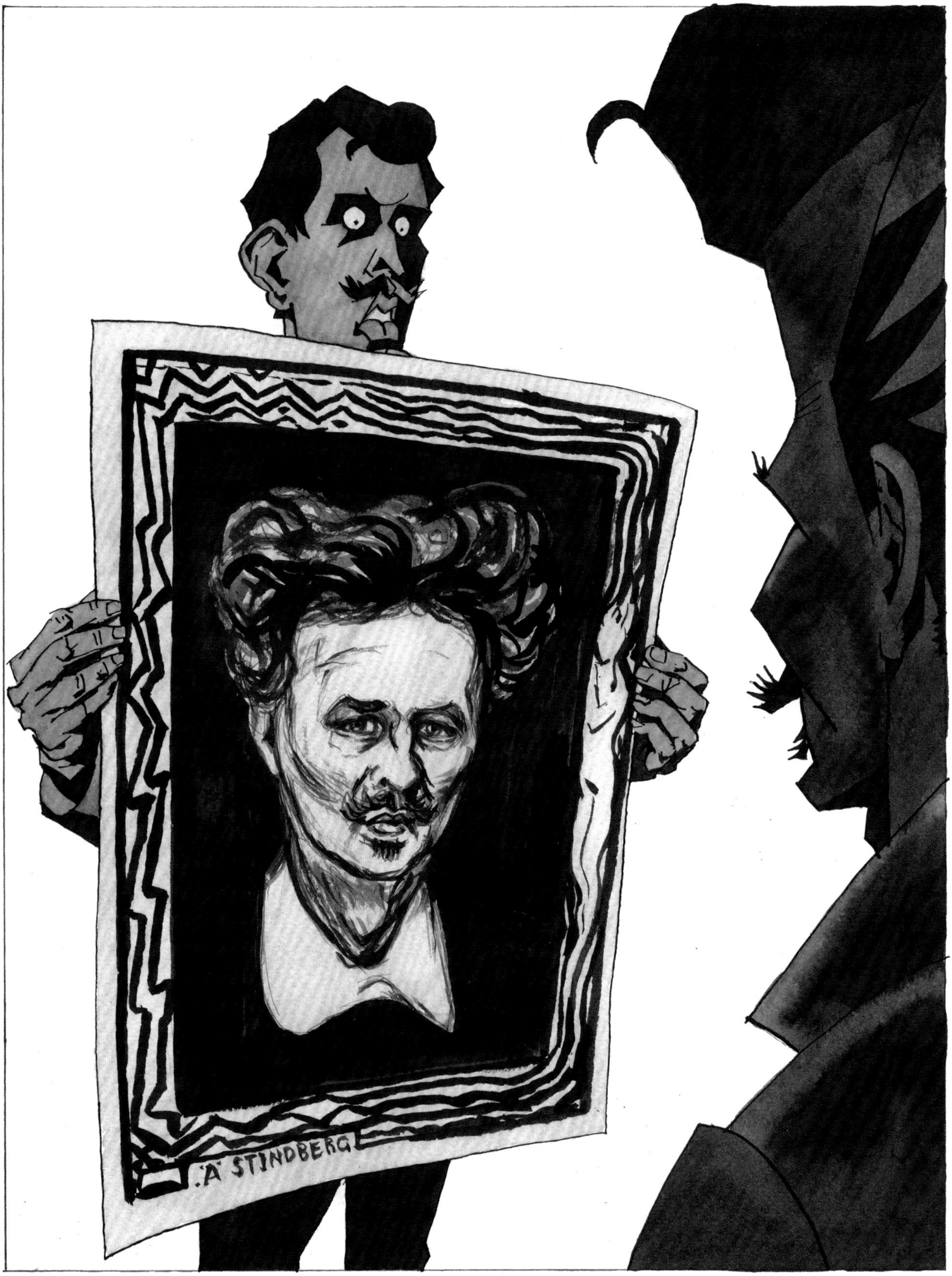
A STINDBERG

STRINDBERG WAS DEEPLY INSULTED BY THE FACT THAT MUNCH HAD INSCRIBED THE FAMOUS LITHOGRAPH WITH HIS NAME SPELLED AS STINDBERG, AND HE WAS EVEN MORE PROVOKED BY THE NAKED WOMAN THAT MUNCH HAD DRAWN IN THE FRAME SURROUNDING THE PORTRAIT.

YOU KNOW THAT I HATE WOMEN, AND THAT IS PRECISELY WHY YOU HAVE DRAPED HER ON MY PORTRAIT!

THE FRAME WAS REMOVED IN LATER REPRINTS.

246

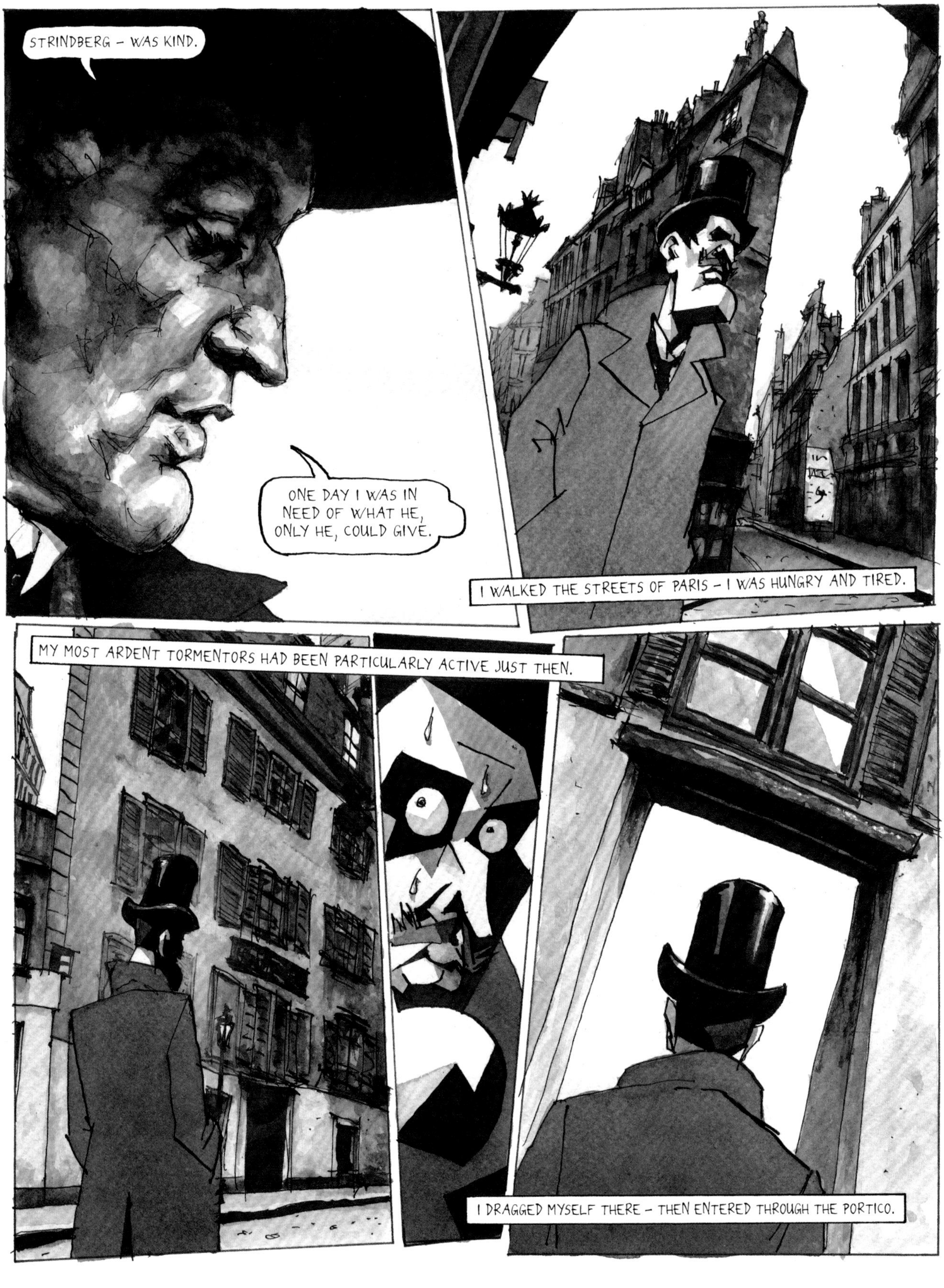
STRINDBERG – WAS KIND.
ONE DAY I WAS IN NEED OF WHAT HE, ONLY HE, COULD GIVE.
I WALKED THE STREETS OF PARIS – I WAS HUNGRY AND TIRED.
MY MOST ARDENT TORMENTORS HAD BEEN PARTICULARLY ACTIVE JUST THEN.
I DRAGGED MYSELF THERE – THEN ENTERED THROUGH THE PORTICO.

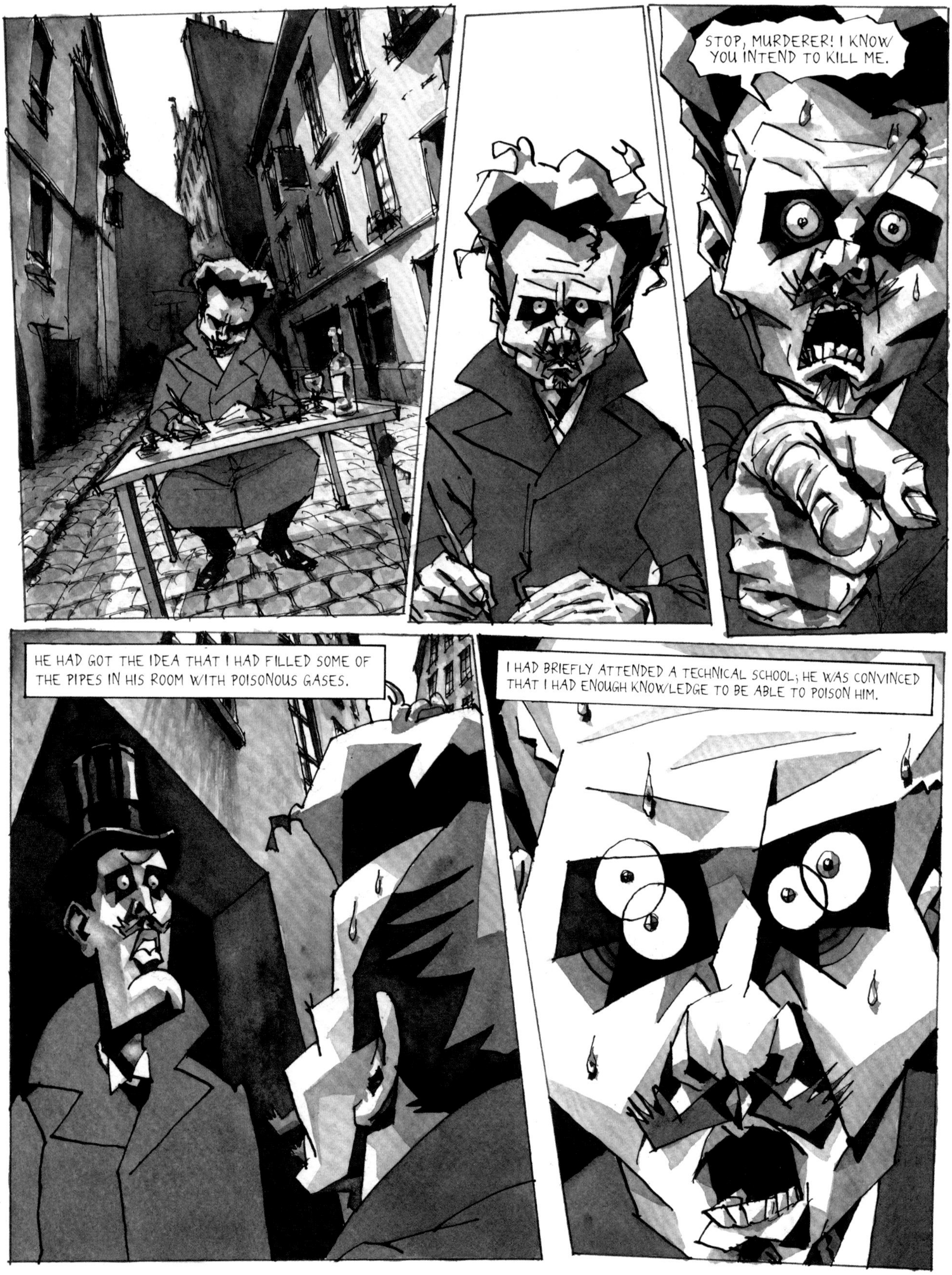
STOP, MURDERER! I KNOW YOU INTEND TO KILL ME.
HE HAD GOT THE IDEA THAT I HAD FILLED SOME OF THE PIPES IN HIS ROOM WITH POISONOUS GASES.
I HAD BRIEFLY ATTENDED A TECHNICAL SCHOOL; HE WAS CONVINCED THAT I HAD ENOUGH KNOWLEDGE TO BE ABLE TO POISON HIM.

THE ONLY PLACE HE FELT SAFE WAS IN THE MIDDLE OF THE COURTYARD.

HE DARED NOT STAY IN HIS ROOM — THERE WERE WATER PIPES THERE — GAS PIPES.

AT FIRST I HOPED IT WAS A JOKE AND TRIED TO LAUGH IT OFF, BUT HE HELD HIS GROUND.

AND I WAS FORCED TO BACK OUT THROUGH THE PORTICO.

FROM THAT DAY FORWARD, WHENEVER MENTION WAS MADE OF STRINDBERG –
AND IT WAS NOT SELDOM – THE EXPRESSION ON MUNCH'S FACE WOULD BECOME
SO PAINED THAT ONE EASILY UNDERSTOOD THAT THE LOSS OF STRINDBERG'S
COMPANY WAS ONE OF THE GREAT SORROWS THAT LIFE HAD BESTOWED ON HIM.

Dear Aunt!   Paris, 1896.
     Strindberg has returned home to
Sweden – he is evidently undergoing
medical treatment for mental illness
– he had so many peculiar ideas –
made gold, discovered that the earth
was flat and that the stars were holes
in the sky.
                    Your devoted E. Munch.

IN MY ART I HAVE SOUGHT TO EXPLAIN TO MYSELF LIFE AND ITS MEANING. I HAVE ALSO INTENDED TO HELP OTHERS TO UNDERSTAND THEIR OWN LIVES.

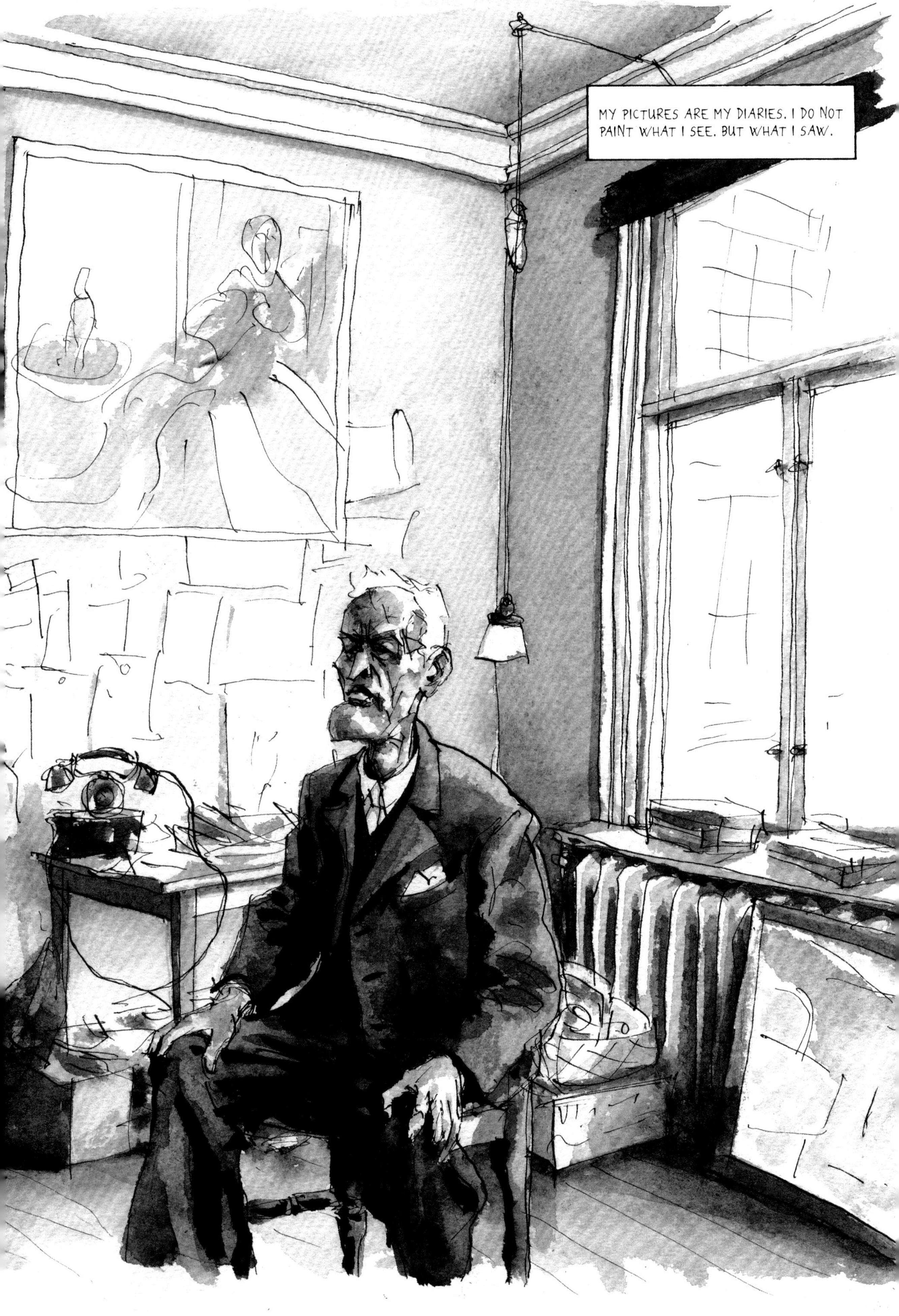
MY PICTURES ARE MY DIARIES. I DO NOT PAINT WHAT I SEE. BUT WHAT I SAW.

ART IS THE OPPOSITE OF NATURE – I DO NOT IMITATE NATURE – I HELP MYSELF TO ITS BOUNTIFUL PLATTER.

THE CAMERA CANNOT COMPETE WITH THE BRUSH OR THE PALETTE – AS LONG AS IT CANNOT BE USED IN HEAVEN OR HELL.

AFTER EDVARD MUNCH'S "SELF-PORTRAIT IN HELL", OIL, 1903.

I SAW ALL THE PEOPLE BEHIND THEIR MASKS — SMILING, PHLEGMATIC — SUBDUED FACES — I SAW THROUGH THEM AND THERE WAS SUFFERING — IN THEM ALL — PALE CORPSES — WHO RESTLESSLY SCURRIED ABOUT — ALONG A TORTUOUS ROAD — WHOSE END WAS THE GRAVE.

DIENER TATTERSALL, BERLIN:

* OLAV GULBRANSSON (1873–1958), NORWEGIAN ARTIST.

256

OUR GREAT PAINTER CHRISTIAN KROHG WAS DEAD.

THE COFFIN WOULD BE CARRIED FROM THE NATIONAL GALLERY UP TO THE CREMATORIUM. MUNCH AND KARSTEN WERE APPOINTED AS HONOUR GUARDS.

KARSTEN PHONED ME IN THE MORNING. HE WANTED ME TO COME INTO TOWN STRAIGHTAWAY, SO THAT WE COULD SPEND A LITTLE TIME TOGETHER BEFOREHAND.

"THE OLD LODGE" WAS A DESERTED PLACE WHERE NOT A SOUL APPEARED ANY MORE.

1925

A SMALL STAIRCASE LED DOWN TO OUR TABLE, AND IF SOMEONE ARRIVED, THE FIRST THING WE SAW WAS HIS LEGS.

AND INDEED TWO LEGS CAME CAUTIOUSLY DOWN THE STAIRCASE AFTER ALL.

WHO COULD IT BE?

IT WAS MUNCH.

THE RECLUSE MUNCH.

HE HAD OF COURSE COME HERE TO BE ALONE.

WE SAT MOTIONLESS.

HE DESCENDED CAUTIOUSLY, STEP BY STEP – LISTENING TO HEAR IF ANYONE WAS THERE.

ALL AT ONCE HE SAW US.

WE DIDN'T MOVE, JUST STARED AT HIM.

AS THOUGH HYPNOTISED, HE CAME TOWARDS US.

HAVE A SEAT!

HE SAT DOWN FEEBLY AND LISTLESSLY.

ARE YOU ALSO GOING TO KROHG'S FUNERAL?

YES, OF COURSE — AND YOU?

WAITER!! A WHISKY AND SODA!

WE DRANK FAST AND COPIOUSLY.

WE SPOKE ONLY ABOUT KROHG — WHOM WE ADMIRED GREATLY.

THE HOURS PASSED.

SUDDENLY KARSTEN STOOD UP AND LOOKED AT HIS WATCH.

THERE — NOW THAT BEARD IS ASHES.

WE HADN'T INTENDED IT THAT WAY, WE SIMPLY FORGOT THE TIME.

DAGNY JUEL, SHE ONLY LIVED TO BE 33, YA KNOW. MUNCH ONCE SAID:

I AM CONVINCED THAT SHE WILL ONE DAY RETURN WITH HIM TO POLAND, BECOME INVOLVED IN NIHILISTIC CONSPIRACIES AND BE HANGED OR DEPORTED. OR PERHAPS SHE WILL DIE OF STARVATION BEFORE THAT.

HE WAS RIGHT ABOUT THEIR MOVING TO POLAND. THE APARTMENT IN KRAKOW WAS CALLED "SATAN'S SYNAGOGUE"!

HOW COSY!

A WEALTHY YOUNG MAN BY THE NAME OF WLADYSLAW EMERYK WAS A CLOSE FRIEND OF BOTH DAGNY AND STANISLAW. HE ADMIRED THEM AND KEPT THE CHRONICALLY DESTITUTE COUPLE AFLOAT.

ON 26 APRIL 1901, HE TOOK DAGNY WITH HIM ON A TRIP TO GEORGIA. STANISLAW PROMISED TO JOIN THEM LATER, BUT NEVER DID.

5 JUNE 1901, GRAND HOTEL, TBILISI.

WHAT HAPPENED?

THERE'VE BEEN A LOT OF LAME THEORIES. FOR INSTANCE, THAT EMERYK SHOT HER BECAUSE SHE LAUGHED AT HIM WHEN HE THREATENED HER WITH A PISTOL. OR THAT HE WAS SUPPOSEDLY CONTROLLED FROM AFAR BY THE SATANIST PRZYBYSZEWSKI. AND SO ON. THE WHOLE BUSINESS IS VEILED IN SMOKE.

WELL ANYHOW, EMERYK SHOT DAGNY IN THE BACK OF THE HEAD, PROBABLY WHILE SHE SAT IN A CHAIR SLEEPING. HE CARRIED HER OVER TO THE BED AND THEN HE SHOT HIMSELF.

ON THE TABLE, HE LEFT FIVE LETTERS, AMONG THEM ONE FOR THE POLICE:
"When I murder Mme Przybyszewska I am in full possession of my senses. Do not blame anyone else for what has happened, the reasons for this will never be known, because they are difficult to understand."

THE SAME YEAR, MUNCH MADE AN ETCHING CALLED "DOUBLE SUICIDE".

HANS JÆGER WAS VITAL FOR MUNCH. MOST OF HIS PICTURES ARE AUTOBIOGRAPHICAL IN ONE WAY OR ANOTHER. IT'S DEBATABLE WHETHER THEY WOULD HAVE BEEN WITHOUT JÆGER.

IN JANUARY 1910, JÆGER LAY WITH HIS STOMACH FULL OF CANCER IN A HOTEL ROOM IN TOSTRUPGÅRDEN IN KRISTIANIA. MUNCH WAS LIVING IN KRAGERØ AT THE TIME, SO HIS GOOD FRIEND JAPPE NILSSEN KEPT HIM INFORMED OF THE SITUATION.

Dear Jappe,

Poor Hans Jæger – he is one of the few I would have liked to see again. He was one of the most sympathetic of the Bohemians and he has written the best Kristiania novel. Give him my warmest regards.

With many regards to you from your old friend Edvard Munch.

Dear Munch!   *Christiania, 1910.*

   Hans Jæger was very touched by your greeting ; I guess he hadn't expected it, thought rather that you were hostile towards him. He asked me to thank you deeply.

Jæger is taking it all unbelievably calmly; he even banters a bit now and then.

But I cannot bear to be up there by his side for long ; it is too sad. And then Jæger barely looks like he is of this world ; death has already fixed its seal on him —

                                   Regards from your Jappe.

HANS JÆGER DIED ON 8 FEBRUARY 1910.   AFTER EDVARD MUNCH'S "THE DEATH OF THE BOHEMIAN", 1917.

MUNCH WANTED TO MAKE A LITHOGRAPH PORTRAIT OF HANS JÆGER, AND SINCE HE HAD HIS OWN PRESS OUT AT EKELY*, I WOULD COME OUT THERE AND PULL PRINTS FROM THE STONE.

Director David Bergendahl:

EDVARD MUNCH'S LAST LITHOGRAPH

THE FOLLOWING WEEK I CAME TO EKELY ALMOST DAILY WITH PRINTS THAT HE EVENTUALLY DISCARDED.

HE FINALLY ACHIEVED A RESULT THAT HE FELT WAS SATISFACTORY, BUT THEN ABRUPTLY CHANGED HIS MIND AND ASKED ME TO SAND DOWN THE STONE. HE WANTED TO MAKE A NEW LITHOGRAPH OF JÆGER.

* MUNCH'S HOME FROM 1916 UNTIL HIS DEATH.

8 O'CLOCK THE NEXT MORNING, MUNCH PHONED. THE LITHOGRAPH WAS COMPLETED, AND HE WANTED TO HAVE A PRINT THE SAME DAY.

HE TOLD ME THAT HE HAD BEGUN THE LITHOGRAPH AT MIDNIGHT, AND FINISHED IT AT 6 O'CLOCK IN THE MORNING.

I ASKED HIM IF HE WAS TIRED, BUT HE ONLY RESPONDED BY SAYING THAT HE DIDN'T SLEEP AT NIGHT ANYWAY.

THE DAY THAT I DELIVERED THE FINISHED PRINTS TO MUNCH, HE DIDN'T LOOK AT ALL WELL.

HE PROMISED ME A PRINT WITH A DEDICATION FOR THE WORK THAT I HAD DONE FOR HIM, BUT SINCE HE DIDN'T HAVE THE STRENGTH TO WRITE, HE WOULD PHONE ME WHEN HE HAD IT READY.

267

I HAD NEVER SEEN HIM SO SICK BEFORE, AND I THOUGHT TO MYSELF THAT HE WOULD PROBABLY FORGET TO SIGN THE PICTURE HE HAD PROMISED ME.

A FEW DAYS LATER HE PHONED AND ASKED ME TO COME OUT TO EKELY.

MUNCH SPENT A LONG TIME INSCRIBING MY PICTURE, WHICH IS PROBABLY THE LAST THAT HE SIGNED.

HE DIED A FEW DAYS LATER {ON 23 JANUARY 1944}.

LUDVIG RAVENSBERG*:

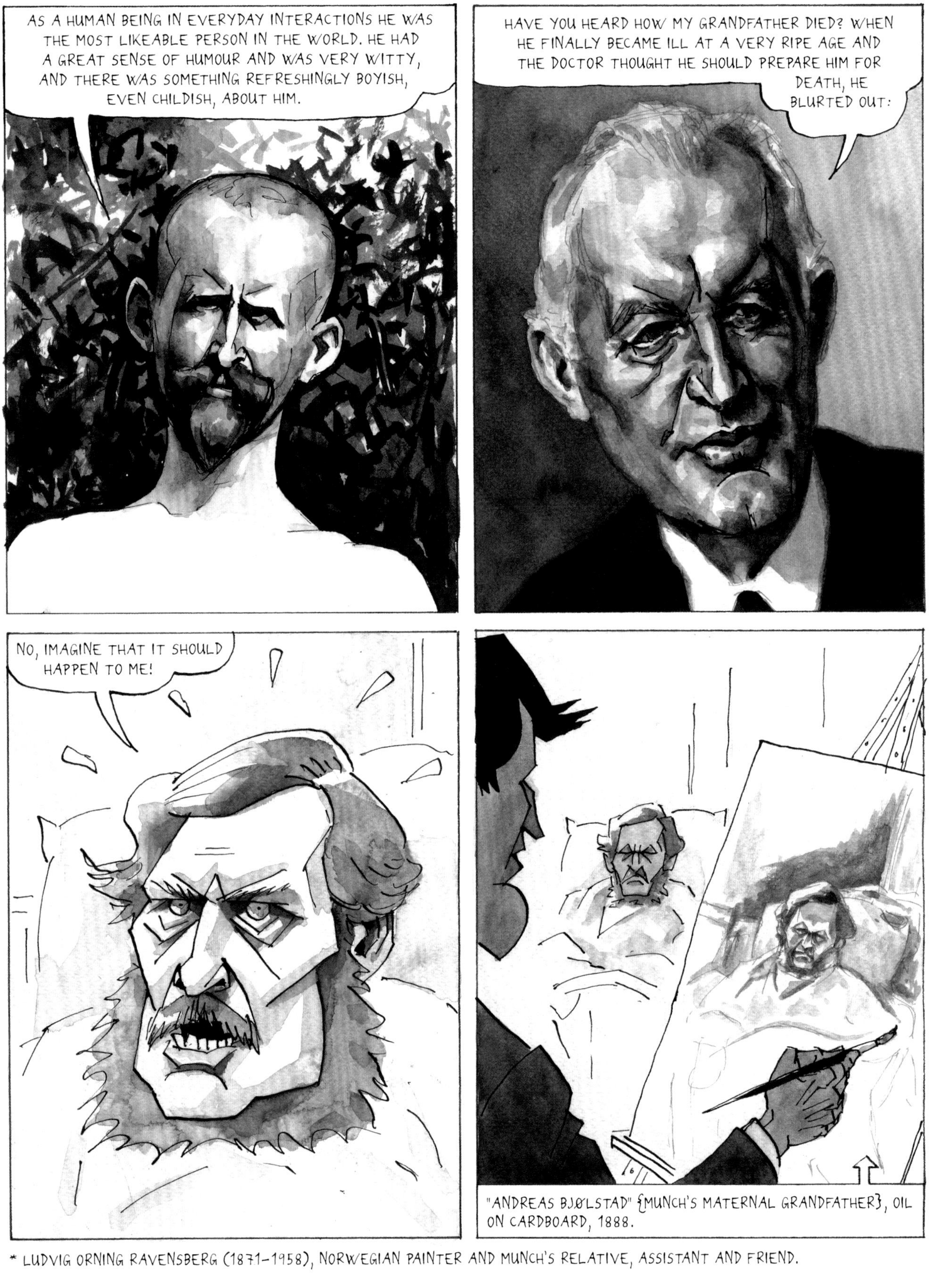
AS A HUMAN BEING IN EVERYDAY INTERACTIONS HE WAS THE MOST LIKEABLE PERSON IN THE WORLD. HE HAD A GREAT SENSE OF HUMOUR AND WAS VERY WITTY, AND THERE WAS SOMETHING REFRESHINGLY BOYISH, EVEN CHILDISH, ABOUT HIM.
HAVE YOU HEARD HOW MY GRANDFATHER DIED? WHEN HE FINALLY BECAME ILL AT A VERY RIPE AGE AND THE DOCTOR THOUGHT HE SHOULD PREPARE HIM FOR DEATH, HE BLURTED OUT:
NO, IMAGINE THAT IT SHOULD HAPPEN TO ME!

"ANDREAS BJØLSTAD" {MUNCH'S MATERNAL GRANDFATHER}, OIL ON CARDBOARD, 1888.

* LUDVIG ORNING RAVENSBERG (1871–1958), NORWEGIAN PAINTER AND MUNCH'S RELATIVE, ASSISTANT AND FRIEND.

HE WAS SO ABSORBED IN HIS ART AND WHAT HE WISHED TO CONVEY WITH IT THAT HE FORGOT TO LIVE,

FORGOT TO EAT HIS DINNER,

EVEN FORGOT WOMEN.

THEY DISTRACTED HIM AND PREVENTED HIM FROM PAINTING.

MUNCH HAD BECOME A MONK WHOSE LIFE WAS DEVOTED TO ART.

271

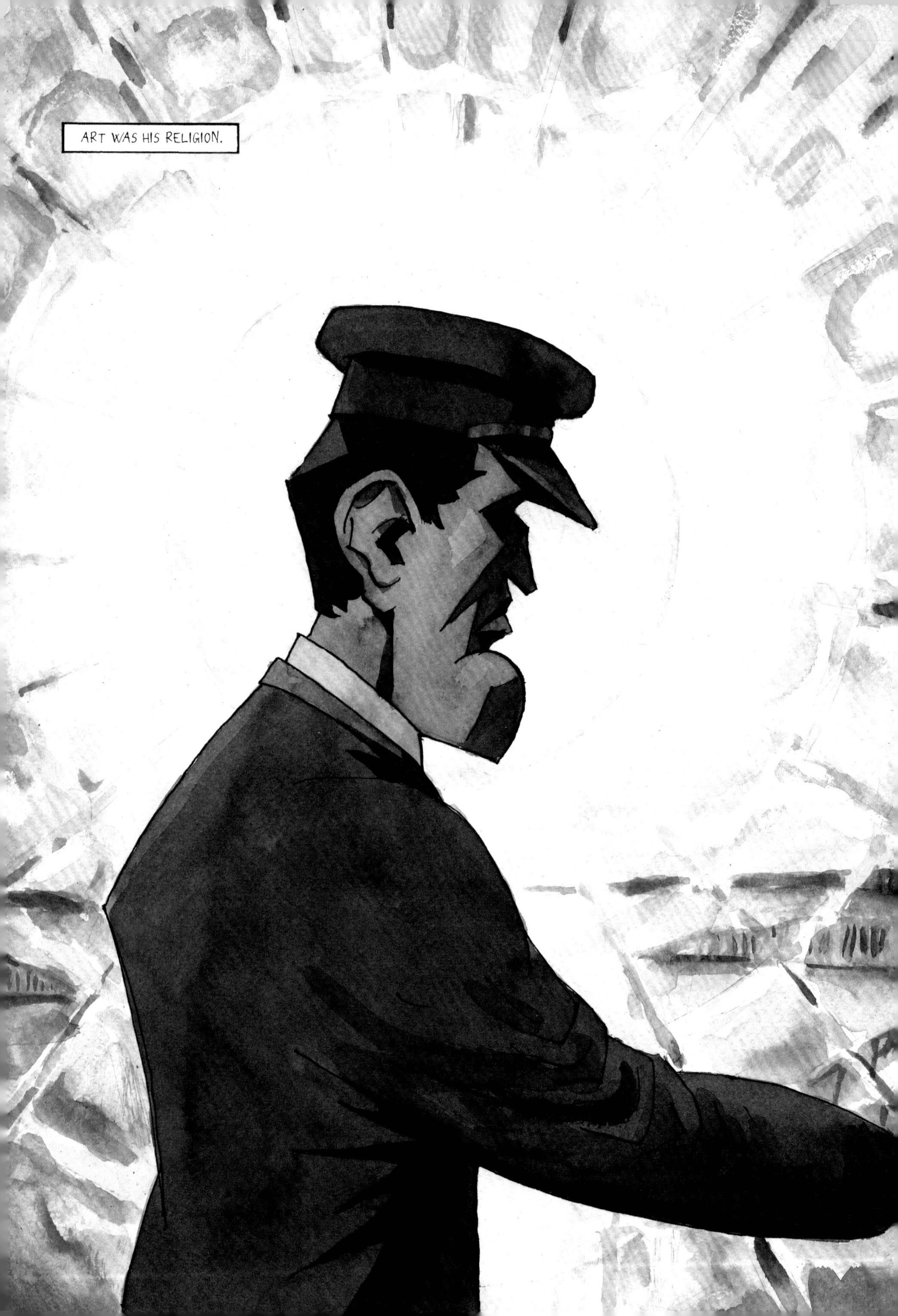
ART WAS HIS RELIGION.

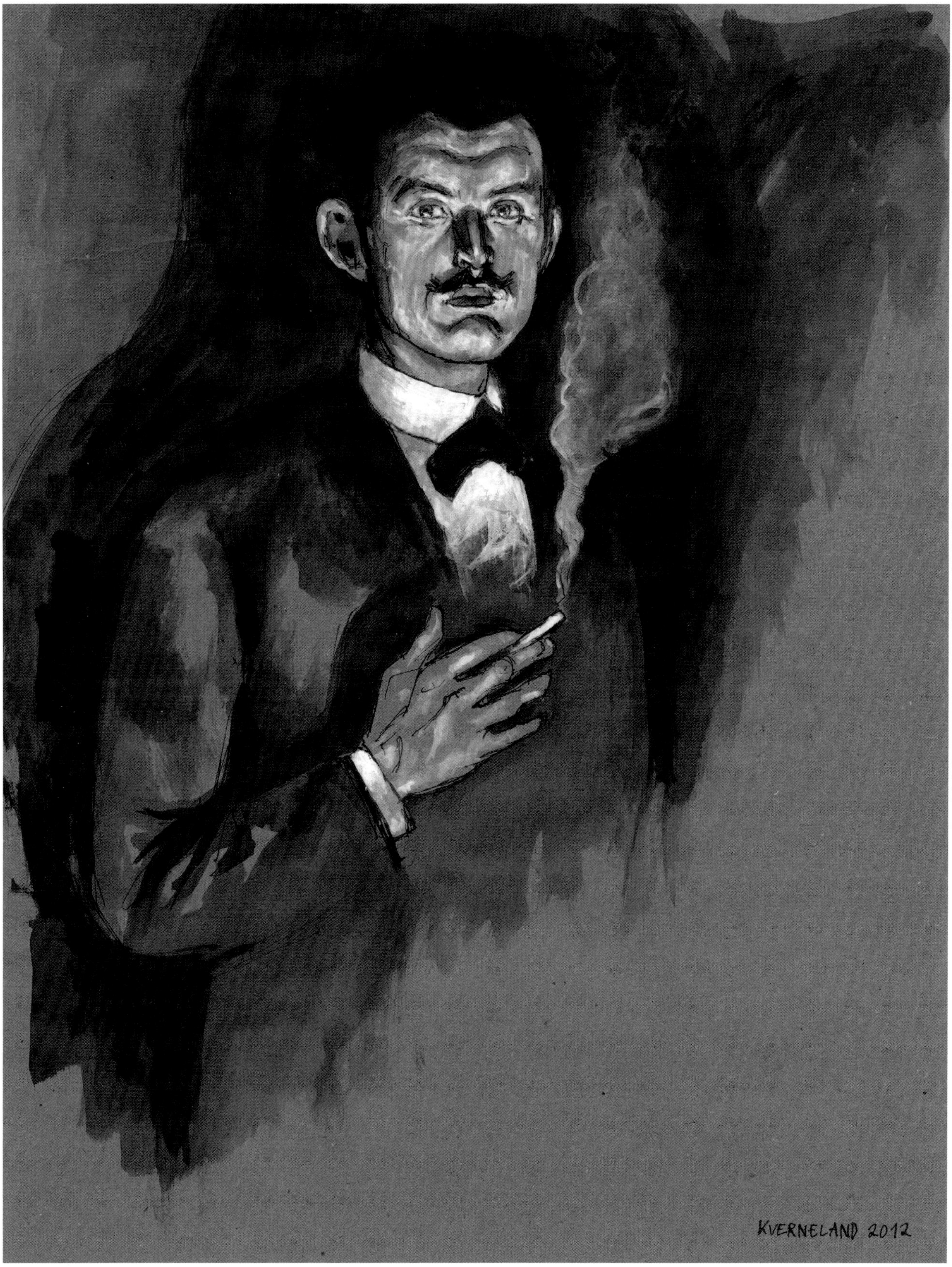
KVERNELAND 2012

SKETCHES, STUDIES AND DIFFERENT
STAGES OF THE MAKING OF PAGE 70

FOLK SKULDE FORSTAA DET HELLIGE, DET MÆGTIGE VED DET OG DE SKULDE TA AV SIG HATTEN SOM I EN KIRKE. —

《ELSKENDE KVINDE/MADONNA》, OLJE PÅ LERRET, 1893

«ELSKENDE KVINDE/MADONNA», OLJE PÅ LERRET, 1893.

«ELSKENDE KVINDE/MADONNA», OLJE PÅ LERRET, 1893.

«ELSKENDE KVINDE/MADONNA», OLJE PÅ LERRET, 1893.

«ELSKENDE KVINDE/MADONNA», OLJE PÅ LERRET, 1893.

Edvard Munch:
Hans Jæger,
1889 (detail)

Sources

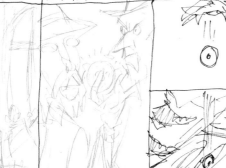

HANS JÆGER VAR BLITT ET UTSKUDD. HAN BLE HÅNET, SJIKANERT OG FORFULGT. MAN SKREMTE SINE BARN MED HAM.

DET FORTELLES AT EN KJENT HØYREREDAKTØR EN DAG GIKK HEN TIL JÆGER OG VISTE HAM EN TOKRONE, OG SPURTE OM HAN HADDE SETT EN SÅDAN FØR, HVORPÅ HAN SLAPP DEN NED GJENNOM KLOAKKRISTEN.

HJEMME I LEILIGHETEN PÅ SCHOUS PLASS 1 VAR CHRISTIAN MUNCH SYK AV ENGSTELSE. VAR DET SANT AT HANS ELSKED SØNN, HANS EGET KJØTT OG BLOD, VAR FORTAPT?

CHRISTIAN MUNCH KJENTE JO TIL ELDSTESØNNENS BEFATNING MED HANS JÆGER OG HANS ALLIERTE I «KRISTIANIA-BOHEMEN». I JÆGERS FENGSELS-CELLE HANG, DESSUTEN ET MALERI AV EN HALVNAKEN KVINNE SIGNERT EDVARD MUNCH.

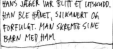

Preliminary ms. sketch, pencil and
magic marker, A4, 2010

Christian Krohg:
Hans Jæger at the
Grand Café
(detail)

HANS JÆGER VAR BLITT ET UTS[K]
HAN BLE HÅNET, SJIKANERT OG
FORFULGT. MAN SKREMTE SINE
MED HAM.

HJEMME I LEILIGHETEN PÅ SCHOU[S]
MUNCH SYK AV ENGSTELSE. VA[R]
ELSKEDE SØNN, HANS EGET KJØ[TT]

Edvard Munch:
Self-portrait in
Hell, 1903
(detail)

Norwegian coin, two kroner, from 1878

Left: Andreas Bloch: Christian Friele, Editor of *Morgenbladet* from 1865–1893 (detail)

 RTELLES AT EN KJENT HØYREREDAKTØR EN DAG GIKK HEN TIL JÆGER OG
AM EN TOKRONE, OG SPURTE OM HAN HADDE SETT EN SÅDAN FØR, HVORPÅ
APP DEN NED GJENNOM KLOAKKRISTEN.

RISTIAN
NS
RTAPT?

CHRISTIAN MUNCH KJENTE JO TIL ELDSTESØNNENS BEFATNING
MED HANS JÆGER OG HANS ALLIERTE I «KRISTIANIA-
BOHÉMEN». I JÆGERS FENGSELSCELLE HANG DESSUTEN
ET MALERI AV EN HALVNAKEN KVINNE SIGNERT EDVARD

Original drawing, India ink, watercolour and opaque white, 42 x 29.5cm, 2010

Studies of model. Kverneland photographed by Liv Braathen

Christian Munch, Edvard Munch's father. Photo on left and Munch's painting on right, ca. 1885

REFERENCES

P.6, panels 3 and 4, and p.7, panels 1 and 2: August Strindberg: *Anvisning att på 60 minuter bliva konstkännare*. Bakhåll 2003. From the foreword.

P.13, panels 1 and 4: Atle Næss: *Munch – En biografi*. Gyldendal Norsk Forlag 2004, p.131.

P. 14-17: Christian Krohg: *Kampen for tilværelsen*. A-gruppen bok og papir A/L 1989 (3rd edition), p.49.

P.19 and 20, and p.21, panel 1: Arne Eggum: *Edvard Munch. Malerier, skisser og studier*. London, Thames & Hudson 1984, p.91.

P.21, panels 2, 3 and 4, and p.22, panels 1, 2 and 3: Nic. Stang: *Edvard Munch*. Johan Grundt Tanum Forlag 1971, p.16.

P.22, panel 4: Bodil Stenseth: *Pakten. Munch – en familiehistorie*. Aschehoug 2004, p.205.

P.23: Marit Lande: *På sporet av Edvard Munch – mannen bak mytene*. Messel Forlag 1996, p.112 and 113.

P.24: Arne Eggum: *Edvard Munch. Malerier, skisser og studier*, p.93.

P.25, panel 1: Marit Lande: *På sporet av Edvard Munch – mannen bak mytene*, p.112 and 113. Panel 2: Arne Eggum: *Edvard Munch. Malerier, skisser og studier*, p.93.

P.25, panel 3, and p.26, panels 1 and 2: Christian Gierløff: *Edvard Munch selv*. Gyldendal Norsk Forlag 1953, p.89.

P.26, panel 3: Bodil Stenseth: *Pakten. Munch – en familiehistorie*, p.206, and Marit Lande: *På sporet av Edvard Munch – mannen bak mytene*, p.114.

P.27, panel 1: Arne Eggum: *Edvard Munch. Malerier, skisser og studier*, p.103. Panels 2 and 3: Arne Eggum, Gerd Woll and Petra Pettersen: *Munch og Ekely*. Munch-Museet/Labyrinth Press 1998, p.151. Panel 4: Atle Næss: *Munch – En biografi*, p.139.

P.27, panel 4, and p.28-32: Jens Thiis: *Edvard Munch og hans samtid*. Gyldendal Norsk Forlag 1933, p.205 and 206.

P.33, 34 and 35 and p.36, panel 1: Rolf E. Stenersen: *Edvard Munch – Nærbilde av et geni of a Genius*. Sem og Stenersen 1994, p.23 and 28.

P.36, panels 2, 3 and 4: Nic. Stang: *Edvard Munch*, p.98.

P.37, 38 and 39: Adolf Paul: *Min Strindbergsbok*. P.A. Norstedt & Söners Förlag 1930, p.53 and p.69 (translated into Norwegian by Steffen Kverneland).

P.40: Rolf E. Stenersen: *Edvard Munch – Nærbilde av et geni*, p.54.

P.41-43: Adolf Paul: *Min Strindbergsbok*, p.57 and 58.

P.44-50: Arne Eggum: *Edvard Munch. Livsfrisen fra maleri til grafikk*. J. M. Stenersens Forlag 1990, p.32, 27, 29, 31, 37 and 39.

P.51, panel 1: Arne Eggum: *Edvard Munch – Livsfrisen fra maleri til grafikk*, p.149 and 155.

P.52: Arne Eggum: *Edvard Munch – Livsfrisen fra maleri til grafikk*, p.155.

P.53: Arne Eggum: *Edvard Munch – Livsfrisen fra maleri til grafikk*, p.142.

P.54, panels 3, 4 and 5: Arne Eggum: *Edvard Munch – Livsfrisen fra maleri til grafikk*, p.176.

P.55, and p.56, panel 1: Arne Eggum: *Edvard Munch – Livsfrisen fra maleri til grafikk*, p.178.

P.56, panel 3: Arne Eggum: *Edvard Munch – Livsfrisen fra maleri til grafikk*, p.160.

P.57 and 58: Arne Eggum: *Edvard Munch – Livsfrisen fra maleri til grafikk*, p.196.

P.59 and 60: Arne Eggum: *Edvard Munch – Livsfrisen fra maleri til grafikk*, p.215 and 216.

P.61, 62 and 63: Arne Eggum: *Edvard Munch – Livsfrisen fra maleri til grafikk*, p.210 and 211.

P.64, 65 and 66: Arne Eggum: *Edvard Munch – Livsfrisen fra maleri til grafikk*, p.181.

P.67: Arne Eggum: *Edvard Munch – Livsfrisen fra maleri til grafikk*, p.25.

P.68, panel 1: Arne Eggum: *Edvard Munch – Livsfrisen fra maleri til grafikk*, p.23 and 5.

P.69, panels 1, 2 and 3: Rolf E. Stenersen: *Edvard Munch – Nærbilde av et geni*, p.27. Panels 4, 5 and 6: Poul Erik Tøjner: *Munch med egne ord*. Forlaget Press 2000, p.143.

P.70: Arne Eggum: *Edvard Munch – Livsfrisen fra maleri til grafikk*, p.185.

P.71: Arne Eggum: *Edvard Munch – Livsfrisen fra maleri til grafikk*, p.187, 188 and 190.

P.74, panel 2: Inger Alver Gløersen: *Den Munch jeg møtte*. Gyldendal Norsk Forlag 1976 (2nd edition, 4th printing), p.45.

P.75 and 76: Arne Eggum: *Edvard Munch – Livsfrisen fra maleri til grafikk*, p.173, 174 and 175.

P.77, panels 1, 2 and 3: Arne Eggum: *Edvard Munch – Livsfrisen fra maleri til grafikk*, p.173, 174 and 175. Panel 4: Ewa K. Kossak: *Irrande stjärna, Berättelsen om den legendariska Dagny Juel*. Bonniers 1978, p.57 (translated into Norwegian by Steffen Kverneland).

P.78, panel 1: Jens Thiis: *Edvard Munch og hans samtid*, p.212. Panel 2: Nic. Stang: *Edvard Munch*, p.91, and Arne Eggum: *Edvard Munch – Livsfrisen fra maleri til grafikk*, p.173, 174 and 175. Panels 3 and 4: Arne Eggum, *Edvard Munch – Livsfrisen fra maleri til grafikk*, p.173, 174 and 175.

P.79, panel 1: Arne Eggum, *Edvard Munch – Livsfrisen fra maleri til grafikk*, p.173, 174 and 175. Panels 2, 3 and 4, and p.80, panels 1 and 2: Mary Kay Norseng: *Dagny Juel Przybyszewska – The Woman and the Myth*. University of Washington Press, Seattle & London 1991, p.151 and 152. Panel 4: Arne Eggum: *Edvard Munch – Livsfrisen fra maleri til grafikk*, p.173, 174 and 175.

P.81, 82 and 83: Hermann Schlittgen, *Erinnerungen*. Stromverlag Hamburg-Bergedorf 1947, p.171 and 175 (translated into Norwegian by Steffen Kverneland).

P.84 and p.85, panels 1 and 2: Frida Strindberg, *Strindbergs andet ægteskab*. Berlingske forlag 1937, p.9 (translated into Norwegian by Steffen Kverneland).

P.86, panels 2 and 3, and p.87: Nic. Stang, *Edvard Munch*, p.96 and 97.

P.87: Frida Strindberg, *Strindbergs andet ægteskab*, p.22, 57 and 58.

P.88, and p.89, panels 1 and 2: Adolf Paul, *Min Strindbergsbok*, p.91.

P.89, panels 3, 4, 5 and 6: Ewa Kossak: *Irrande stjärna*, p.103.

P.90, panels 1 and 2: Frida Strindberg: *Strindbergs andet ægteskab*, p.109. Panel 3: Olof Lagercrantz: *August Strindberg*. Wahlstöm & Widstrand 1979, p.284 (translated into Norwegian by Steffen Kverneland). Panel 4: Adolf Paul: *Min Strindbergsbok*.

P.91, panels 1 and 2: Adolf Paul: *Min Strindbergsbok*, p.91.

P.91, panels 3 and 4: Frida Strindberg: *Strindbergs andet ægteskab*.

P.92 and 93: Frida Strindberg: *Strindbergs andet ægteskab*, p.109.

P.94, panel 3: Arne Eggum: *Edvard Munch – Livsfrisen fra maleri til grafikk*, p.18.

P.96: Facsimile from Christian Gierløff: *Edvard Munch selv*, p.114.

P.97-102: Adolf Paul: *Min Strindbergsbok*, p.93, 94 and 95.

P.103 and 104: Arne Eggum: *Edvard Munch – Livsfrisen fra maleri til grafikk*, p.104 and 105.

P.105, panel 1: Arne Eggum: *Edvard Munch. Malerier-skisser-studier*, p.117. Panel 2: Inger Munch: *Edvard Munchs brev – Familien. Et utvalg ved Inger Munch*. Johan Grundt Tanum Forlag 1949, p.127.

P.106: Inger Munch: *Edvard Munchs brev – Familien*, p.129 and 130.

P.107, panel 1: Inger Munch: *Edvard Munchs brev – Familien*, p.133. Panels 2 and 3: Arne Eggum: *Edvard Munch – Livsfrisen*, p.116.

P.108, panels 1 and 2: Arne Eggum: *Edvard Munch – Livsfrisen*, p.116. Panel 3: Arne Eggum: *Edvard Munch – Livsfrisen*, p.14 and 15, and Arne Eggum: *Edvard Munch, Malerier-skisser-studier*, p.96. Panel 4: Arne Eggum: *Edvard Munch, malerier-skisser-studier*, p.129 and 130.

P.109, panel 1: Ewa K. Kossak: *Irrande stjärna*, p.98 and 99. Panels 2 and 3: Mary Kay Norseng: *Dagny Juel Przybyszewska – The Woman and the Myth*, p.51.

P.110, panel 1: Mary Kay Norseng: *Dagny Juel Przybyszewska – The Woman and the Myth*, p.51 and 65.

P.111-113: Nic. Stang, *Edvard Munch*, p.88, and Pola Gauguin: *Edvard Munch*. H. Aschehoug & Co 1946, p.116, 117 and 118.

P.114: Rolf E. Stenersen: *Edvard Munch – Nærbilde av et geni*, p.55.

P.116, panel 1: Adolf Paul: *Min Strindbergsbok*, p.156. Panel 2: Kossak, *Irrande stjärna*, p.111. Panels 3 and 4: Adolf Paul: *Min Strindbergsbok*, p.119.

P.117: Adolf Paul: *Min Strindbergsbok*, p.149 and 114.

P.119: Olof Lagercrantz: *August Strindberg*, p.284.

P.120 and 121: Frida Strindberg: *Strindbergs andet ægteskab*, p.119, 120 and 121.

P.122: Ewa K. Kossak: *Irrande stjärna*, p.111, and Adolf Paul: *Min Strindbergsbok*, p.91.

P.123: Olof Lagercrantz: *August Strindberg*, p.284.

P.124 and 125: Frida Strindberg: *Strindbergs andet ægteskab*, p.152-156.

P.126 and 127: Rolf E. Stenersen: *Edvard Munch – Nærbilde av et geni*, p.25.

P.128-130: Jens Thiis: *Edvard Munch og hans samtid*, p.221.

P.131: Inger Munch: *Edvard Munchs brev – Familien*, p.133 and 131.

P.133, panel 3: Inger Munch: *Edvard Munchs brev – Familien*, p.122. Panel 4: Inger Munch: *Edvard Munchs brev – Familien*, p.126.

P.134: Inger Munch: *Edvard Munchs brev – Familien*, p.159 and 160.

P.135, panels 3 and 4, and p.136, panels 1 and 2: Arne Eggum – *Livsfrisen fra maleri til grafikk*, p.280.

P.136, panel 3: Arne Eggum: *Edvard Munch – Livsfrisen fra maleri til grafikk*, p.283.

P.137: Arne Eggum: *Edvard Munch – Livsfrisen fra maleri til grafikk*, p.280 and 281.

P.138, panel 2: Arne Eggum: *Edvard Munch – Livsfrisen fra maleri til grafikk*, p.288.

P.139, panels 1 and 2: Rolf E. Stenersen: *Edvard Munch – Nærbilde av et geni*, p.10. Panel 3: Arne Eggum: *Edvard Munch – Livsfrisen fra maleri til grafikk*, p.238.

P.140, and p.141, panel 1: Arne Eggum: *Edvard Munch – Livsfrisen fra maleri til grafikk*, p.260 and 261.

P.141, panels 2, 3 and 4, and p.142, panels 1 and 2: Arne Eggum – *Livsfrisen fra maleri til grafikk*, p.269.

P.142, panels 2 and 3, and p.143: Arne Eggum – *Livsfrisen fra maleri til grafikk*, p.259.

P.144: Inger Munch: *Edvard Munchs brev – Familien*, p.47.

P.145: Nic. Stang: *Edvard Munch*, p.39.

P.146 and 147: Jens Thiis: *Edvard Munch og hans samtid*, p.78.

P.148, panel 1: Arne Eggum: *Malerier – skisser og studie*, p.39. Panel 2: Nic. Stang: *Edvard Munch*, p.39.

P.149, panel 1: Jens Thiis: *Edvard Munch og hans samtid*, p.166. Panels 1, 2 and 3: Marit Lande: *På sporet av Edvard Munch*, p.79.

P.150, panel 1: Øyvind Storm Bjerke: *Style and Technique as Strategic Devices Used by 'the Middle Generation' 1882-86*. From Ingebjørg Ydstie and Mai Britt Guleng (ed.): *Munch Becoming Munch – Artistic Strategies 1880-1892*. Munch-museet/Labyrinth Press 2008, p.51. Panel 2: Nils Messel: *Edvard Munch og hans kritikere i 1880-årene*. From *Munch blir Munch*, p.159.

P.151: Christian Krohg: *Kampen for tilværelsen*, p.47.

P.152: Jens Thiis: *Edvard Munch og hans samtid*, p.98, and Arne Eggum: *Edvard Munch – Livsfrisen fra maleri til grafikk*, p.244.

P.153, panels 1, 2 and 3: Arne Eggum: *Edvard Munch – Livsfrisen fra maleri til grafikk*, p.243. Panels 3 and 4: Jens Thiis: *Edvard Munch og hans samtid*, p.137.

P.154: Arne Eggum: *Edvard Munch – Livsfrisen fra maleri til grafikk*, p.244.

P.155 and 156, and p.157, panels 1 and 2: Arne Eggum: *Edvard Munch – Livsfrisen fra maleri til grafikk*, p.247 and 248.

P.157, panel 3: Pola Gauguin: *Edvard Munch*, p.67.

P.158, panel 1: Poul Erik Tøjner: *Munch med egne ord*, p.145. Panels 1, 2 and 3: Jens Thiis: *Edvard Munch og hans samtid*, p.136, 137 and 138.

P.159: Pola Gauguin: *Edvard Munch*, p.69 and 32.

P.160, panel 1: Øystein Sørensen: *1880-årene, ti år som rystet Norge*. Universitetsforlaget 1984, p.88. Panels 2, 3 and 4: Pola Gauguin: *Edvard Munch*, p.36. Panel 5: Bodil Stenseth: *Pakten, Munch – en familiehistorie*, p.129 and 130.

P.161: Bodil Stenseth: *Pakten, Munch – en familiehistorie*, p.125.

P.162-165: Hans-Martin Frydenberg Flaatten: *From 'Fragmentary Notes for a Novel' to Prose Poem – Edvard Munch and the Medusa Head of Modern Pessimism*. From *Munch Becoming Munch*, p.113 and 114.

P.166: Bodil Stenseth: *Pakten – en familiehistorie*, p.145.

P.167: Bodil Stenseth: *Pakten – en familiehistorie*, p.145, 146 and 147.

P.168: Bodil Stenseth: *Pakten – en familiehistorie*, p.147 and 149. Jens Thiis: *Edvard Munch og hans samtid*, p.172.

P.169: Nic. Stang: *Edvard Munch*, p.63.

P.170, and p.171, panel 1: Poul Erik Tøjner: *Munch med egne ord*, p.67.

P.171, panel 2: Inger Munch: *Edvard Munchs brev til familien*, p.63.

P.174: Edvard Munch: *Livsfrisen*, Blomqvist 1998 (1918), p.2, and Marit Lande: *På sporet av Edvard Munch*, p.89.

P.177-181: Rolf E. Stenersen: *Edvard Munch – Nærbilde av et geni*, p.154 and 155.

P.185: Arne Eggum: *Malerier – skisser og studier*, p.61.

P.186 and 187: Inger Munch: *Edvard Munchs brev til familien*, p.68 and 69.

P.188, and p.189, panels 1 and 3: Poul Erik Tøjner: *Munch med egne ord*, p.84 and 85.

P.189, panel 4: Inger Munch: *Edvard Munchs brev til familien*, p.74.

P.190: Poul Erik Tøjner: *Munch med egne ord*, p.84 and 85.

P.191, 192 and 193: Poul Erik Tøjner: *Munch med egne ord*, p.86 and 87.

P.194: Nic. Stang: *Edvard Munch*, p.28 and 29.

P.195 and 196: Poul Erik Tøjner: *Munch med egne ord*, p.85.

P.197, 198 and 199: Atle Næss: *Munch – en biografi*, p.96 and 97.

P.200 and 201: Arne Eggum: *Edvard Munch – Livsfrisen fra maleri til grafikk*, p.241.

P.204: Poul Erik Tøjner: *Munch med egne ord*, p.131.

P.208 and 209: Vilhelm Krag: *Nat. Digte i Prosa*. John Griegs Forlag 1892 (cited from an article by Hans-Martin F. Flaatten, *Morgenbladet* 28 July 2006).

P.210-214: Christian Skredsvig: *Dager og netter blant kunstnere* (4th edition). Gyldendal Norsk Forlag 1970, p.119-124.

P.215: Lasse Jacobsen: *Edvard Munch's Travels and Sojourns in France in the Period 1885-1892*. From *Munch Becoming Munch*, p.241.

P.216 and 217: Christian Skredsvig: *Dager og netter blant kunstnere*, p.119-124.

P.218 and 219: eMunch.no: *MM T 2367*, Munch Museum. Dated 1892. Note.

P.221: Arne Eggum: *Edvard Munch – Livsfrisen fra maleri til grafikk*, p.222 and 223.

P.235, 236 and 237: www.artscandinavia.dk.

P.238, 239 and 240, panels 1-4: *Avskrift av referat fra møte i Studentersamfunnet 9. 11.1895* (photocopy courtesy of Lasse Jacobsen, Munch Museum).

P.240, panel 5: Christian Gierløff: *Edvard Munch selv*, p.102.

P.241, panels 1 and 2: Rolf E. Stenersen: *Edvard Munch – Nærbilde av et geni*, p.18.

P.241, panels 3 and 4, and p.242, panels 1, 2 and 3: Marit Lande: *På sporet av Edvard Munch*, p.133.

P.242, panels 4 and 5, and p.243 and 244: Jens Thiis: *Edvard Munch og hans samtid*, p.224 and 225.

P.244, speech bubble: postcard from August Strindberg to Edvard Munch, posted Paris 19.7.1896. Munch Museum.

P.246, top of page: Nic. Stang: *Edvard Munch*, p.96.

P.246, panels 1 and 7: Jens Thiis: *Edvard Munch og hans samtid*, p.225.

P.247-250: Inger Alver Gløersen: *Den Munch jeg møtte*, p.91.

P.251: Inger Munch: *Edvard Munchs brev til familien*, p.160.

P.252: Poul Erik Tøjner: *Munch med egne ord*, p.128 and 72.

P.253: Poul Erik Tøjner: *Munch med egne ord*, p.134.

P.254: Poul Erik Tøjner: *Munch med egne ord*, p.98.

P.255: Arne Eggum: *Edvard Munch – Livsfrisen fra maleri til grafikk*, p.219.

P.257-260: Dagny Bjørnson Gulbransson: *Olaf Gulbransson – hans liv fortalt av Dagny Bjørnson Gulbransson*, p.124. Dreyers Forlag 1969, p.120.

P.261, panel 1: Ewa K. Kossak: *Irrande stjärna*, p.99 and 100.

P.263, panel 2: Ewa K. Kossak: *Irrande stjärna*, p.228.

P.264, panel 3: Erna Holmboe Bang (ed.): *Edvard Munch og Jappe Nilssen – efterlatte brev og kritikker*. Dreyers Forlag 1946, p.52.

P.265: Erna Holmboe Bang (ed.): *Edvard Munch og Jappe Nilssen*, p.70 and 71.

P.266, 267 and 268: David Bergendahl: *Edvard Munchs siste litografi*. From *Edvard Munch som vi kjente ham – vennene forteller*. Dreyers Forlag 1946, p.107.

P.269, panel 1: Ludvig O. Ravensberg: *Edvard Munch på nært hold*. From *Edvard Munch som vi kjente ham – vennene forteller*. Dreyers Forlag 1946, p.190.

P.269, panels 2 and 3: Jens Thiis: *Edvard Munch og hans samtid*, p.48.

P.270, 271 and 272: Ludvig O. Ravensberg: *Edvard Munch på nært hold*. From *Edvard Munch som vi kjente ham – vennene forteller*, p.214.

The "volcano theory" on pages 206, 207, 223 and 224 were inspired by the theories and research done by Don Olson, Russell Doescher and Marilyn Olson, Texas State University.

The hypothetical scenes on pages 208 and 209 were inspired by Hans-Martin Frydenberg Flaatten's theories and research.

ROLF E. STENERSEN: EDVARD MUNCH – CLOSE-UP OF A GENIUS

ONE SUMMER, THERE WAS A GREAT FIRE NEAR EKELY.

MUNCH CAME RUNNING WITH HIS CANVAS AND PAINTBOX AND WENT TO WORK.

HE HAD POSITIONED HIMSELF SO CLOSE THAT A FIREMAN ASKED HIM TO MOVE.

CAN'T YOU SEE THAT I'M WORKING?

COULD YOU PLEASE WAIT A MOMENT BEFORE USING THAT HOSE OVER THERE?

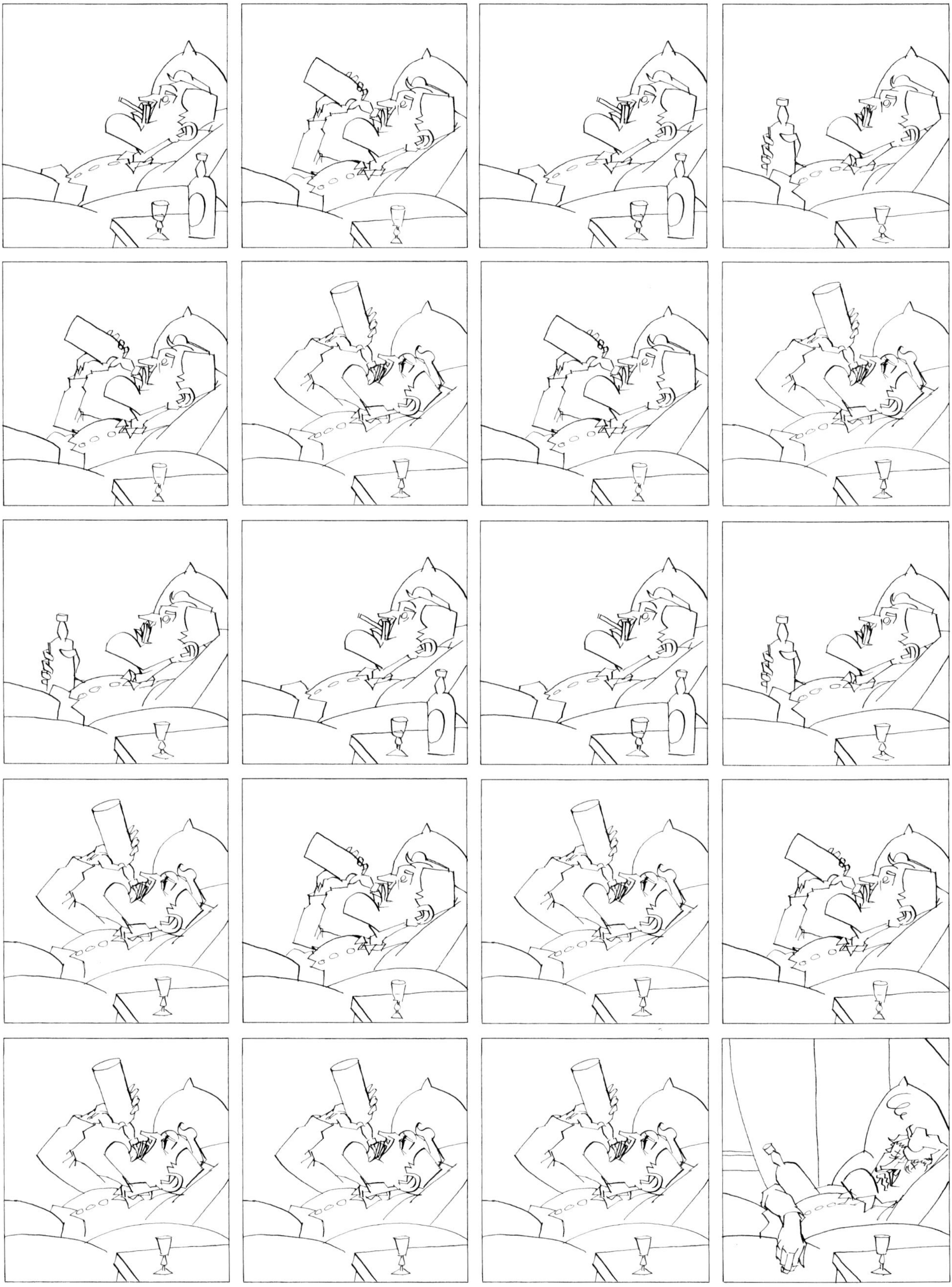